TOO CLOSE TO THE SUN

SARA
WHEELER

RANDOM HOUSE
TRADE PAPERBACKS
NEW YORK

TOO CLOSE TO THE SUN

THE AUDACIOUS LIFE AND TIMES OF DENYS FINCH HATTON

2009 Random House Trade Paperback Edition

Published in the United States by Random House Trade Paperbacks,
an imprint of The Random House Publishing Group,
a division of Random House, Inc., New York.

RANDOM HOUSE TRADE PAPERBACKS and colophon are
trademarks of Random House, Inc.

Originally published in Great Britain by Jonathan Cape, London, in 2006.

Subsequently published in hardcover in the United States by
Random House, an imprint of The Random House Publishing Group,
a division of Random House, Inc., in 2007.

Permission credits for previously published material that appears
in this work are located in the Acknowledgments section beginning on page 277.

LIBRARY OF CONGRESS CATALOGING-IN-PUBLICATION DATA

Wheeler, Sara.
    Too close to the sun : the audacious life and times of Denys Finch Hatton /
Sara Wheeler.
       p.   cm.
    ISBN: 978-0-8129-6892-7
    1. Finch Hatton, Denys George, 1887–1931.   2. British—Africa, East
    —Biography.   3. Africa, East—Social life and customs.   4. Africa, East—History.
    I. Title.
    DT365.75.F56W44 2007
    967.6'030092—dc22   2006048349

www.atrandom.com

*Title page photos: (top left) Denys's custard-yellow Gypsy Moth;
(bottom left) Denys on safari with Edward, Prince of Wales, in 1928;
(right) Denys in Kenya in the 1920s. All courtesy of the family collection.*

Book design by Barbara M. Bachman

147468846

For W G W *and* R G W

CONTENTS

EAST AFRICAN CAMPAIGN 1914-16

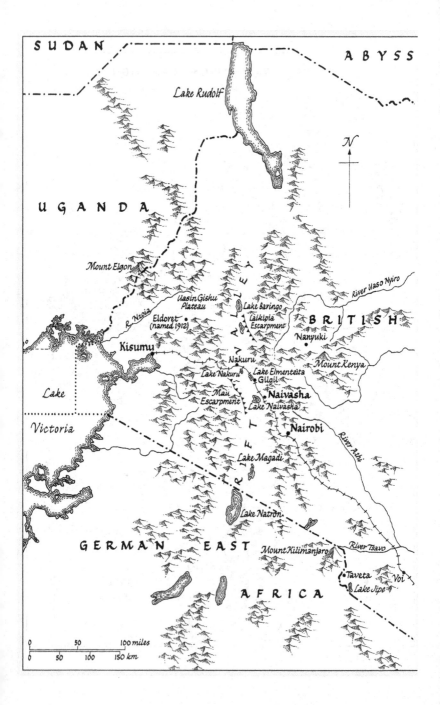

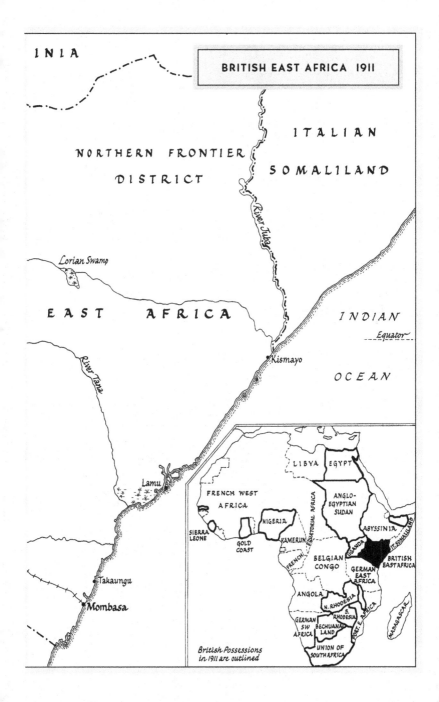

BRITISH EAST AFRICA 1911

INIA

ITALIAN

SOMALILAND

NORTHERN FRONTIER

DISTRICT

River Juba

Lorian Swamp

EAST   AFRICA

INDIAN

Equator

•Kismayo

OCEAN

River Tana

Lamu

LIBYA   EGYPT

FRENCH WEST
AFRICA

ANGLO-
EGYPTIAN
SUDAN

NIGERIA

ABYSSINIA

SIERRA
LEONE

KAMERUN

UGANDA

IT. SOMALILAND

GOLD
COAST

BELGIAN
CONGO

GERMAN
EAST
AFRICA

BRITISH
EAST AFRICA

•Takaungu

ANGOLA

N. RHODESIA

•Mombasa

GERMAN
SW
AFRICA

S.
RHODESIA

BECHUANA-
LAND

*British Possessions
in 1911 are outlined*

UNION OF
SOUTH AFRICA

GEORGE WILLIAM
10th Earl of Winchilsea &
5th Earl of Nottingham
(B. 1791, D. 1858)

m. 1 GEORGINA MONTROSE   *m.* 2 EMILY BAGOT   *m.* 3 FANNY RICE

GEORGE JAMES
11th Earl of Winchilsea &
6th Earl of Nottingham
("The Gambling Earl")
(B. 1815, D. 1887)

MURRAY
12th Earl of Winchilsea &
7th Earl of Nottingham
(B. 1851, D. 1898)

m.
EDITH HARCOURT

MURIEL
(B. 1876, D. 1938)

m.
ARTIE PAGET

GEORGE EDWARD
Viscount Maidstone
(Maidy)
(B. 1885, D. 1892)

THE FINCH HATTON FAMILY

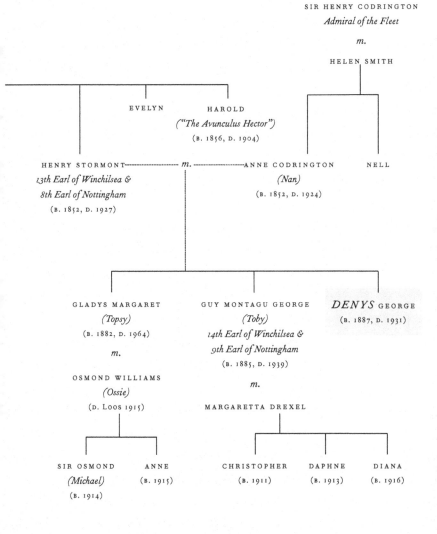

SIR HENRY CODRINGTON
Admiral of the Fleet

m.

HELEN SMITH

EVELYN   HAROLD
            ("The Avunculus Hector")
            (B. 1856, D. 1904)

HENRY STORMONT ·············· m. ·············· ANNE CODRINGTON   NELL
13th Earl of Winchilsea &   *(Nan)*
8th Earl of Nottingham   (B. 1852, D. 1924)
(B. 1852, D. 1927)

GLADYS MARGARET   GUY MONTAGU GEORGE   *DENYS* GEORGE
(Topsy)   *(Toby)*   (B. 1887, D. 1931)
(B. 1882, D. 1964)   *14th Earl of Winchilsea &*
                            9th Earl of Nottingham
m.   (B. 1885, D. 1939)

OSMOND WILLIAMS   m.
(Ossie)
(D. LOOS 1915)   MARGARETTA DREXEL

SIR OSMOND   ANNE   CHRISTOPHER   DAPHNE   DIANA
(Michael)   (B. 1915)   (B. 1911)   (B. 1913)   (B. 1916)
(B. 1914)

I HAD SPENT YEARS THINKING ABOUT THE ANTARCTIC, AND MORE THAN half of one living in it. Then I went to Africa. After so many long white nights in a place where the sun never set, I balked at the balsamic colors of an equatorial sunset, and after the biological haiku of the South Pole I was overwhelmed by the cauldron of life that foamed in East Africa. Kenya, Tanzania, Somalia, Uganda, Ethiopia: I followed Denys Finch Hatton there, though those countries had been called by different names when he trekked across them. I had first noticed him in his lover Karen Blixen's poetic memoir *Out of Africa*. His mysterious otherness caught my attention: he appeared as the eternal wanderer. I quickly discovered that he left few traces, and that I was at the end of a long line of women searching for the real Denys. But the real Denys had escaped into legend. (In the Hollywood version of Blixen's book, Robert Redford even gave him an American accent.) As he left no diaries and only a couple of dozen short letters, his inner life remains opaque. He died in 1931, so there is no one alive with adult memories of him. "The real Denys" is unknowable. But through literature—*Out of Africa*, Beryl Markham's *West with the Night*—he has become an iconic figure in the inner lives of millions. My aims in writing his life were threefold: to depict a figure in a landscape, to explore the universal themes threaded through his story, and to find out why he was an engine of myth. The character who emerged at the end of my researches was not the buccaneering adventurer I expected.

This is an ordinary story of big guns and small planes, princes from England and sultans from Zanzibar, roulette, a famous divorce case, a Welsh castle and a Gilbertine priory, marauding lions, syphilis, bankruptcy, self-destruction, and the tragedy of the human heart. It moves from the smoky orange lights of the Café Royal to the geometry of the desert hills in the Northern Frontier District, and it is infused alternately with the whiff of cordite, of elephant spoor, and of a bucket of eau de cologne tipped over onto the linoleum of an Eton schoolroom. The action shifts between London, Paris, Mesopotamia, and the steppes of the Rift Valley from Lake Baringo to Maasailand—what Martha Gellhorn described as "the paradise section of Africa." Denys was there during the short-lived colonial phase, a period in which a previously protean assemblage of tribes was frozen into unnatural suspension by an imperial administration. I tried to see East Africa through his eyes. He responded profoundly to landscape, and many of the significant relationships of his life were with places rather than people. But he never really settled in Kenya; he kept coming and going. Abrupt scene changes appealed to him, as did cultural chiaroscuro. He was divided by his love for worldly things and his desire to escape them, as I am. In terms of a career—positions held, books published, the shibboleths of success one lists in *Who's Who*—there was nothing. Six feet three and a superlative athlete, Denys was vital and restless, and in his apparently paradoxical fusion of the rebellious and the traditional he was a curiously eighteenth-century figure. (In fact, he was born in 1887.) Elegant and boisterous, simple and sophisticated, with a gift for gracious living and for the parsed existence of the wilderness, he would have been as comfortable in Hogarthian London as he was in the broken blue foothills of Mount Meru. He was a loose-limbed heartbreaker, and his defining characteristic was charm—he went about disarming the world before it could engage with him. "Charm," Anthony Blanche warns Charles Ryder in *Brideshead Revisited*, "is the great English blight. . . . It spots and kills anything it touches." In Denys's case it killed ambition and purpose, at least until the final years. But he was not flighty, or in any sense superficial, and he had an immense capacity for friendship. He had a powerful effect on everyone he met. "The man with about the most impressive personality I have ever known," wrote Bertie, Lord Cranworth, who fought alongside him and knew his share of big personalities. Again and again, acquaintances spoke of Denys's individuality; the usually weak adjective "unforgettable" was applied regularly, but nobody ever did forget Denys. His servants spoke lovingly of him for decades after his death, in England, Wales, and Kenya. Seventy-five years on, his reputation rests chiefly on the romance of the white hunter, a beguiling enough subject for investigation, and on the portrait painted by Blixen in *Out of Africa*.

Working for three years with only the dead for company, I excavated the sources, searching for clues among the unending clutter of hours and years. I was looking for scraps of illuminating detail among huge heaps of negligible things, something that would release currents of energy connecting Denys Finch Hatton to me, and his world to the one we inhabit. In this book I have sought to integrate the rainbowlike intangibility of personality with the solidity of fact. I followed Denys on a journey of self-realization until he finally found some kind of purpose, and patterns did emerge from the mosaic of his life. But I had to subject the material to a process of rigorous questioning in order to sort myth from reality. Denys achieved legendary status in his lifetime, and as a result anecdotes were ceaselessly retailed and recycled, facts were reinterpreted, and versions of Denys—oral and written—were layered one on the other like a palimpsest. He was a figure buried under his own reputation. But when I looked only at the primary sources, he rose to life again. Sifting through the versions, discarding the unreliable and the unprovable, I asked myself what we can know of a man, and increasingly I came to see the lack of material not as a biographical handicap but as a cipher for the unknowability of anyone else's inner life (or of one's own, for that matter). The absence of data itself stood for that fumbling search for certainties which so often stalls before arriving at a conclusion. This sustained me when I heard little but the sound of trees crashing across my path. Acceptance of the unknowable is a vital step on the human journey.

Denys lived through tumultuous times—from Lord Salisbury, the patrician prime minister, to the sensational fictional heroine Lady Chatterley. As the son of a peer (his father was the thirteenth Earl of Winchilsea and the eighth Earl of Nottingham), he witnessed at first hand the marginalization of his class when agricultural interests were overtaken by economic modernization. Throughout his life, almost all the male members of his family struggled to shift their resources out of land, with varying degrees of success. Old privileges were eroded, and so were the social certainties of the first three-quarters of the nineteenth century. (When I went to inspect the family's town house in a venerable London square, I found a Ferrari parked outside, with a personalized license plate.) The lack of conventional structure in Denys's own adult life was a paradigm of modernism: fragmented, disordered, and, for many years, ostensibly sterile. He went to look for a new world, and in Kenya found the colonial overspill of assumed suzerainty. It was neither the dream of fortune that drew him there nor the quest for identity. It was a desire for freedom and danger. In the end, he found something more profound and infinitely more valuable. Tragically, it turned out to be too late.

An unknown war slices through the middle of the story. Our notions of the First World War derive primarily from images of sodden trenches in France and Belgium—an iconography burned deep into the national imagination. The same war was fought for more than four years in East Africa, though not with tanks and mustard gas, and not on a line where success was measured in yards per week. It was an old-fashioned war involving bayonets, nineteenth-century smoking guns, and hundreds of miles of unmapped bush in which men were as likely to be routed by a rhino as by the enemy. It was also a unique theater, with its own particular horrors. British East Africa was the only part of the empire to be invaded by the Germans, and the campaign that ensued—as bitter and killing as all war—lasted longer than anywhere else in the fighting world, as news of the Peace failed to reach the distant East African battlefields until after the armistice. It was typical of Denys to find an obscure and unregulated front. Even the diligent official history cites "exceptionally scanty material," as many nonregular units of the kind in which Denys began his military career kept no records at all. It happened like that not by chance but because people who liked filing reports tended not to scarper to Africa. "We found accounts of battles [in East Africa] which differed not only as to the hour, day and even week when they occurred, but also in every other possible detail," wrote a desperate historian toiling in the Official War History office in London.

As far as the psychic landscape was concerned, I thought it was important to uncover layers of emotional and imaginative experience as well as the factual kind. Denys's romantic life in particular can be viewed at best through a glass darkly, but I know that he never crossed that odd line between affection and addiction, and that seemed worthy of consideration. Karen Blixen, who found global fame as a fiction writer under the pen name Isak Dinesen, played an important part in the last decade of his life, and she left a detailed record of their relationship, published and unpublished. At first I disliked her intensely. But as I dug deeper I saw that, like many monsters, she had a lovable heart. Of Denys's spiritual life I had a clearer glimpse, at least of its darker moments: at times he was almost pathologically convinced that life is stale and weary. But this is a story, too, about the redemptive power of landscape. The deep joy with which Denys responded to nature took him close to the mystery of it all, and gave him a gratifying awareness of the human need to reach out to the transcendental.

Many of the topographic descriptions in the book come from my own African travels. I wrote those passages late at night, when tiny comet-tailed geckos invaded the pages of my notebook and ostriches boomed in their peculiar hollow way not far from our camp. It was only when I flew low in a small plane over banks of purple delphiniums on the slopes of the Aberdares that I understood what it meant to Karen Blixen to take wing with Denys. Like landscape, grand passion can redeem. "It is worth having lived and suffered, been ill, and had all the *shauries* [difficulties], to have lived for this week," she wrote once after Denys had been on her farm between safaris. He left her; went off with someone else; was killed. But it was his love that enabled her to write a masterpiece. She had learned from the classics that misery was the food of ancient heroes, bestowed by the gods to be transmuted into something noble. Most people who fail, as Karen Blixen did in Africa, by any worldly standards, do not go on to smelt art from the crucible of disappointment. This was her great achievement. She recognized it. "No one came into literature more bloody than I," she once wrote.

Apart from the fieldwork, both in Africa and in Europe (and a couple of times in the United States), I worked with such written material as there was, among documents and shadows, and developed those of the emerging themes that interested me. Chief among these was the gap between character and accomplishment, being and doing. Almost everyone who knew Denys spoke of his greatness, yet he did little. I wondered if we are tyrannized by the need for achievement. I was also interested in the universal human dilemma between going and staying, a theme that Denys's story seemed to throw into relief. It was the age-old choice between four walls and the open road, security and freedom, or, as Karen Blixen put it, the lion hunt and bathing the baby—a dilemma that dogged my own life for many years. My cast of characters, from the Marlovian Bror Blixen to the future Edward VIII, all made different choices at different times in their lives, as most of us do. But Denys never wavered. He was the open road made flesh.

TOO CLOSE TO THE SUN

CHAPTER 1

OUT OF TRIM

I saw him first fingering a pistol in a Nairobi gun-shop, with the casual interest that men of action will show for such toys, and well I liked the look of his scholarly appearance, which had also about it the suggestion of an adventurous wanderer, of a man who had watched a hundred desert suns splash with gilt the white-walled cities of Somaliland.

—LLEWELYN POWYS, *Black Laughter*, 1925

WHEN HE HEARD THAT DENYS FINCH HATTON HAD BEEN KILLED ON the plains of Africa, Alan Parsons reflected that his friend had been "like one of his forefathers of Elizabethan days—a man of action and a man of poetry." It was the first Sir Christopher Hatton who had raised the family to the sunlit uplands of the English aristocracy, and they languished there through the pleasant centuries while their nation prospered. Denys inherited the charm of his Elizabethan ancestor, but not his taste for the gilded baits of conventional success. A Northamptonshire man, ruffed and sharp-bearded, Sir Christopher had worked his way into court and dazzled Queen Elizabeth with his dancing. She showered him with money and honors until he was Lord Chancellor. At thirty-five, he was able to purchase Kirby Hall in East Northamptonshire, one of the great Elizabethan houses, a model of proportion replete with cupolas, pergolas, and ninety-two fireplaces. But Sir Christopher had many mansions, and for five years he was too busy to visit Kirby.

By the time Denys was born three centuries later, the family was heading in the other direction (down), as his uncle George, the eleventh Earl of Winchilsea, had gambled away several fortunes. After disposing of most of the family paintings, he sold the lead from the roof of Kirby Hall. His widowed stepmother, meanwhile, was quietly bringing up three sons and a daughter at Haverholme Priory in Lincolnshire. Frances "Fanny" Rice became the tenth earl's third wife in 1849; their second son, Henry Stormont, was Denys's father. At Haverholme, Henry and his siblings grew to love the pared-down landscape and the winds that sped across the flatlands freighted with the chill of the North Sea. The three boys went out with their uncles, shooting partridge in the gravel pits, pigeons in Evedon Wood, and rabbits everywhere. They caught pike up and down the Slea and dace in the section between Haverholme Lock and Cobbler's Lock, and played golf and cricket in the park. (In the untroubled 1860s, the Priory had its own cricket team.) After boarding school Henry went up to Balliol, the Oxford college favored by the ancestral earls. At nineteen, his hollow-cheeked Renaissance face was framed by sideburns the color of sweet sherry. His nose was long and sharp, his eyes deep-set, and a prehensile mustache dipped and clung to his chin below his lower lip.

Finch Hattons were speculators and adventurers. By the 1870s, young men from the landed gentry had started heading south to Australia—many were hired as jackaroos on the cattle stations—and after a year Henry gave up on Balliol and steamed to the subtropical northern tip of Queensland. He rode a horse down to Mackay, a huddle of shacks quietly sweltering among the sugar plantations 150 miles north of the Tropic of Capricorn. There he joined a maternal uncle who had sailed to Australia six years earlier. Knowing little of sugar, the pair determined to set themselves up as stockmen, and reconnaissance took them to the well-watered cattle country around Mount Spencer, forty-five miles inland. They purchased four hundred square miles of bush, at first sleeping on canvas stretchers in a hut overlooking a lagoon. Henry had a table for his tin basin and a fragment of looking glass balanced on a pair of nails driven into a post. At night, he read in the sallow glow of a fat-filled jam tin wicked with a twist of tweed from his trousers.

The lure of the frontier was in the blood, and within a year Henry's younger brother, Harold, had arrived in Queensland to assist the fledgling family firm. On his first night, he found an eleven-foot carpet snake coiled in his cot bed. But it would have taken more than a snake to deter Harold, a figure of buttonholing vigor and the most voluble of the Finch Hattons. With his brother and his uncle, he turned Mount Spencer into a comfortable village of houses and huts, and the station into a going concern with twelve thousand cattle and a permanent staff of stockmen and boys. It was hard work all around. Simply chopping timber for fences was a Sisyphean task that involved pulling a crosscut saw and swinging a maul under a vertical sun, the thermometer often reaching 110 degrees in the shade. "But if a man is thoroughly sound," Harold wrote, ". . . it is odd if he does not look back to the time when he was splitting rails for ten hours a day as the happiest in his life." A man with a powerful sense of public duty, Harold was quickly appointed a Queensland magistrate and later became the voice of judicial authority at the goldfields, granting (or, more often, refusing) alcohol licenses. He was a model of moral seriousness and egregious self-confidence—an imperial *beau idéal*.* In his spare time, he learned to throw the boomerang; he included this among his achievements in *Who's Who* ("only white man who could ever throw the boomerang like the blacks of Australia"). He never married. In later years, he was close to his nephews and nieces, and Denys, the youngest, worshipped his uncle Harold, the archetypal man of action. Denys loved hearing stories of the magnificent landscapes, dizzying scale, and hazards innumerable that characterized the pioneering experience of the white men who battled the Australian bush in the last decades of the nineteenth century. For those made of the right material, it was a Garden of Eden. Thirty-five years later, Denys was to find a similar paradise on the plains of East Africa.

DENYS'S MATERNAL GRANDMOTHER, Helen, had married Admiral of the Fleet Sir Henry Codrington, KCB (Knight Commander of the Bath), in 1849. His father had captained the *Orion* at Trafalgar. After fifteen years

---

* A Finch Hatton township, named after the brothers, still processes cane in the lush hinterland south of the Clarke range.

of marriage, the admiral sued for divorce on the grounds of his wife's multiple adulteries. The Codringtons had been living in Malta, where Sir Henry held the position of admiral-superintendent of the dockyard. Since its acquisition in 1814, Malta had been one of the great British naval bases and the home of the Royal Navy's Mediterranean fleet. Perks of the job included a high-specification gondola, and at the divorce trial in London the gondolier testified that when Lady Codrington was escorted home by a certain officer he regularly observed his vessel "getting out of trim" due to excessive movement in the cabin. Day after day, jurors heard a litany of alleged activities, including a lesbian affair and flights from private detectives—all subsequently recounted in minute detail in the pages of *The Times*. It was the soap opera of the moment, and through the dog days of summer in 1864 the denizens of the Establishment gasped for the next installment. The admiral, suggested Lady Codrington in a robust counterattack, had once entered her bedchamber and groped her lady companion. Lawyers read out copious extracts from diaries and letters and, in his summing-up to the jury, the judge expressed his concern that they should not be influenced by the sheer number of charges brought against Lady Codrington—"so many imputations of criminal intercourse . . . all more or less sustained by evidence." He pointed out that even a thousand weak links did not make a strong chain. But the jurors thought the links were strong enough, and on November 23 they found Lady Codrington guilty. Her daughters, Denys's mother, Anne—known as Nan—and her sister, Nell, were eleven and ten. The admiral got his decree nisi. But the verdict was disputed, and, to the delight of the nation, the case rolled on. Like one of the admiral's ships in full sail, it took a long time to stop.

The two little girls, meanwhile, were shunted among relations, friends, and governesses, absorbed enough in the private world of childhood but uneasily aware of the hostilities that lay beyond its frontiers. Their mother had emerged from her husband's testimony as a figure of lewd vulgarity. In reality, Helen Codrington, hemmed in by an existence over which she had no control, had chosen the only means of self-renewal available to her. She could not leave, so she tried to make staying tolerable; it was her way of seeking a better world. The affair was never spoken of in the family, even after many years. Denys never knew his grandmother; she died before he was born. It was a pity, as in him she would have found an ally at last. He had her affinity for waywardness, and his heart, too, never settled.

HENRY FINCH HATTON met Nan Codrington when he returned from Australia on leave in 1879. Three years later, when both were thirty, they married. The bride had copper pre-Raphaelite hair, aspirin-white skin, and large gray eyes that sheltered under broad red brows. Her friends were artists and musicians, and she brought a gentle bohemian glamour to the closed and traditional Winchilsea clan. She was intimate with Ellen Terry, an actress of the grand manner who had won the country's heart during her twenty-four-year stage partnership with Sir Henry Irving. Known to her circle as Nellie, Terry was five years older than Nan and devoted to her—a stream of genuine affection plain to see amid the thespian gush. In her memoirs, Nellie said that once, as she was preparing to play Beatrice in a new production of *Much Ado About Nothing*, she "began to 'take soundings' from life for my conception of her. I found in my friend Anne Codrington what I wanted. There was before me a Beatrice—as fine a lady as ever lived, a great-hearted woman, beautiful, accomplished, merry, tender. When Nan Codrington came into the room, the sun came out." Many would later note the same ineffable specialness in Nan's son Denys. John Craigie, a university friend, recalled in old age, "He has remained with me as an almost unique personality. Completely fearless, he showed kindness in all his deeds. A king among men, he never did an unworthy action."

Eleven months after their marriage, and by now back in Australia, Henry and Nan had a daughter. The proud parents could not agree on a name, so the infant was christened Gladys Margaret, names never liked by anybody, with the result that she was known, from the outset, as Topsy. Two and a half years later, a son was born: Guy Montagu George, always known as Toby. The expanding family returned to England, and there Henry and his elder brother Murray focused on their bank balance. "Everything in the family financially at as critical a point as can be imagined," Henry wrote in his diary on January 1, 1887. The large sums that should have been available had been dissipated by their half brother, George, the eleventh earl (he had found a fresh source of revenue at the pawnshop, where he deposited his wife's jewelry). In addition, rents nationally had fallen by a quarter between the mid-seventies and the mid-eighties, denting the income of the entire landed class. The family business in Australia had failed to bring in money and now descended into crisis. Harold, the boomerang-throwing third brother, had returned from Queensland in 1883 and embarked on a financial career in the City, so he was unable to go back to try to salvage at least some of the initial investment. It was agreed that Henry should return to Australia alone "to see to things." This was a difficult decision, as Nan was pregnant again. She and the two children were to live in rented accommodations in London until the new baby arrived, then move up to a property on the Haverholme estate in Lincolnshire. It was a typical Finch Hatton plan; the compulsion to move house bordered on the pathological.

In February 1887, Henry moved his brood into 22 Prince of Wales Terrace, a new town house in a Kensington cul-de-sac that he had taken at six guineas a week until the end of May. Haverholme Priory had to be tenanted. "Alack, HP is a thing of the past," Henry wrote in his diary the day the maids unpacked the trunks. But it wasn't. He held on to Haverholme for another forty years. When he really did have to let it go, the grief of it killed him.

On March 9, Henry left England, comforting himself on the steamer with Thompson's *History of the Paraguayan War*. Almost as soon as he arrived in Queensland, he realized that the financial prognosis was disastrous. Back in the 1870s, he and Harold had started a mining company in addition to the cattle station. Since the California rush of 1849–50, the prospector had been a familiar figure in the imperial landscape. When a vigilant opportunist from New South Wales recognized, in the Californian seams, rock formations similar to those at home, he returned to the mountains of his youth, found a mine, and triggered the Australian gold rush. After yellowy glints were spotted in a creek running off Mount Britten, on the western fall of the coastal range, Harold and Henry sank money into a mill at the diggings. With land in England no longer a gold mine—even without a gambling earl—the Finch Hattons were speculating on any possible fresh source of income. But Henry returned to find that all efforts to float the company had failed. "No sale is possible now at almost any price," he concluded.

It was not all bad news that year. Back in Prince of Wales Terrace, baby Denys was born on April 24, 1887. His eyes were topsoil-brown, and he was long. The news reached his father by cable sixteen days later. "Hurrah at last!" Henry wrote in his diary that night. "No words to express the relief and delight." But Henry was suffering from rheumatism in his shoulder and a bad case of homesickness. "My darling Nan," he wrote on August 15, after receiving the mail, "I thank everything [*sic*] seems cosy and happy . . . I do long for her so dreadfully." Although his rheumatism turned into sciatica ("Never had so much torture in my life"), Henry managed to keep up his fishing trips, got in a spot of possum shooting, and even had a pop at the cockatoos. He was glad to see the back of the year, notwithstanding the acquisition of another son. "So ends 1887, and I hope 1888 may have more luck in store for us all," he wrote in his diary on December 31. "It's been a vile year for me on the whole, away from home and bothered with station affairs and minor anxieties—and mostly alone." Then, on June 15, he learned by cable that his gambling half brother, George, had died at the age of seventy-two. "Poor dear old W. [Winchilsea]," Henry wrote in his diary. "I hope he knew how fond of him we all were. But he was always thinking we must hate him for ruin brought on the family by him. We didn't." George's only son had predeceased him, and the title—but not the money, as most of that had gone to the bookmakers—passed to his half brother Murray, who was thirty-six.

WHEN DENYS WAS a few weeks old, Nan and the children moved up to the Haverholme estate in Lincolnshire. Situated a hundred miles north of London, where the torso of England flattens out and slims down, the village on the estate, which was called Ewerby, was populated by tenant farmers and agricultural laborers. The single road that wound in and out was rarely troubled by motor vehicles (until 1896 the open-country speed limit was four miles an hour and each car, preceded by a man with a red flag, required a crew of three). The Winchilseas owned almost the whole village—the pub was called the Finch Hatton Arms—and Nan and the children could walk to the Priory without leaving family land. Their new abode, the Cedars, was the Haverholme dower house. It was a solid red-brick structure overly decorated in the late-Victorian fashion, with shardy potted palms in every recess and porcelain gewgaws on dark, heavy side-boards. But the servants had been with the family for many years, and Nan was a natural homemaker. Purple loosestrife was still blazing around the pond when she and the children moved in, and blackberries lolled from the bushes in Evedon Wood. Denys, nicknamed Tiny, was wheeled in his perambulator along the lanes north of the village and on to the Priory, past the clay pits of the brickworks and through the cow parsley and creeping cinquefoil of the deer park, where the air, damp from the Slea, was scented with water mint.

Henry's elder brother Murray was much in evidence on the estate. A trim and determined man with a handlebar mustache, Uncle Murray was a towering figure in the world of egg collecting. He had the finest collection of eagles' eggs in the country, all stolen from the nest personally. In 1875, he had married Edith Harcourt, granddaughter of the second Earl of Sheffield. The flighty Edith was proud of her eighteen-inch waist—one can hardly imagine, looking at photographs, where her organs were stored. She lived in the grand manner, sending out stiff dinner invitations printed with the instruction "Decorations," and at her London residence footmen served beluga caviar on solid silver platters, followed by *Suprêmes de Turbotin Grand Duc, Carré d'Agneau Pré Salé*, cold pineapple soufflé, and roe on toast. Murray, on the other hand, was a deeply serious figure who worked tirelessly to discharge his civic responsibilities, whether he was investing in drainage in Ewerby, setting up schemes to assist farmers and their laborers, or presiding over meetings in his role as high sheriff of Lincolnshire. When he inherited the title from the Gambling Earl, he found that checks signed "Winchilsea" were hard to cash, and immediately set about retrenchment. The land portfolio stood at just under thirteen thousand acres, and this he reduced to eight thousand through the sale of Eastwell Park, a Kentish estate with a particularly dazzling mansion. It took Murray years to untangle the problems George had bequeathed. According to *The Times*, "the succession led to a vast network of legal difficulties upon which, it is stated, no fewer than 22 firms of lawyers were engaged at different times." At the end of it, finances were savagely depleted, but nobody was going to starve. Rents were still flowing in from different parts of the country, even if they had fallen.

Murray was fascinated by the development of the motor vehicle; this, he was sure, would catch on, and he foresaw its potential contribution to farming methods and distribution. Many were still hostile to the introduction of cars, largely because the landed class had invested heavily in the railway. But Murray, one of the strain of male Finch Hattons who did not favor half measures, was among the first to celebrate when, in 1896, an act of Parliament recognized a class of road machine weighing less than three tons and exempted it from the three-man-crew rule, at the same time raising the speed limit to twelve miles an hour. In honor of this development, champions of the internal combustion engine organized the first Motor Car Tour from Whitehall to Brighton. On November 14, Murray inaugurated the rally by burning a red flag at the starting line, and he drove the route himself, presiding over the official dinner at a hotel the same night. But Murray was to regret his involvement in motoring. He had become chairman of the Great Horseless Carriage Company. This outfit, based on a good idea, was managed by a rogue named Harry J. Lawson, a bicycle maker turned motor trader who had learned a few tricks about making money during the bicycling boom of the 1890s. He had started a syndicate that was to acquire the rights to all cars sold in Britain. After hauling in thousands of investors, Lawson juggled shares and accounts and took anyone who appeared to be infringing his patents to court. There was a loud din of publicity when the whole rotten edifice came tumbling down, and Murray lost his entire investment. It was a trickster's market, with so many peers struggling to diversify, and in 1898 *Punch* ran a cartoon of a lord displaying a sandwich board advertising the Bust Tyre Company. Another fraudster actually paid Murray and two other peers to join his board—a fact he freely declared during his bankruptcy proceedings (all reported in *The Times*), stating quite truthfully that with lordly names on his prospectus he was able to recruit subscribers.

ON AUGUST 6, 1888, Henry left Australia for good. He and Nan had been apart for almost eighteen months. Nine weeks later, at the Cedars, he picked up his second son for the first time. Denys's hair, at first light brown, had darkened to the same sweet-sherry color as his father's. He had inherited, too, his father's long nose, but not his gloomily deep-set eyes: Denys's eyes were wider apart, and shaped like large almonds. Both he and his sister, Topsy, with her flaxen-gold hair, were angelically hand-some. Toby was the odd one out. He had a wider face and a squarer chin, and less of his mother's streamlined fluidity.

The children's lives were enmeshed with those of their Haverholme cousins—Murray and Edith's children Muriel, six years older than Topsy, and George, Viscount Maidstone, known as Maidy, who was the same age as Toby. The five chased one another along the warm gravel paths of the Priory, followed the undergardener as he trenched celery, and netted spar-rows in the ivy after dark. They nursed finches by the kitchen range, cor-nered the butler in the pantry to solicit arrowroot biscuits, and trapped mice in the passages, stuffing their bodies into matchboxes then forgetting they were there. When the cedars were dumb with snow, the cousins threw paper darts from the window of the day nursery and pored over pic-ture books in the firelit library. In spring, they floated homemade rafts down the Slea, picked off the snails that stuck to the tendrils of the water buttercups, and built crow's nests in the yews, which they reached by rope ladders and stocked with chocolate creams. In August, the whole family decamped to rented villas in the genteel resort of Felixstowe in Suffolk, Granny Fanny in attendance with her own army of servants and Uncle Harold coming and going from town by train. "Chix having a fine time by the briny," Nan reported to her diary in June 1891. But in March 1892, Maidy died of influenza in Cannes. He was seven. Denys was not quite five. This death changed everything. Provided Edith had no more sons, when Murray died the earldom would pass to Denys's father. Henry went to Sleaford Station to meet the little coffin, and walked behind it all the way to the Priory.

When Denys was six, the family moved back to the capital. Both the Priory and the Cedars were let, and for a decade London was their main residence. The volatile existence of the Finch Hattons reflected the uncer-tain times. In the 1890s, agriculture was so depressed that landed families regularly let their piles and squatted in town houses. There was little stigma attached; it was part of the social, political, and economic upheaval of an uneasy decade in which landowners found themselves displaced from property that had been in the family for centuries. When the Liberal chancellor introduced death duties in 1894 (and on a graduated principle, too), the breakup of the huge estates quickened pace. Few great houses were built, and hundreds were sold or demolished in the new trend toward liquidation as opposed to accumulation. Like many, Henry persevered in his quest to find new sources of revenue. In 1890 and 1891, he went prospecting in Ireland, without success. On January 1, 1892, Nan wrote in her diary, "I wish us all joy—as much happiness and rather more prosperity than last year." But life was still good for the rich in the richest city of the richest country in the world. The poorest of the poor, meanwhile— some as young as six—fashioned matches at the Bryant and May factory in London's East End for eleven and a half hours a day. They were fined if they dropped a match, and many developed bone cancer from the phosphorus fumes. One-third of Londoners lived in poverty. In 1889 the dockers, who broke their backs unloading freight shipped in triumph from all corners of the empire, had gone on strike. While Denys was busy growing up, the world that had sustained the great landed fortunes was dissolving in the acid bath of labor disputes. In 1902, when Lord Salisbury resigned as prime minister for the last time, an era died. Many, unwilling to change with the times, were to seek a new world elsewhere, or, at least, to seek the old world in a new setting.

NINETEENTH-CENTURY EXPLORERS had brought Africa into the drawing room. When Henry and his siblings were playing cricket at Haverholme, explorers were the celebrities of the age, and their books, illustrated with naked bodies and comical headdresses, were bestsellers. Catalogs offered buffalo-hoof "door porters" with brass handles, buck-horn toasting forks, and corkscrews fashioned from tusks. Eager decades of "discovery" then culminated in an undignified sprint to carve up the continent. Salisbury noted that when he left the Foreign Office in 1880 nobody thought about Africa, but when he returned to government as prime minister five years later the principal nations of Europe were quarreling obsessively over the division of the continent. It was the sudden acquisitive interest of other countries that transformed an indifferent poking around into an urgent search for colonies. (The Germans had a word for it: *Torschlusspanik*, panic over the door-closing. Lord Derby called it the Scramble for Africa.) The Belgian king, Leopold II, a catalyst of sorts, was prepared to spend his money—"*Il faut à la Belgique une colonie*"—and he searched for tropical territory for two decades before he found the Congo basin. Colonial pressure groups sprouted in France and Germany, expeditions were dispatched, and the *tricolore* was soon flapping on the banks of the Niger. At the West Africa Conference inaugurated in Berlin at the end of 1884, there was lofty talk about civilizing the dark continent, but in reality it was simply imperative to stop other countries from gaining a trading monopoly. Colonial sovereignty was a kind of commercial protectionism. Politicians indicated that there was money to be made from the new territories, but for many settlers, Karen Blixen among them, life in Africa was to be one long struggle with the bank manager. As for Africans, they were perceived as a dark, inert mass: people who, if they were well behaved, would benefit from the civilizing effects of mechanization, commerce, and trousers.

IN 1893, THE FINCH HATTONS rented a villa in Sydenham, a prosperous residential district in the burgeoning London suburbs. Henry played golf at Mitcham while the children and Nan went to the pantomimes and flower displays at the Crystal Palace, Sir Joseph Paxton's iron-and-glass masterpiece that had been moved pane by pane from its original home in Hyde Park. Nan filled the house with books. The children read Mrs. Ewing's soldier story *Jackanapes*, the historical romances of Charlotte Yonge, and Kingsley's classic *The Water Babies*. While Topsy lingered over *Little Women*, the boys moved on to the manly novels of G. A. Henty (these appeared at the rate of three or four a year until the industrious author expired in 1902). Henty fostered the heroic ideal of the Briton dining in black tie in the Punjab or raising his hat to a compatriot in the murderous heat of the Nullarbor Plain, and the boys ate it up. Their appetite for the outdoor life was stimulated by a diet of *Treasure Island*, *The Swiss Family Robinson*, and *Around the World in Eighty Days*, as well as the sensational new *Jungle Book* and its sequel. After tea, the children sang songs in the parlor with their mother. Nan, a talented musician, was often at the piano with one of a succession of pet jerboas—furry rodents with large ears and long hind legs—listening on her shoulder. ("Oh," Nellie Terry wrote to her passionate admirer George Bernard Shaw in 1896 during a difficult period, "all the time I was just dying to go away to some quiet place—to you, or to hear some music from Nan Finch Hatton. . . .") All three children had inherited her musical ability, and there were frequent family concerts with guest appearances from Terry and Nan's other theatrical friends. Denys was surrounded by strong, artistic women in his childhood, and their influence persisted in his adult relations. The family revolved around Nan. Remembering the tensions of her own childhood, she was determined that her children should always know how much they were loved. "She was so unselfish," her desolate husband wrote after her death, "that everyone who knew her loved her dearly."

London had its attractions, but the hearts of the Finch Hattons remained in Lincolnshire. Between Priory tenancies everyone boarded the train and rattled up to Sleaford, where they were met by the Haverholme brougham and conveyed to the one home to which Denys felt a lifelong emotional attachment. A crenellated extravaganza with thirty bedrooms, the Priory was Victorian mock Gothic of the purest order, and hideous. Despite a row of delicate arches that lent the ground level an ecclesiastical aspect, the overall effect was warlike; there were slits through which teams of imaginary archers could aim their bows, and the pargeted chimneys jostled cowled shoulders against the watery fen sky. The house was surrounded by a low, balustraded stone wall that formed a rectangle, and the whole lot had been plonked in the middle of the flatlands like an overdesigned toy castle resting on a tea tray. But its poetry absorbed its absurdity. It was said locally that the Priory was the model for Chesney Wold in Dickens's *Bleak House*. It looked bleak, though it warmed up when you got within the low wall and considered it from close range. Then the texture of the stone and the scope of the architectural detail softened the façade. Inside, a touch of the monastery lingered. Even on the brightest days the rooms were dark, and the long corridors lined with marble busts of Roman emperors were positively stygian. The cold, high-ceilinged drawing room was silent save for the sound of great clocks all ticking together, and the interminable journey to the nursery, dimly lit by flickering oil lamps that brought suits of armor to life, was peopled in the children's imagination by a phantasmagoric cast of monks, knights, and fairies. Once in bed they listened for the resident ghost, a Gilbertine canoness whose footsteps could be heard on the path under the tower window.

For the children, the park was paradise. They played in the monks' burial ground and near the pigsties and among the watercress beds by the old river Slea. Wherever they went, it was windy. Cricket stumps had to be drilled deep, and blankets and rugs securely weighted by members of a familiar tribe of outdoor servants. Indoors, only the cook, Mrs. Rook, had equal status with the butler. A monumental square-jawed figure with the physique of a wrestler, Mrs. Rook was permanently swathed in acres of black and ruled her territory like a despot, tyrannizing her kitchen maids with booming orders that were underscored by the rumble of the massy brick furnace in the windowless Still Room, and by the orchestrated plumbing of the condenser.

Haverholme was not an obviously lovable estate. The Cistercian monks who had settled there in the twelfth century had not cared for it: too flat, damp, and marshy (*"locus vastae, solitudinis et horroris"*). But Denys responded deeply to the numinous light and the sense of space of the flatlands, and later tried to find those characteristics in other land-scapes. His love of Haverholme, rooted early, was nourished by images of egg hunting in the nests of ancient yews; of collecting mosquito larvae from the filmy surface of the water butt behind the grape house; of racing Toby on the towpath along the north bank of the Slea on their Sunbeam bicycles. Haverholme was the setting for all the significant rituals of their early years. In the South Hall, on Christmas Eve, village children gath-ered with their mothers to receive presents. The untroubled world of pre-ordained classes might have been tottering, but its traditions flourished. There was no sense of patronage on either side when, after the villagers had left, the servants crowded into the hall, each man with a capacious red-and-white-spotted handkerchief that he unrolled on a trestle table so juvenile Finch Hattons could set upon it a hunk of raw beef and a packet of raisins sprigged with holly. Church was an inalienable component of these feudal rituals. Winchilseas and Finch Hattons worshipped at the fourteenth-century St. Andrew's among relations entombed inside and out. They filed into their own pew, eyed by a congregation of tenants and employees, and during the Reverend Grayson's incomprehensible ser-mons the children watched the reticulated tracery of the stained glass cast patterns on the pocked flagstones of ancestral graves.

Like God, guns and animals were always part of their lives. Even be-fore he could walk, Denys was loaded into the dogcart with his brother and sister and taken to watch his father shooting at partridge or rabbits. On one occasion, they went to a tenants' shoot at Haverholme. Some guns were still muzzle-loaded despite the fact that breechloaders had appeared in 1865, and a ramrod was accidentally left inside one. A tenant, aiming at a hare put up between him and the cart, missed his target and peppered the cart with shot as the forgotten ramrod penetrated one side, whizzed between the children's legs, and emerged on the other side. "My God, man," spluttered Henry. "If you must kill my children, then pick one, but don't brown the lot." As far back as he could remember, Denys's spirits rose at the sight of the racks in the gun room and the powder horn that hung on a nail. On shooting mornings, he and Toby ran out to find keepers and beaters stamping their feet in the stable yard while the head keeper, Mr. Garrod, a Pickwickian figure with white sideburns, a bowler hat, and a velveteen coat, stood, legs wide, fastening the leads of three curly-haired retrievers to a strap attached to his waistcoat. The boys carried the cartridge bag and walked behind the line as it rustled through the September foliage, while keepers cracked partridge skulls with their teeth. By the time he was eleven, Denys was allowed to go out alone to shoot rabbits with a twelve-bore, and the satisfaction of watching them tumble head over heels was one that he recaptured on a larger and larger scale as an adult until he saw the whole picture and realized that the killing could not go on forever.

AT THE BEGINNING OF 1896, Toby and Denys went off to prep school, to warm them up for Eton, the royal establishment twenty miles west of London where generations of family males had been educated. Henry and Nan had settled on a place in Eastbourne, a prosperous resort on the Sussex coast sheltered from the prevailing southwesterlies by the bulk of Beachy Head (the benefits of sea air were heavily touted by the school's proprietors). Nan was distraught at the prospect of her chicks' departure. "Last day, last walk," she noted sadly in her diary the day before they left. "Everything seems hateful." At the end of her first visit, she concluded, "Horrid cold place. It was dismal leaving them."

Uncle Harold, meanwhile, remained a favorite with Denys. Despite his bachelor status, he was a dedicated family man, deeply involved in the affairs of his clan. It was he who stood up to Edith when she became un-reasonably histrionic, and he who took control of a wedding or a funeral when arrangements careered off the rails. He influenced everyone. Harold put a golf club into Denys's hand when he was still wearing a sailor suit, Harold taught him to stalk deer, and Harold, more than anyone, instilled in him a passion for field sports. The Avunculus Hector, as Denys called him, was a huntsman and a crack shot, and uncle and nephew often tramped together through Evedon Wood or rode to hounds side by side. But it was not just a sporting bond. Harold was his own man, and Denys admired the independent spirit. As a teenager, he often sat alongside his uncle in the red-walled dining room at White's Club in St. James's, breathing in the cigar smoke and languid, lordly grandeur while riffling through the gun section of the latest Army & Navy catalog. Harold em-braced the Establishment but refused to submit to convention for its own sake, a duality that impressed his nephew. Years later, a school friend re-membered Denys speaking frequently of "the 'Avunculus Hector' whose life excited him to emulation."

In 1885, Harold had written a book called *Advance Australia!*, an en-tertaining mixture of autobiography and imperial polemic. To celebrate publication, he had a silk coat of arms woven depicting the heraldic Finch Hatton griffin boxing with a kangaroo, and when the book went into a second edition the fact was added to the announcement of the author's boomerang prowess in *Who's Who*. At the same time, Harold had em-barked on a marathon attempt to win a seat in Parliament, and in 1895 he was finally elected Conservative Member for the Newark Division of Nottinghamshire. (It was the year after the octogenarian Gladstone re-tired, having seen his last efforts to force through home rule for Ireland defeated in the Lords.) Harold was an active parliamentarian. He kept a house in London at 110 Pall Mall East and went for a run around Hyde Park each morning before walking to the Palace of Westminster to join a debate. Although he was a Conservative in his bones, like all Finch Hat-tons, he was an independent one, and in 1898 resigned his seat in protest against policies that he felt were at odds with Conservative principles.

Through all the twists and turns of his career, Harold couldn't stay still for long. He was continually getting on and off trains to Lincolnshire or Kent, or, beginning in 1891, Harlech in Wales. He had inherited several hundred acres in North Wales from a distant relation. It was an unexpected acquisition but an intriguing one, and it was to shape the lives of everyone in the family for the next two decades.

WHERE ONE FINCH HATTON broke a trail, others followed, and by the end of the 1890s Henry and his young family were regular visitors to Harold's main Harlech property, Y Plas, or "the Big House," a gabled granite-and-shale building that was once a popular coaching inn. Wales was a foreign land to the children—the exotic double consonants of Welsh were unintelligible and the toponyms positively hieroglyphic. The servants were on first-name terms with sprites and elves that danced in pointy hats under a woodland moon, and the peaty hills behind the town were lively with Bronze Age cairn circles, standing stones, Neolithic burial chambers, holy wells, and other sacred sites. Denys loved the proximity of the sea, the washed dun colors of the hills, and the way the fields flecked with sheep glowed lime-green when the sun fell. To a child with his temperament, inured to the jaundiced fogs of London and the saturnine fens of Lincolnshire, the unruly Welsh landscape was an exhilarating release. For Denys, with adulthood still a distant land, a pattern of almost constant movement between opposing environments had already been established.

Harlech was a small town nestling in the lee of the Lleyn peninsula, the northern claw of the Welsh coast. Up in that isolated corner, the country's most rugged mountains slid off Caernarvonshire and sank into the Irish Sea. On a summer's day, it was a dreamy landscape of purple and cadmium hills and fleshy pink inlets streaked with blue. Above the town, the thirteenth-century castle erupted from the rock like a tooth, one of a ring of fortresses built by Edward I to keep the Welsh in order. Between Tremadog Bay and the castle, nearly a mile of reclaimed salt marsh sprouted with gorse, broom, buttercups, dog roses, mustard, and orchids, and at the coastal edge a dromedary line of forty-foot sand dunes fell away to a sandy beach. The low bosomy hills behind Harlech, spotted with gray stone farms, merged into the Rhinog Range and eventually collided with the outer rim of Snowdonia. One could walk there for fifteen miles without crossing a road or passing a farm. Agriculture was at subsistence level, and when Uncle Harold inherited the estates most Harlech men worked at the slate caverns of Blaenau Ffestiniog, a short distance inland. At its height, in the 1890s, the industry employed more than six thousand people. The gray-blue slate was loaded onto the wagons of the narrow-gauge Ffestiniog railway and carried to Porthmadog, where Western Ocean Yachts shipped it around the world. But in 1900 the North Wales Quarrymen's Union went on strike at Lord Penrhyn's mine at Bethesda. The miners were asking for fairer conditions. Lord Penrhyn refused to recognize the union, or to meet its representatives; he simply closed his quarry. It was one of the longest disputes in British industrial history, and it culminated, in 1903, in the surrender of the quarrymen. After three years of devastating hardship, several hundred strikers were blacklisted. The industry never recovered. A fresh source of income, however, had unexpectedly presented itself. In the last two decades of the nineteenth century, Harlech was discovered by the landed classes of both Wales and England, and by the time Harold appeared the town had developed into a fashionable resort. Besides the attractive setting, and the recreational activities offered by both mountains and sea, Harlech enjoyed a mild climate, warmed by the Gulf Stream and protected from the east winds by a curtain of hills. In addition, despite its remote position it was easy to reach; by 1890 Cambrian Railways ran a service to England every two hours, and twice on Sundays.

While practicing his boomerang technique on the salt marshes, the inventive Harold noted that the reclaimed turf under the castle would make an ideal golf links. He was a strong competitive golfer, and within a short time had laid out a course. Soon an aged gardener was employed as greenkeeper and given a scarlet tailcoat by a supporter who had recently retired from hunting. St. David's Golf Club opened in the rain on November 2, 1894, with Harold as its first president. The club quickly established itself as the premier links in Wales, a mecca for moneyed Edwardian aristocrats. But the scarlet-coated greenkeeper took to the bottle and was found recumbent on the course so often that a rule was instituted allowing a golfer to move a ball lying near him a club's length away—but not closer to the hole—without penalty.

Denys and his clan spent stretches of every winter in Wales. In December, the children waited with mounting anticipation for the day when the mechanical wax woman appeared in the window of Griffith Jones

Williams's shoe shop, maniacally whirring the feathers from a goose until her arms dropped in exhaustion and Williams wound her up again. In the spring, the whole family walked to the flat-fronted St. Tanwg's Church for the eleven o'clock Easter Sunday service, the only one in English. Other visitors drew up in broughams and landaus with uniformed postilions, and Welsh children sat on the wall opposite to watch ladies stepping out in their ostrich-feather hats, veils, and boas, vivid plumage among the indigenous grays and blacks. Summers were immensely sociable, with enormous beach picnics at which lords and ladies and their nubile progeny dined off hampers of boned chicken, whole hams, sherry cake, and fruit compotes. The bathing ritual involved voluminous green serge costumes donned within a caravan-like contraption, which a pair of nags towed out into the bay while troupes of minstrels strummed in the dunes or the town band belted out "Men of Harlech."

EARLY IN 1897, Uncle Murray, the twelfth earl, fell ill and was ordered by his doctor to the south of France. There were quiet hints within the family that the histrionic Edith was bad for his health. She was a hypochondriac, an affliction that had rubbed off on him, and neither could survive long without sickness. Murray had been badly affected by the debacle of the Great Horseless Carriage Company. He died at the Priory on an exceptionally hot September day just a month after the bankruptcy case and eleven years after succeeding his half brother. He was forty-seven. The title passed to Henry, Denys's father. Toby became Viscount Maidstone, Denys was an earl's son, and, to the postman's horror, there were now four countesses of Winchilsea.

The burden of family finances now transferred to Henry. In addition to the title, he had inherited eight thousand acres but no cash. Murray's will was proved at £16,000 gross, nil net, and there was still £24,500 due in respect of a mortgage on the Haverholme estate. The Priory had to be let again. This latest batch of Winchilseas remained in London. In 1897, they had left their rented house in Sydenham and bought a late-eighteenth-century town house in Kensington Square. Laid out around a rose garden in 1685, the square was among the oldest in the capital, and in recent decades residents had included Sir Edward Burne-Jones, William Makepeace Thackeray, and John Stuart Mill. No. 29, a five-story terraced house, was sandwiched between the worldly clamor of Kensington High Street and the pious quietude of the Convent of the Assumption. Soon after Henry and his family moved in, Queen Victoria celebrated her Diamond Jubilee. The country exploded with displays of patriotic joy, crowds surged through the streets, and the plane trees of Kensington Square were decked with bunting and illuminations. The greatest empire on earth was at its zenith, and everyone was glad—or almost everyone. "Imperialism in the air," the author and socialist reformer Beatrice Webb wrote in her diary that day. "All classes drunk with sightseeing and hysterical loyalty."

At about this time, the whole clan began to go on fishing holidays in northern Norway, where Granny Fanny's youngest brother had built a house and invested in a sawmill. (Later, Denys embarked on his first trading venture by exporting timber from the mill.) Sailing from either Hull or Newcastle, Winchilseas and Finch Hattons hopped up the Norwegian coast from Stavanger to Bergen and transshipped for Ålesund and Trondheim and on overland to the Rice house deep in fjord country. There men and boys fished for sea trout and everyone went on exploratory walks, joined by an amoebic mass of relations who seethed back and forth across the North Sea. Nan had by now had enough of Eastbourne, and on their return from Norway in 1897, in the same hot month that their father assumed the earldom, Denys and Toby started at a new school above the rolling Hampshire Downs. West Downs Preparatory School, outside Winchester, had been founded two years earlier by the headmaster, Lionel Helbert. Situated not far from the prison, the barracklike brick buildings caught the full force of the east winds. One mother said the school corridor was the only place where her hat had ever blown off indoors. The balding Helbert was a man of cadaverous aspect, with a vast domed forehead and sunken eyes. He was humane—still a novel concept in the educational field—and to those in his charge he was "a sympathetic, fatherly and boyish friend." Nan took to him, and to his school, just as she had taken against Eastbourne. When she enrolled Toby and Denys, West Downs had twenty-five pupils, ranging in age from eight to fourteen. Staff and boys walked arm in arm over the chalky downs, and in the dining room everyone squeezed together on benches as Cook loomed through the steam in the hatch, her bosom obscured by a menacing bulwark of spotted dick. The curriculum focused unblinkingly on the classics. Boys even had to ask if they might go to the lavatory in Latin ("Please, sir, may I go to *foricas?*"). Math was taught, but not science, which wasn't introduced to West Downs until 1964, four years after the launch of Britain's first nuclear submarine. On the *mens sana in corpore sano* principle, Helbert was obsessed with the health of his charges, leading them on runs—often at night—even in February and sometimes in the rain. A doctor visited every morning, gargling with an unidentified pink liquid was a daily requirement, and bowel movements were monitored, Matron stalking the dormitories before lights-out wielding a jeroboam of syrup of figs. But if a boy was properly ill Helbert sat with him all night.

In 1899, Toby went off to Eton. Denys followed a year later, but before leaving West Downs he was found to have a minor heart condition. Treatment involved physiotherapy and daily immersions in mineral salts at a London clinic. Whatever the condition was, it failed to impair his sporting record, but it never went away and in his adult life it was apparently aggravated by cold weather. Despite this, he was more robust than Toby, and at the age of twelve already taller. The pair were different in every way. Denys had inherited the Codrington panache, as well as his mother's finely tuned aesthetic sensibility. Toby, figuratively as well as literally the smaller of the two, was more of a stolid Winchilsea. Essex Gunning, a third cousin who spent much of her childhood at Harlech and Haverholme, reflected that "Toby had great charm but he could hurt! I never knew Denys to lose his temper, a word or a look was enough, unlike Toby who could be short tempered." Henry and Nan's brood were, in Essex's opinion, "a wonderful family, quite unlike anyone else." In particular, she savored Denys's sense of fun, and his gentleness. "He had such understanding and sympathy," she said. Essex recalled, too, Denys's "immense reserves of affection." Despite his charm and sociability, he could also be solitary, and often sought out quiet places, with the result that his cousin likened him to the cat in Kipling's *Just So* story: "The Dog was wild, and the Horse was wild, and the Pig was wild—as wild as wild could be—and they walked in the Wet Wild Woods by their wild lones. But the wildest of all the wild animals was the Cat. He walked by himself, and all places were alike to him."

The bronchitic Henry, his mustache advancing farther downward and gripping the point of his chin, sat in the Lords for the first time on August 3, 1899, eleven months after inheriting the title. He was a member for twenty-seven years, and never spoke. His political ideology was characteristic of his class: he was opposed to the change and reform promulgated by the Liberal enemy, and he had nothing to say that had not been said already. In Henry's worldview, the existing order was not to be troubled. At the time that he took his seat, the British Empire covered more than a quarter of the land surface of the earth. But at home the rising forces of democracy so distrusted by Lord Salisbury were becoming harder to ignore. The Independent Labour Party had been created in 1893. In 1899, the dockers went on strike again, action that led, eventually, to the organization of industry-based trade unions for unskilled workers. Henry viewed the world from an ultra-Conservative perspective, as Denys was to do, but whatever one's vantage point, there was something disquieting in the existing order. Independent-minded young men were to think increasingly of escape.

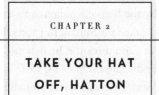

CHAPTER 2

TAKE YOUR HAT OFF, HATTON

Did the sun always shine at Eton in those days?
Or was it only that, when Denys was there,
it seemed to shine?

—*Eton College Chronicle*, MAY 2, 1931

THE DAMPLY UNPROMISING MONTH IN WHICH DENYS ARRIVED AT ETON
coincided with a period of intense chivalric patriotism. The school, like
the country, was transfixed by events in southern Africa. Five years earlier, the Jamestown Raid had fanned the enmity smoldering between the
Boers of the Transvaal and the British of Cape Colony. Britain was determined to win control of the gold and diamonds in the southern cone, and
in order to do so aimed to create a united South Africa under the Union
flag. The scramble for a slice of the African cake had almost reached its
conclusion, and this final victory, it was hoped, would ensure British preeminence.

When the Boer War began in 1899, the country swelled with elation.
Many boys at Eton were related to the men running the campaign, and
flags moved over classroom maps as masters tracked the fighting with
near-hysterical excitement. It brought Africa close. Then came the first
rumble of defeat (British forces were routed in three battles in a row), and
even doubt—that most un-Victorian of sentiments. An immobile army of
red-faced retired colonials began to snort over reports of British weakness. In April of 1900, even Henry wrote to *The Times,* ranting over the

military incompetence that had facilitated Boer successes. In response to the long guerrilla campaign, the British tactic was to herd women and children into concentration camps devised by the heroic Kitchener, an Irish-born military hero who had already vanquished the Sudan. But something akin to riots erupted in the schoolyard at Eton after the British military post at Ladysmith was finally relieved, and again on May 18, 1900, when the seven-month siege of the garrison at Mafeking was lifted. Not all boys were taken in. "Most of us know that Mafeking is a glorious pretext for a whole holiday and for throwing off all discipline," John Maynard Keynes wrote to his parents on May 19.

At the beginning of 1901, while the war thundered on, Denys found himself shivering on the grounds of Windsor Castle as the entire school lined the last leg of the route of Queen Victoria's funeral cortege. She had died on January 24. "So the blow has fallen," Aunt Edith wrote theatrically to her daughter Muriel, "and we are without her! The greatest Queen the world has ever known, and the most perfect woman the world has ever loved!" But the histrionic Edith was in touch with the mood of the country. The Queen occupied a central place in the national identity, and bells tolled up and down the land; Osbert Sitwell, who arrived at Eton the year Denys left, heard them in Scarborough. The loss, he said, "was something in which no man, born and brought up in that long reign, could altogether believe." At Windsor, bluejackets drew the coffin up the hill with ropes white with pipe clay, and the boys strained for a glimpse of the plumed helmet of Victoria's grandson the kaiser wobbling among the crowned heads.

Denys's housemaster, Herbert Tatham, was a benign and sympathetic figure. Gentle and adventurous at the same time, he had a solid face, deep-set eyes, and a drooping mustache that made him look like a good-natured walrus. He was a Cambridge classicist and, like many schoolmasters of his vintage, a mountaineer, flogging regularly up the foothills of the Eiger in stout boots and tweed knickerbockers.* On Sunday evenings the whole house gathered in the classroom, and in the glow of the fire Tatham read aloud stories he had written himself—tales of derring-do involving knap-sacks, wizards, and hunters, God always lurking in the background. Denys liked listening to stories, but in the classroom he showed interest

---

* Tatham fell to his death off an alp in 1909.

only in literature, history, and music, and even these he preferred to study on his own, rejecting anything that whiffed of institutional learning. He was already an enthusiastic reader, especially of poetry, and by the end of his school career was widely read in the major Romantic poets as well as the full classical battalion and had made inroads into the English nineteenth-century novels of the tombstone variety. He read what he wanted to read and neglected his homework, shaking off the consequences with the supple ease that was to be his trademark. Failing to produce an assignment one day, he diverted Tatham's attention by pretending to spot a mouse in the classroom. The housemaster joined in the hunt with a poker, upsetting a jug of water in the process. When he discovered the deception, he forgave everything in what one observer described as "a gust of Tathalmic laughter." It was brattishness by any other name, but it illustrated the reach of Denys's charm. Once released from the classroom, he wandered barefoot through Cloisters learning Bengali puns from the son of the maharaja of Cooch Behar, or languished at Little Brown's tea shop teasing Bunko, the Mistress Quickly of the High Street. His practical jokes were legendary, and his vendetta against Henrietta, a master's unshorn poodle, was endlessly reported over cutlets and apple charlotte. As for games, they were a cult, and the athlete a hero. The alliance between physical and moral courage that produced Muscular Christianity exemplified a classic manliness, and boys yearned to multiply the caps hanging from the corners of their sporting prints (each cap signified selection for a school team). Once won, the caps were worn with careless indifference, as it was important at Eton to hide feelings and disguise ambition. Denys was an outstanding athlete, captaining numerous teams and sauntering out onto the hallowed turf of Lord's for the annual Eton-Harrow cricket match. The grounds were pied with top hats and waistcoats, sisters paraded the light-blue Eton ribbons in their boaters, and mothers glided around in long white gowns and alarming floral millinery. Ritual rioting in front of the pavilion marked the end of the match.*

* The Winchilseas were proud of the role played by a distinguished ancestor in the making of English cricket. In 1787, the ninth earl, a generous sporting patron, had been the chief backer of Thomas Lord when he opened a private cricket ground on Dorset Fields in London's Marylebone. (Lord moved the ground to its third and present site in 1814.) Winchilsea had guaranteed Lord's investment, and without his support neither Lord's, arguably the most famous cricket ground in the world, nor the hallowed Marylebone Cricket Club would have come into existence.

—

AT THIRTEEN, DENYS wore his hair greased and parted over his left eye, a style that made his big ears look enormous. The pronounced dip in the middle of his top lip meant that the ends of his mouth appeared as if they were always about to turn up into a smile, and, like his mother, he had such a graceful way of moving that people said it was difficult not to look at him when he came into a room. Older boys indulged him, and, as he progressed through the school, younger ones worshipped him with unwavering devotion.

His most fervent admirer at Tatham's was a small lisping aesthete with a French accent and a huge fortune. Philip Sassoon was descended from Baghdadi Jews who had accumulated their wealth in India from the opium trade, and his family was in the vanguard of the social and cultural elite— an indication of the extent to which the old landed order was losing preeminence. Dark-skinned, heavy-lidded, and moonfaced, Philip had inherited from his French mother, a Rothschild, flawless taste and an attenuated sensibility. He was both fastidious and frenetic: someone once wrote that "he might have been strung on electric wires," and when a bad smell pervaded the drafty top floor of the house he tipped a bucket of eau de cologne over the linoleum. The other boys didn't like pansies, and without Denys's protection Sassoon would have been badly bullied. His gratitude veered toward the ludicrous. On one occasion, he visited a flu-ridden Denys bearing gifts of ruby shirt studs and diamond cuff links. On Sassoon's departure, Denys threw them into the unlit grate, only to think better of his gesture and recover the gems for Topsy. Although he jibbed at conspicuously vulgar opulence, he was naturally attracted to aesthetes and intellectuals and could see beyond the prejudices of the group. Sassoon, as it turned out, was no ordinary underdog.

Throughout his Eton career, Denys's closest friend was the dazzling Guy Buxton, the youngest of a tribe of gifted siblings referred to by a contemporary as "that family of fabulous good looks and charm." On school holidays, Denys often went to stay at Dunston, the Buxton estate on the river Tas in Norfolk. The redbrick faux-Elizabethan mansion had fifty bedrooms and two bathrooms, and was as cold and drafty as Haverholme. But once the fires roared, the rooms filled with cigar smoke, and the click of billiard balls ricocheted down the passages, everyone forgot about drafts. In summer, the grounds were ideal for hurling cricket balls, a competitive sport pursued by all junior Buxtons, including the one girl, the tomboy Rose, with whom Denys was to fall in love. Like all the great estates, Dunston was maintained by a fleet of servants bred never to reason why. A French boy once stayed at the same time as Denys, and, struck down with a migraine, he retired to his room. In the early evening, Mrs. Buxton sent a footman up to ask if he wanted a cup of tea. The boy had just returned from a long spell in Germany, and, half-asleep, replied drowsily, "*Nein*." The footman retired, only to reappear ten minutes later bearing a tray laid with nine cups of tea.

It was at Dunston that Denys first heard about British East Africa. Guy's eldest brother, Geoffrey, had emigrated there, and was farming one of the first plots in the Wanjohi Valley. On Geoffrey's visits home, Denys and the others listened in amazement as he described the Shangri-la he had found on the equator.

EAST AFRICA HAD NOT begun to interest foreign powers until the last phase of the Scramble, and then only because of the access it offered to the El Dorado of the Great Lakes. Livingstone, Speke, Stanley, and others had all reported the existence of fertile tracts of country around Lakes Victoria and Tanganyika; some enthusiasts even claimed there was a new India there for the taking. In 1895, after more than a decade of vacillation and failed initiatives, London mandarins declared the existence of the Protectorate of British East Africa, now Kenya.* Land to the west had already been designated the Protectorate of Uganda. For many years, both the British government and private entrepreneurs were far less interested in Kenya than they were in landlocked Uganda, as they indulged in the geopolitical fantasy that whoever controlled Uganda controlled the White Nile, the river that originates at Lake Victoria, joins the Blue Nile in the Sudan, and flows on to Egypt. Control of the Nile therefore meant control of the Suez Canal, the jugular of empire. But Uganda was so hard to

* British East Africa was not named Kenya until July 1920. To avoid confusion, however, from now on the territory will be referred to in these pages as Kenya.

reach. Every imperial filing cabinet had to be carried on a porter's head for three months from the coast, and every tusk the same distance back. This was why the British government decided to finance a five-hundred-mile rail link between Mombasa and Lake Victoria, a characteristic act of late-nineteenth-century bravura. It was such an extravagant and impractical scheme, fraught with so many engineering challenges, that *Punch* dubbed it the Lunatic Line. Thirty-two thousand Indians were shipped in to build it. They put up 35 viaducts and 120 bridges and culverts while fleeing man-eating lions and scooping scorpions from their tents by the bucketful. When indigenous people objected to what was happening to their land, they were shot. The Lunatic Line cost British taxpayers £5.5 million. (The total government expenditure for 1899 was £133 million.) The eastern segment of the track ran within fifty miles of German East Africa— territory to the south of Kenya that was to become Tanganyika and then Tanzania—a proximity that would have a profound influence on that little-known epic of guerrilla action, the Great War in East Africa.

Meanwhile, in the closing years of the nineteenth century, white men had been leading caravans through Kamba and Maasai country, establishing depots on the main trading routes. In 1893, the Reverend Stuart Watt, his wife, and their five children walked fifty miles through the Taru Desert to set up home at Fort Smith, the first brick fort on the continent. One of the children was a three-month-old baby. Like Geoffrey Buxton, the Watts marveled at the limitless pasturelands and the superb hunting. Life was not as hard as it was for the settlers beating the Canadian wilderness into submission, as there was no native labor in Canada. But it was hard enough, and there were problems with manpower, too. At Limuru, not far from Nairobi, a pair of pioneering brothers setting up a sawmill faced the challenge of shifting hundreds of tons of earth without mechanical assistance. They imported a consignment of wheelbarrows, but when they inspected the works they found laborers filling the barrows and carrying them to the dumping grounds on their heads. This was interpreted as behavior of unfathomable stupidity. But it illustrated the gulf between two ways of thinking.

BACK AT ETON, at the end of the first week of June 1902, Ronnie Knox, a brilliant boy who went on to become a famously elitist Catholic priest, was soaping himself in the bath when he heard a commotion below. Rushing down clasping a towel around his milky waist, he cried, "Is it peace?" It was. Someone hung a Boer flag from a window at Mr. Broadbent's house and seven panes of glass were smashed in the mêlée. But beyond the schoolroom the stories that had been emerging from Africa since the glories of Mafeking dampened the mood of the country. Twenty thousand women and children were among Boer casualties, many of them victims of the disease endemic in Kitchener's camps. Tens of thousands of British men had perished from cholera and enteric fever. The British had burned farms, starved families into submission, and destroyed the livelihood of entire communities as they followed orders to "sweep the veldt clean." Nobody even knew how many Africans had died. No war is heroic on the ground, but this one was less heroic than most. The teenage Denys, caught up in school celebrations, could not have foreseen that in the next war—one in which so many of his capering Eton peers would be killed— he would be commanded by one of the Boers now languishing in defeat.

A year later, the school itself was literally consumed by fresh tragedy. In the early hours of June 1, 1903, a fire broke out at Mr. Kindersley's house, a two-hundred-year-old structure of wood, lath, and plaster adjacent to the chapel. Most of the forty boys escaped through the windows of their rooms by climbing down the friendly wisteria. (Among them was Hugh Dalton, the future chancellor of the exchequer, who singed his hair.) But two boys had bars at their windows, and, as the others huddled in the courtyard below, they watched a pair of small white faces caged behind the glass. Kindersley climbed a ladder and struggled with a crowbar, but both boys burned to death. The head panted to the scene in a gray dressing gown and shortly after, standing in his private quarters, dictated a telegram to the boys' parents as tears slid down his cheeks: "Very grave news. Come at Once." One of the fathers traveled down from the north of Scotland, and when he changed trains in London he read the news in an evening paper.

BY THE TIME DENYS was sixteen, he exceeded six feet and weighed more than thirteen stone. Julian Huxley, who was to evolve into a distinguished biologist, was among his intellectual friends. According to him, Denys was "without doubt the handsomest boy in the school." His hair, no longer greased, rolled away from its parting in waves that broke over the tops of his ears. "I remember seeing him on my return from a before-breakfast Sunday run, standing on top of College Wall in a red silk dressing-gown—an unforgettable Antinous," Huxley wrote.* Another contemporary described him "in full sunshine crossing the street . . . with his peculiar, slouching, rolling gait, half gamin and half seraph. His hat is tilted back, forehead quizzically wrinkled, eyebrows raised, eyes dancing with amusement, and his queer, wide, flexible mouth curling at the corners in that enchanting smile!" Denys's vitality and restlessness pulled people to him like a centripetal force. Physically, he fitted the hero mold; in the last years of the Edwardian era, the time was ripe for unconventional heroes. In an age that was becoming increasingly mechanized, Denys's free spirit leaped out from the crowd like a flame. His admission to the Olympian heights of Pop was a foregone conclusion. Although the Eton Society (its proper name) was originally devoted to debating, by the start of the twentieth century it was simply a self-elected club of two dozen senior boys voted in on grounds of popularity, sporting prowess, elegance, vitality, and charm. Denys embodied the Pop ideal of wit, urbanity, and physical favor, and for his last two years he was elected president of this influential social oligarchy.

In this period, Denys consolidated his friendship with a group of fabled young men who came to represent the gilded, gifted best of the generation swallowed by the trenches. They formed, in retrospect, a magic circle that epitomized the values and rebellions of Edwardian society. One was Julian Grenfell, the son of an Olympic fencer who was raised to the peerage as Lord Desborough in Julian's penultimate year at Eton. Grenfell was a Byronic figure who rebelled against the socialite lifestyle of his mother, the beautiful Ettie, and wrote a book excoriating it. When she used her influence to prevent publication, he lay on a sofa for six months with a shotgun by his side. Another was Patrick Shaw Stewart, an odd, freckly creature with marmalade hair and a long nose who went on to have

---

* Antinous was a Greek servant boy who became a favorite lover of the emperor Hadrian. He was beautiful, intelligent, witty, a great hunter and athlete—just like Denys. But he drowned in the Nile before he was twenty. In his grief, Hadrian had him deified—a poor boy transfigured by love, and the last great god to emerge from the Roman Empire.

an affair with Grenfell's mother. At Eton he, Julian, and Denys were close to Lord Ribblesdale's son, Charles Lister. Tall and bony, with a pear-shaped face framed by curling molasses hair, Charles caused a sensation when he joined the Independent Labour Party while he was still at school. (His parents, mildly curious, consulted the prime minister about this aberrant behavior. Arthur Balfour, philosopher king of the glamorous and aristocratic Ribblesdale circle, calmly announced that it was preferable to keeping an actress.) Lister went on to organize a trade union among the shop assistants on High Street. But in general there was little social awareness. "Keir Hardie in his cloth cap was a joke," wrote Denys's contemporary L. E. Jones. Pupils were taught to feel sorry for the poor, and trooped in dutiful batches to the school Mission at Hackney Wick, "but it could never have entered our heads that some of the boys we met there might well, in our lifetime, be among her Majesty's Ministers." Despite the shift in labor relations and the debacle in South Africa, there was no tremor of the social earthquake to come. "We rode on the backs of the workers," Jones continued, "with the insouciance of the man who sat on the back of a whale, believing it to be an island."

Denys's peers were not the only ones who judged him someone special (although that was striking enough, since, as children, they were not an impressionable group and they lived lives of unimaginable privilege). The masters did, too, despite his unattractive adolescent stunts. This was unusual. Bertie Cranworth, who was an important friend to Denys in the African years, noted, "The headmaster used to . . . consult Denys on matters concerning the conduct and wellbeing of the school, and it is even a fact that during his last summer he [Denys] gave a supper party on a houseboat on the river, naturally contrary to every known rule, and that more than one master actually accepted and enjoyed his hospitality." The head asked him to stay on for an extra year in the hope that he would bring on the younger boys. Although it was customary for pupils to remain until their nineteenth birthday, permission to stay on much beyond that was rarely granted. But Denys was a special case. Twenty-five years later, when news reached England that he had been killed, an anonymous contributor wrote an obituary in the school magazine. "Denys was a great figure," it read, "not only to Masters and Boys, but to the Eton population at large, human and animal . . . Autocrat and democrat, an adored tyrant." Acknowledging his sporting excellence, the obituarist went on to note that "athletics were never his preoccupation or his ambition; they were taken in his stride: his real Eton life was in his friends, his mock antipathies, his laughter and his jokes, his catchwords ('Not a fool at all of course') and his escapades. And underneath it all, one always knew there was something fine and spacious. How else could he have dominated the school as few boys can ever have dominated it, before or since?" The piece concluded on a poignant note: "It is many years since we have had to do without him, and to think of him happily as going his gay and gallant way in wider and sunnier spaces than we can enjoy. And we must just go on thinking of him like that."

Overwhelming social success can have a deleterious effect on character. In Denys it promoted the sense, already present, that there was no need for effort. Others learned to disguise ambition at Eton. In Denys's case, Eton destroyed ambition. He did not leave until he was nineteen and a half. It was the only place he stayed too long.

IN MAY OF 1904, the Avunculus Hector dropped dead of heart failure on the doorstep of his Pall Mall house as he returned from his morning run around Hyde Park. He was forty-eight. The night before the funeral, Toby, Denys, and their father stayed with the bombazined Edith at the Cedars. "It is very nice having Henry and the boys till Thursday night, when they have to go back to Eton," she wrote to Muriel. "Denys is over 6 foot now and a wonderfully good looking boy. . . . I do hope they won't be spoilt—but it is bad for boys to be so good looking."

Uncle Harold left his entire estate—later valued at £18,998—to a settler's wife in Australia. Nobody in the family had ever heard of this woman. But she had predeceased him, as had his eldest brother, Murray, so Henry got it all—including the Harlech estate. The Winchilseas were already sharing the Plas with Harold: they had been visiting regularly for years, and in 1902 Henry had shifted the family permanently to Wales. Harold's death consolidated their position. The earl and the countess naturally adopted their usual feudal role. Nan took the children to visit the sick in candlelit cottages that smelled of onion resin and herb poultices. When they had tea on the back lawn and children peeped from the gardens of the narrow houses of Tryfar Terrace, she sent a footman over with a plate of cakes and fruit. The new countess was admired by the people of Harlech. Henry was considered austere, but he was a decent landlord, and that was the most important thing. As for the children, Toby and Denys became famous, singing comic duets at concerts and gallantly stepping in to read the lesson at St. Tanwg's when the vicar had a sore throat. But it was Denys who won all hearts. Elsie Williams, a young servant at the Plas, could still picture him in her eighties. Her mother had also been on the staff. "I remember Denys so well," Elsie said. "He was tall, extremely handsome, witty and affectionate. He was loved by all Harlech, especially the children, for he would always stop and talk to them. He used to come into the kitchen at the Plas to amuse the staff, often picking mother up into his arms and teasing her unmercifully." But it was not all cakes and tease. Welsh men who went to sea—and many did, working as crew on mer- chant schooners—were away for two or three years at a time, sometimes forever. Education for the poor was even worse here than it was in En- gland. Although Welsh was the first language, all teaching was conducted in English. Schools were overcrowded, not least because of the large size of many families. Two households in a village near Harlech had twenty- six children between them, and they all walked into school with a package of bread and dripping and a bottle of cold tea.

IN HARLECH, A DASHING young man named Ossie Williams hurtled into the Winchilsea orbit. Four years older than Denys, the dark-haired Ossie was tall, with full lips and eyes like blue gas jets. All junior Winchilseas adored him. Their parents were less impressed, as the Williamses were committed Liberals. Their seat, Deudraeth Castle (pronounced *Die-dreth*), occupied a wooded promontory that jutted out into the sands at Penrhyndeu- draeth.* To get to Harlech, nine miles away, it was necessary to cross the estuary on the railway bridge and follow the serpentine road up to the town—except at low tide, when one could walk across the sandy bottom of the Dwyryd. In 1901, Ossie started soldiering, and before he turned

---

* In 1933, the Williams family sold the rocky, romantic peninsula to a cousin, Clough Williams- Ellis. On it, he built Portmeirion, the celebrated Italianate village designed to prove that develop- ment of a naturally beautiful site need not lead to its defilement.

nineteen he had served in the South African war, returning to Harlech with a DSO (Distinguished Service Order) to thrill Topsy, Toby, and Denys with stories of bivvying on the veld. The three young men careered between the Plas and Deudraeth, surging with high spirits, shooting, skating, and staying the night wherever they ended up.

Twenty-two-year-old Topsy was not permitted to sleep away from home. (She was allowed to take her shoes off when prawning, but not her stockings.) Taller than the less-favored Toby, she had grown into a fine-featured woman with her mother's figure and a wistful expression, and she had Denys's cool temperament. The pair were close; both of Topsy's children recalled, many years later, the "special bond" that existed between them. As the tragedy of Topsy's life unfolded, she and Denys became closer still, and the tie drew him back from Africa. By 1903, Topsy's hair had gone up and her skirts had come down, but she had few companions in Harlech and spent many hours in her room at the top of the house with her dog, a smooth-haired white fox terrier called Billy. Her cousin Essex Gunning felt sorry for her and considered that she had a "rotten social life" in Wales. But in 1906 it emerged that Topsy had not been entirely left out after all, and the consequences precipitated a family crisis: she and Ossie had fallen in love. Henry disapproved of the match on political and social grounds, considering the Williamses to be middle-class Welsh country squires as well as Liberals. It was bad enough that in February the Liberals had swept to victory in the general election. Now they were infiltrating the family. This was agonizing for the shy, sensitive Topsy, but she would not give him up. There was something introspective about the Winchilseas, whereas Ossie and his clan were extrovert, and liberal in both senses of the word. According to Topsy's son, Michael, this was "a breath of fresh air" to his reserved mother. The year they became engaged, Ossie was obliged to retire from his regiment after a polo accident. He got a job in railway construction and spent several years in Chile and Bolivia. Topsy waited for him. At balls, she would hide under the table rather than dance with anyone else. Denys was her main source of support. When she got engaged, he sent her a book from school inscribed "There is no good in arguing with the inevitable. The only argument available with an East wind is to put on your overcoat."

—

DURING SCHOOL HOLIDAYS, Denys voyaged stealthily between Harlech, Haverholme, London, and, in August, the Scottish grouse moors. He liked the abrupt change of landscape and the contrasting rhythms of town and country. His restless spirit never tired of either. In the capital, he spent his time with school friends, among them the hospitable Philip Sassoon. The size of one of the larger department stores, the Sassoon residence at 25 Pall Mall featured cathedral-height ceilings, towering porcelain urns, and bowlegged French furniture topped with cupids. Everything seemed to be encrusted with gilt, and the sheeny surface of ten-foot oil portraits of assorted Sassoons quivered with the reflection of a forest of chandeliers. Besides such urban excitements, there was a constant flow of country-house parties—an essential sideshow in the Edwardian carnival. Denys would arrive to find a card inscribed with his name slotted into a little brass frame on a bedroom door, and before cocktails a water man brought kettles suspended from a wooden yoke balanced across his shoulders. At seven, a duchess "received," lit up with jewels and attended by liveried footmen in house colors, and later silver grape scissors did the rounds at the conclusion of a ten-course dinner while maids waited in the passages struggling to stay awake.

AT NINETEEN, DENYS thought that he could get away with anything. In the autumn of 1906, he sat for the Balliol scholarship at Oxford. Candidates were required to write an essay on what they would do if they were given a million pounds. Julian Huxley argued that he would buy up as much of the British coastline as possible for conservation purposes. Denys stated that he would pension off the older Balliol dons. Huxley got a scholarship; Denys didn't even get a place. It had always been assumed that he would go up to Oxford. His father, Uncle Murray, and the Avunculus Hector had matriculated at Balliol, all the dead earls were Oxford graduates, and Toby was prospering at Magdalen. Balliol was the obvious choice for a boy as brilliant as Denys: public schools still reckoned their status by the number of their Balliol scholars. But an unconventional streak had already emerged. Even at school, Denys wore eccentric clothes as an expression of nonconformism, in his final year favoring trousers made from a material in minuscule dogtooth check commonly used for sponge bags. Alan Parsons, who knew Denys intimately for three decades, reflected in 1931, "Even as a boy Denys was utterly different from other boys of his age. It was not merely a question of unconventional attire . . . but of unconventional outlook. I always thought that the twentieth century did not suit him." He was known especially for his headgear, an association that was cemented when he wore a sun hat of coarse beeswaxy straw into class and the master shouted, "Take your hat off, Hatton." But, however little Denys cared for Balliol, the truth was that Oxford was the nearest thing to Eton on offer. ("To pass from Eton to Oxford in October 1906 was a slight change," Denys's friend and contemporary Ronnie Knox wrote.) So, like many agreeable personalities who were lacking in ambition, Denys chose Brasenose, a placid college that topped the university golf table but failed to trouble its academic counterpart.

Founded in 1509, Brasenose took its name from a brazen (brass or bronze) door knocker in the shape of a nose. Denys was billeted on staircase nine in New Quad, which was still new then—the High Street frontage wasn't completed until the college's 1909 quatercentenary. Designed to reflect the asymmetry fashionable in the High Victorian era, the quadrangle, with its angled gate turret, was austere compared with the honey-colored Early Tudor Old Quad and the college gatehouse on Radcliffe Square. Denys's second-floor room overlooked the spire of St. Mary's, the university church, and, beyond the dome of the Radcliffe Camera, the dreaming Hawksmoor towers of All Souls. As the staircase was adjacent to the kitchens, in summer odors of cabbage and ham offered proleptic intimations of luncheon.

Denys started off reading law, but in his second year he switched to modern history, reckoning that there was no point in submitting to the tedium of the law reports since he was never going to practice. Nobody seemed to mind what he did. The college's attitude toward work was reflected in the fact that undergraduates weren't permitted to enter the library until 1897, the same year that heat and light made an appearance. A contemporary of Denys's has written of "the roomy, uncrowded years" when an Oxford college was like "a small Utopia"; but it has never been crowded at Brasenose. The college was less a bastion of scholarship than a sporting club in which young men in gray flannels and Harris green coats could loaf at leisure, and most rules could be broken as long as one knew whom to pay. The supremacy of sport was unchallenged, and within weeks of arrival Denys got his first half-blue, traveling up to the Royal Liverpool Golf Club at Hoylake to compete against Cambridge. Between the ages of seventeen and twenty-three, he played golf nearly every day. The counterbalancing demands of strength and intricacy appealed to his imagination, and so did the way the links glowed greenly as his whole body worked in anatomical harmony. He grew addicted to the grandeur that blossoms out of a well-lofted slice, the dizzy instants of whiz, hover, and fall, the clipped satisfaction of a bunker chip slashed in an arc of sand. Open space compelled him, and golf is a sport welded to landscape. At St. David's, his home course, he was in touch with the altered perspectives of the changing seasons. In spring, he could tell where the plovers' eggs nestled in the gorse. He knew the deepening rough of June, the patchy greens and thunderstorms of August, the wet October smell of foliage as the links ripened and the lower angle of the sun brought the contours of the fairway into fuller relief. Golf satisfied his restlessness in many ways, from the quiet concentration required to solve a problem alone in the long grass to the shared slow drama of the foursome and the camaraderie at the nineteenth. It was a sport that exploited sharp eyes and finely tuned coordination, the same gifts that later enabled Denys to save clients' lives on safari, and to kill Germans.

Denys was to play twice more in the Varsity match, and in his final year captained his team. At the Easter meeting of 1909, he also won the President's Cup at St. David's. (It was presented to him by the president—his father.) But despite his championship potential, golf, like everything else in his life, was never more than a game to Denys, and his attitude reflected his mysterious antipathy toward achievement. During one university match, a don among the spectators watched him concede a yard putt to his opponent. "Remember," snorted the don, "you are playing not for yourself but for your university." "Remember," flashed the reply, "that you are playing for neither." Denys was the apotheosis of the amateur. He was competitive only to a point, and too much winning would have been vulgar. At Oxford, he gave up cricket and soccer altogether. "He did not appear to take games seriously," Alan Parsons recalled. Many years later, Karen Blixen based the character Lincoln Forsner in her short story "The Dreamers" on Denys. "I had myself been fairly keen for competition as a boy," says Forsner as the dhow in which he is sailing tacks from Lamu to Zanzibar under a monsoon moon. "But even while I had been still at school had lost my sense of it, and . . . unless a thing was to my taste, I thought it silly to exert myself about it just because it happened to be to the taste of others." A report of Denys's football skills in the Eton magazine confirms the point, as well as inadvertently catching his character: "The Hon. Finch Hatton, when not charged, is apt to be careless. . . . When charged, he rises to the occasion and is very hard to get past."

Building on his Eton career as a romantic anarchist, Denys moved out of college toward the end of his first year. He had worked out that it would be easier to circumnavigate the rules governing hours, guests, and entertaining if he did not have to get past the porter in his gatehouse cubbyhole. Inquiries and emollients secured ample lodgings at 117 High Street, a terraced house directly behind Brasenose that was supervised by an unscrupulous landlord by the name of Goodall. Denys filled the bedrooms with friends and, as house scout, installed the aged Feltham, a servant he and Toby had taken over from their father. (Employed as Lord Winchilsea's butler, Feltham had been sacked after leading a shooting party to the wrong place.) A diligent, if unusual, scout, Feltham was the object of mirth at No. 117, and Philip Sassoon once referred to him with intriguing obscurity as "a tiara of hair and a mixture of Dr Nikola and Sherlock Holmes." (Dr. Nikola was a popular fictional archvillain.) During all-night gambling sessions, Feltham was on hand with supplies of champagne, caviar, and pâté de foie gras sandwiches, and on Sunday mornings he cleared up the debris while the young men slept it off, oblivious to the bells of St. Mary's and the dumpy horse omnibuses clattering down the High. Denys's circle of friends extended far beyond the "gown" sector of Oxford, and the house and its tuneless piano soon became famous for well-oiled gambling sessions. John Langley was a regular guest. A bookmaker and the mayor of the neighboring town of Marlow, Langley was popular with sporting undergraduates, as he allowed them to settle debts with non-cash payments such as fur coats. Denys, who was often short of cash, frequently availed himself of this service. The provenance of the furs remains unknown.

When Denys grew bored with gambling, he went off to the college chapel alone to play the organ, and when he grew bored with that he went roof climbing, an urban substitute for mountaineering. Under cover of darkness, he maneuvered his long feet around corner tiles to find an accommodating waterspout; glissaded down the pillars of the Ashmolean; and conquered the north face of Trinity clock, commemorating the achievement by setting the hands to a new time. He was invited to join the Phoenix, a Brasenose dining club founded in the 1780s (and credited now as the oldest Oxford dining club still in existence). Eight times a year, twelve Phoenix men and their guests quaffed vintage Pol Roger and expressed their joy by hurling crockery down the stairs.* But despite the reckless buccaneering, like Ronnie Knox, Denys felt that "Oxford was always a very poor second best" to Eton. He kept up with school friends spread throughout the university, crossing the cobbled courtyard of the Bodleian to Balliol staircases unchanged since his father's day to catch Julian Grenfell striding out with his black greyhound, Slogbottom. He dined with Ronnie Knox, and made fun of Charles Lister, who still had his shoulder to the socialist wheel, organizing an Anti-Sweating Exhibition to publicize the plight of industrial workers and marshaling the female staff of the university's Clarendon Press in a strike. Denys was bored by party politics. He had a naturally speculative mind, but it ran free, yoked only to the wings of imagination, and it could not be trammeled within the cage of theory. In preference to a night of debate at the Union, he went out drinking and fighting. "The only time I saw him rouse himself and that cynical smile leave his remarkably handsome face," noted Alan Parsons, ". . . was in a street fight in Abingdon. He set about his opponents for twenty minutes or so and enjoyed himself hugely, gigantic and triumphant." But his nonchalance concealed a state of mental alert. "Under a guise of laziness and even slovenliness," Parsons continued, "Finch Hatton never let his keen brain rest idle for a moment."

At the bookmakers or around the roulette table, Denys thrived on risk.

---

* They were still at it when the author was a Brasenose undergraduate, though the vintage Pol Roger had long since been glugged.

Inheriting the family gene that ruined his uncle George, he had begun betting at school, and quickly found that it took him to a place where reality was blotted out and adrenaline hijacked his functions. Besides danger, he craved the visceral thrill of winning and the challenge of outwitting his opponents. Naturally, he was keen to fill No. 117 with gambling partners. When, in the winter term of his final year, a vacancy came up, he wrote to John Craigie asking if he would like to fill it. Craigie, a bluff golfer three years Denys's junior who had kept a betting syndicate at Eton, was about to go up to Magdalen. "Denys was such a celebrity," Craigie recalled, "that Dr Herbert Warren, president of Magdalen, allowed me as a freshman to say yes to this, and forgo my first year in college." Craigie shared many of Denys's delinquent tendencies, but even he could not always keep up. He remembered one particular roulette session at No. 117 attended by the mayoral bookmaker John Langley, Count Felix Elston, whose real name was Prince Yusupov, and C. T. Chu, a convivial little man who liked to bruit about the observation that he was "the 52nd heir to the Chinese emperor." Craigie bailed out halfway through and was awakened the next morning by a gray-faced Feltham announcing, "It's 'arf past seven, sir, the ball is still rollin' and the Chinaman's lost two 'undred." In a single session, Denys had lost and retrieved his entire annual allowance of £300.

"In a long life, Denys has remained with me as an almost unique personality," Craigie recalled in old age. "Above all was the remarkable individuality with which he said and did things, including games . . . [in golf] even his swing was unique. He was generous to a degree and greathearted, popular, loyal and forthright. A non-sufferer of fools, he always amusingly chaffed them."

By the time Denys left Oxford, he was gambling so ferociously that he was poised over the abyss of self-indulgence—a Prince Hal fallen into the hands of his own Falstaff. But the risks were, over time, to grow exponentially. The terrestrial pleasures of gambling failed to hold Denys down. He took to the air, where the stakes were higher.

THE YEAR DENYS turned twenty, he fell in love with Catherine Bechet de Balan, a pretty young Frenchwoman a daring five years his senior. Known as both Kitty and Pussy, she spoke English and German without an accent and could hold her own in Spanish and Italian as well. At the age of sixteen, she had moved to London and lived with an aunt who was a friend of Nan's. Petite and fragile, her skin almost transparent, like a shrimp in sunlight, she had an exotic side, as did many of Denys's girlfriends, and once traveled around North Africa dressed up in the brocaded costume of a Moroccan beauty. Denys danced attendance when Pussy visited the Winchilseas in Harlech or stayed with Topsy at the family town house, and one summer he and she spent two months walking and fishing in Norway. But she was not his only girlfriend. Through Alan Parsons, he became close to Viola and Iris Tree, whom he met while he was at Eton. The girls were daughters of the actor-manager Herbert Beerbohm, who took the additional name of Tree. Although his half brother Max was more famous, Herbert was among the most influential figures in the theatrical world. He and his wife kept a fashionable house in London, and their three daughters—Viola, Iris, and Felicity—moved in the young aristocratic set that circled around the Ribblesdales, Asquiths, and Desboroughs. The asthmatic Parsons was an intimate member of this group, but he was poor (he was the son of a Surrey vicar), and when he began to court Viola her parents made their disapproval clear. When the pair became secretly engaged in 1908, Denys promised to be Alan's best man. But he was more interested in Iris.

Born the same year as Denys, Iris was a dogged bohemian; according to her biographer, "romance was the star she followed until the end of her days."* With red-gold hair and freckles, she described herself, not unreasonably, as *jolie-laide*. She studied at the Slade School of Fine Art and in 1913 was one of the first girls in England to appear with bobbed hair after snipping off her long plait on a train and leaving it on the seat. Voluptuous and outré, she puffed at a cigarette in a long holder, wore clunky amber and turquoise beads, and walked with a swagger. Epstein sculpted her, helmet-haired, and she wore dresses designed by members of the Bloomsbury group—Duncan Grant and Vanessa Bell even wrote asking her to be photographed in one of their garments. Iris stood out for her reluctance to conform, like Isadora Duncan and the sculptress Kathleen Bruce. She was

---

* John Julius Norwich counts Iris as "the only true bohemian I've ever met."

not especially intelligent or talented. She wrote bad poetry and later tried acting (she appeared as herself in Fellini's *La Dolce Vita*, reading verse). But she inspired enthusiasm. Iris had been invited to house parties at the Plas, and once Viola became close to Alan, Denys saw more of her. He preferred bohemian women to society beauties. She, according to one of her sons, "was a romantic, and from what I now know about Denys Finch Hatton I can imagine how easily his personality would have fitted her concept of a hero in that epoch." On warm June nights, he took the train to London and escorted Iris to the opera, where they heard Caruso from the back of the gods for five shillings, and afterward drank coffee behind the louche custard-yellow blinds of the Eiffel Tower on Soho's Percy Street.

"Denys has taken a season ticket to London and spends all the time on the train," Julian Grenfell reported to his mother in 1908. He was already finding the schoolboyish custodial regulations of Oxford too restrictive. Undergraduates were required to be at their billet before midnight, a rule that applied whether they lived in college or in digs. (The last train to arrive in Oxford from London in time to reach one's room by the deadline was known as the Flying Fornicator.) The punishment for a tardy return was a gating, a period of confinement within college grounds. It was a landlord's duty to submit a daily time sheet of his tenants' hours to their respective colleges. After a short round of negotiations, Goodall, the landlord at No. 117, agreed to falsify reports in return for a rent supplement of fifteen shillings a week "for matches." Denys was therefore able to return from the capital on the last train, known as the Post-Fornicator. Meanwhile, on Saturdays he and Iris went to Belvoir Castle, the ancestral home of the Duke of Rutland, for house parties at which a gong-beater with a waist-length white beard called guests to dinner along corridors still lit by candles, as both electricity and gas were considered vulgar (along with oranges and bananas, and oblong envelopes). Denys found it easy to seduce. He was not promiscuous, leaving instead, in many hearts, the tender pain of unfulfilled possibilities. His temperament was a devastating combination of the poetic and the classically masculine. "With his grand physique and his slow crooked smile, Denys was enormously attractive to women," Bertie Cranworth observed. "Indeed, nature had presented him with more gifts than were the fair share of one man." At about this time, however,

Denys developed a fixation about the one physical characteristic that pierced his self-confidence: he had gone almost completely bald. His scalp had never recovered from an experience at the hands of a trichologist after he and Toby shaved their heads before a Norwegian fishing holiday. When Denys's locks refused to grow back, his father sent him to a specialist, who applied ammonia. His schoolboy hat habit now became an obsession, and for the rest of his life he hated to be seen bareheaded.

IN THE WET SUMMER of 1902, after Lord Salisbury left Downing Street with victory over the Boers in his pocket, his languid nephew Arthur Balfour was the first prime minister to go to Buckingham Palace in a motorcar and to the House of Commons in a homburg hat. In 1905, the motor omnibus arrived in the capital, followed two years later by motorized taxicabs. The telephone was proliferating (a line was even installed at the Plas in 1909), electricity was showing promise, and, most significant, attitudes were altering. There was a freedom to breathe not enjoyed by the Victorians. Bertrand Russell was born in 1872. Contemplating the tone of the generation born in the eighties (as Denys was), he wrote, "It is surprising how great a change in mental climate those ten years had brought. We were still Victorian; they were Edwardian." But 1910, the year Denys went down from Oxford, turned out to be a traumatic one for the nation. The previous April, Lloyd George had introduced his People's Budget, the most radical in history. It specifically taxed land and unearned income, imposing, among other measures, duty on mineral royalties such as those reaped by the Winchilseas from quarries they owned in Northamptonshire. The budget aroused furious resentment in the whole of the landowning class, and after seven months of splenetic struggle it was thrown out by the Lords. An election was called, in which the Liberals clung to power with a greatly reduced majority. But even if the Liberals held the Commons, the Conservatives, if they felt threatened, could fall back on the veto power of the Conservative Lords, as they had done in 1893 to block Gladstone's bitterly disputatious Home Rule Bill. The Liberals were determined to destroy this absolute power, and in April 1910 the House of Commons approved legislation to remove the Lords' right to veto decisions of the lower house. The Conservatives were equally determined to preserve their last rampart of privilege. The Liberal government was still set on home rule for Ireland, so the idea was floated, in order to prevent the House of Lords from again exercising its veto, of creating a new batch of Liberal peers. Henry and his fellow Lords were faced with the prospect of losing either the veto or their majority in the House. Either spelled disaster for their class. In the middle of this maneuvering, Edward VII expired. "I am miserable that the king should have died," Denys's freckly contemporary Patrick Shaw Stewart wrote to their mutual friend Diana Manners. "He was my favourite institution. There will be no more fun now of any sort."

In the chambers of government it was open warfare, not fun. Throughout that summer, Parliament, and the establishment that supported it, focused on the constitutional crisis. The unpopular new king, George V, persuaded Asquith to fight another election before taking radical action. The fact was, however, that although Liberal fiscal reforms were draconian, they were a logical continuation of a process that had its roots in the Victorian age. The ground was shifting. The complexion of the House of Lords was changing, and, to a certain extent, so was that of the Conservative Party itself. Between 1886 and 1914, two hundred and forty-six new titles were granted, seventy of them in recognition of success in business or industry (several new Lords were brewers, and as a result the whole lot were known to the Old Guard as the beerage). The landed aristocracy in the House, and in power, was being watered down. On another front, there was a further assault on the status quo: in 1910 the Suffragettes entered their militant phase. It was time to leave.

In the spring of the same year, his work at Oxford done, Denys went up to Liverpool and called on Toby aboard the *Lusitania*, as he was about to sail to New York. Toby had been courting Margaretta Drexel, the daughter of Anthony J. Drexel, Jr., a Philadelphia-based financier from a family of distinguished money brokers and entrepreneurs. (The railroad magnate Jay Gould was Margaretta's great-grandfather on the maternal side.) The Drexels were Europhiles, maintaining residences in both Paris and London, and the courtship had proceeded smoothly, with transatlantic visits on both sides. Now the couple were officially engaged, and Toby was heading west for a round of prenuptial festivities. As for Henry, Ossie Williams would not do, but this match was all right; he approved of an injection of American cash into the depleted Winchilsea reserves. Marrying American money had been a popular solution to the problem of dwindling wealth for two decades, adumbrating the relationship between new American cash and the old world order; but this was a love match, of sorts at least, and Toby was no Gilbert Osmond.

As soon as they returned from America, Toby and Margaretta were married ("crowd and heat appalling," the groom noted in his diary). Ten bridesmaids carried Margaretta's brocade train up the aisle. The church, banked with lilies, was thronged with duchesses, ambassadors, and American plutocrats. But Denys had refused to be best man. He said, hurtfully, that he couldn't be bothered. But it was Topsy whom he didn't want to hurt. She had been denied a wedding and was still sitting it out alone.

In the month that Toby married, Denys learned that he had been awarded a fourth-class degree.* It was a spectacularly unheroic performance, but he could not have cared less. The prospects of formal employment bored him. All he could think about was getting away. "England is small, much too small," he told Cousin Essex. "I need space." Immediately after the wedding, he went to Wolverhampton to visit Cousin Muriel and her husband, Artie Paget. They were a pair of affable, unconventional golfers, and Denys was fond of them both. Artie had read chemistry at Oxford, later deploying his scientific expertise in his work as a patent lawyer. Denys had enjoyed following the progress of a motorcar with a push-pull steering column on which Artie had collaborated, and had watched from the window as Muriel was taken for a jerky tour in this innovative machine. Like everyone else in the family, the Pagets invested considerable energy into moving house as often as possible. They had recently come to rest at Old Fallings Hall, in Bushbury, north of Wolverhampton in the West Midlands. Using this early-Georgian brick manor as their headquarters, they followed the Edwardian season, traveling down to London for the choicest parties before departing again to India or the Sudan, where Artie would attempt to flog his latest invention to colonial governments and private companies. Now they had their sights set on South Africa. In 1901, Artie's sister Dorothy had married Herbert Gladstone, the youngest son of the late prime minister. After thirty years as an

---

* The Fourth ceased to exist in 1967.

MP, early in 1910 Gladstone had abruptly been created viscount and bundled off to South Africa as the first governor-general of the newly constituted Union. He and Dolly had sailed out on a lavender-hulled Union-Castle mail steamer and landed in Cape Town in May. Muriel and Artie were eager to visit, especially as a Paget brother was on Gladstone's staff and a sister was living in Johannesburg. Artie also hoped to interest South African railways in an exciting automatic buffer coupler. They were sailing in July.

Denys, meanwhile, had been mulling over escape routes. Africa was a natural choice. He was a willing outcast with a vagrant's heart, and sought a place where he would not have to conform. He had been brought up on stories of derring-do on the Dark Continent. To boys of his background, Africa was a stage on which Europeans enacted their fantasies or lived out the heroic ideal. Tatham had read out essays on Livingstone and Gordon and others who had slashed their way through malarial swamps or parleyed with Maasai chiefs in feathered headdresses. "What do we mean by a hero?" Tatham had begun his description of Gordon. While Denys could take or leave the idealization of Gordon as a symbol of Christian civilization, and was by temperament antipathetic to the conformism of the military, he warmed to the lack of restraint that characterized Africa— even to the savagery suggested by G. W. Joy's often-reproduced oil *General Gordon's Last Stand*. The pursuit of large animals had come tantalizingly alive through the exploits of big-game hunter Allan Quatermain, the protagonist of Rider Haggard's *King Solomon's Mines*, the first popular novel in English to be set in Africa. ("The thirst for the wilderness was on me," Quatermain proclaimed when he abandoned England.) More personally, there had been the talk of Kenya during days and nights with the Buxtons at Dunston.* Much of East Africa was undeveloped, as Queensland had been when Denys's father and the Avunculus had taken their chances. Africa represented the open space that he craved, both liter-

---

* Denys still went to drafty Dunston, but it had become a sad place. Guy had gone up to Trinity College, Cambridge, and at the end of the first summer term traveled up to Scotland as usual for a week of salmon fishing on Loch Shin with his father. One morning, with a fish on the line, the twenty-year-old Guy lost his balance and fell heavily into the shallows among the boulders. The gillie panicked and rushed along the bank to fetch Guy's father. When they got back, Guy was dead.

ally and metaphorically. He decided to go to South Africa with Muriel and Artie and spend a short time on the Cape before sailing back to Mombasa to take a look up-country.

THEN DENYS FELL IN LOVE with planes. When he turned up at Old Fallings, he found his cousins in the grip of aviation mania. Artie was chairman of the organizing committee for a flying meeting on Wolverhampton racecourse at the end of June. The dream of flight, so long cherished, was becoming a reality before the eyes of the young men of Denys's generation. The Wright brothers had been toiling in the back of their bicycle shop in Dayton, Ohio, learning from the pantomime-style efforts of nineteenth-century aeronauts, and in 1903 they fixed a small engine on the gossamer frame of a machine they called simply the Flyer. They hauled it out to the dunes of Kitty Hawk, North Carolina, and got it to stay up, with Orville in it, for twelve seconds. In August 1908, the unflappable Wilbur brought a flying machine to Le Mans. The following year, crash-prone Louis Blériot made the first crossing of the English Channel, and soon after, in Rheims, the first major international air show provoked public scenes of near-hysteria. Artie's event was trumpeted as the first all-British flying meeting. Aviators inveigled to Old Fallings included Claude Grahame-White, who in April had made the first London-to-Manchester flight in a biplane box kite, and Charles Rolls, who had just become the first person to fly both ways across the Channel without stopping.*

The weather was poor for almost the entire week. Even when the sheep had been removed, the Dunstall Park racecourse was too small, and it was inconveniently surrounded by trees. In addition, the lesser-known pilots refused to participate because of a dispute over their hotel bills. On the last day, when the principal prizes were on offer (categories for minor awards included one for "bomb-throwing"), the weather was so bad that Grahame-White did not even attempt to fly but, instead, drove his plane round and round the field, tooting and waving as he circled the crowd. After tea the clouds lifted and all the aviators went up, with the usual re-

---

* An aristocrat who descended to trade, Rolls had imported French cars into Britain before teaming up with the engineer F. H. Royce and forming a manufacturing company.

sults. By the end of the day, airplane fragments lay in all corners of the racecourse, though for once nobody was killed. Grahame-Wright won the £1,000 endurance prize, with a cumulative total of one hour and twenty-three minutes airborne. Captain Scott and his wife, the sculptress Kathleen Bruce, were among the spectator-guests. Scott was in the news, as he had just seen his ship, the *Terra Nova*, off on her journey south for his second expedition to the Antarctic. He and Kathleen were sailing to join the ship later. No passenger flights were scheduled, but Muriel persuaded Grahame-Wright to take her up. It was considered dangerous for women to fly, as their hats blew off and became entangled in the propeller. Artie, who was judging and knew nothing of Muriel's plan, was at the far end of the course inspecting a machine when he looked up and saw his wife's legs dangling from the front edge of the lower part of the biplane. Never to be outdone, Kathleen Bruce also went for a spin, gushing to reporters afterward, "It was simply splendid. The feeling as one sails smoothly through the air is most exhilarating. . . . I was not a bit nervous." The day ended with the consumption of a giant rum-filled cake in the shape of a plane, and a valedictory chorus from the tubas of the Wolverhampton Military Band. Ten days later, Rolls was dead; his plane crashed in an air show at Bournemouth. Denys had just turned twenty-three, and the three defining themes of his life had emerged: Africa, flying, and bohemian women.

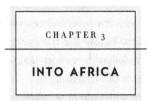

> London always seemed rather too small
> for Denys Finch Hatton.
>
> —*Evening Standard*, MAY 15, 1931

THE SHIP DOCKED AT CAPE TOWN IN DECEMBER 1910. IT WAS NINETY-FIVE degrees in the shade. Denys and the Pagets stayed with Governor-General Gladstone at his official residence, an old Dutch house in the forested shadow of Table Mountain. For the next three months, Denys practically lived outdoors. The gilded hostesses of the expatriate elite competed for his presence, but he avoided their cocktail parties. South Africa was too sophisticated. In early March of 1911, he said goodbye to Muriel and Artie and took a ship up the east coast to Kenya, still then the land of the pioneer.

As the ship crawled up the bony flank of eastern Africa, Denys was finally alone. He was anxious to get to Nairobi. Until Dar es Salaam, the trading posts on the coast were thin enough. But at the end of the second day of the voyage the scent of cloves and spices overlaid with shark meat floated from Zanzibar on warm southwesterlies. The shark, which had arrived by dhow from Arabia, had been deposited in vats to be salted before being reexported to the African mainland. The island had become the most prosperous port between Durban and the Suez Canal, and its sultan also claimed an impressive empire on the mainland. But in living memory Zanzibar had been a clearinghouse for slaves. Royal Navy vessels on anti-slave-trade patrol were once coaled and bunkered there by slaves, an appropriate image of the double standards often at work when the white man intervenes in Africa.

At Mombasa, passengers disembarked in a rowboat and entered a tin customs shed behind a line of bald baobabs. Below the fretworked balconies of close-packed coral-lime houses, rickshaw boys with teaky backs pulled carts teetering with the graying boards of dried kingfish. The hard red mud of the street was steaming. Women with gold nose studs squatted behind ziggurats of limes, guavas, and Zanzibar oranges; Arabs in flowing garments rode Muscat donkeys; and turbaned Somalis led camels toward a sun-bleached minaret. The low elephant grief of a ship's horn rose above the din of Kiswahili banter and, at dusk, when the sun set far off below the plains, on the walls of the Mombasa Club the cobalt hues of agama lizards died with the light.

Denys took the Uganda Mail train to Nairobi, the administrative center of the Protectorate and the focus of settler activity. Through the Rabai Hills the coaches jolted so violently that passengers with false teeth were advised to remove them in advance. At every fuel and water stop, Swahili vendors thrust baskets of bananas and gourds of gruel up through the glassless windows, and if someone wanted to stop between stations to shoot a photograph or a gazelle he had only to ask the driver. After the fertile coast, the train entered the Taru Desert, where extremities of climate had reduced the landscape to a vegetable equality. Regulars took out goggles as clouds of red dust billowed through the window openings, and when they looked out it did not seem so very long since slave caravans had trekked through on their death-laden journey from the Great Lakes. At dusk, a railman walked along the roof, opening a trapdoor over each carriage and lighting the oil lamps from above before the sun went down in its equatorial haste and velvety stillness enveloped the bush. At Voi, the darkened plains erupted in crazy conical peaks, unnaturally symmetrical volcanic extrusions that no one from Europe could ever imagine might exist on the earth. Denys was twenty-four years old, and his future turned to rock before his eyes.

The train stopped at Voi for first-class passengers to dine at a corrugated-iron dak bungalow. Like some magic box, the third-class carriages, with their wooden benches, disgorged more people than it seemed possible for them to contain. Families sat down around baskets of yams, while in the bungalow white-jacketed stewards served soup, boiled beef, mashed potatoes, and cabbage, followed by tinned fruit and custard, all embedded with a variety of winged insects. After brandy and cigars on the veranda a bell sounded, indicating that the train was ready, though only rookies swallowed their drinks in haste. The black air filled with sparks and embers, with the mating calls of the tree hyrax, and with the smell of Africa—dry, peppery, and deep.

At dawn, the foothills of Kilimanjaro flushed flamingo beyond fresh young grass stained with billowing cumulus. Rain had recently ended three years of drought, and the land was alive. Kudu cows in big-bellied panic careered across the Athi Plains while flocks of gilded green guinea fowl skittered into an acacia thicket. Buffalo, ostrich, a fugitive band of lyre-horned hartebeest—on the pottery-colored steppe the air still vibrated with the bark of a hundred thousand zebras. The Uganda Mail was "a railway through the Pleistocene," according to Teddy Roosevelt, who had ridden it two years before Denys. The air burned with the smell of wild sage as the engine curved through the acacias and puffs of cetacean steam leaped free of the branches to dissolve in the blue. The grasslands rose imperceptibly through the lambent heat. Then the train reached the marshy flats at the southern end of the Kikuyu uplands, one degree south of the equator, and for the first time Denys looked out at the grape-purple contours of the Ngong Hills.

In 1911, the year Denys arrived in Kenya, some Africans still had virtually no contact at all with whites—the elusive Dorobo, for example, said to be the country's oldest inhabitants. Like other diminutive hunters, the Dorobo, who haunted the forest fringes, were despised by taller tribes. They were the best trackers in East Africa and could skin a buffalo in five minutes. But the British administration was already in the process of imposing its baleful apparatus on the tribes by establishing departments and municipalities, and although among Africans the flight to the towns had not begun to any significant degree—there were hardly any towns— a growing number were living and working in quasi-feudal arrangements with white settlers, their working conditions appalling at best. Pastoral and primarily pastoral people like the Maasai, the Kipsigi, and the Nandi still remained outside the new system, but this did not mean that they were left alone. These three tribes practiced a traditional kind of grazing that meant that much of their land lay empty for long stretches. If Europeans built on it, as they increasingly did, they restricted the movement of men and herds. If fertile land was occupied, settlers expropriated it. Districts had already been set aside as "African areas," and a lengthy government report in 1909 had recommended a system of defined reserves to which Africans could be dispatched in order to keep them off more productive land. The Maasai had already been moved once en bloc, and within months of Denys's arrival they were to be shifted again. No wonder most Africans viewed their new "rulers" with a jaundiced eye. While the white man's medicine was still widely revered, few continued to believe in the kind of white magic that had spawned the belief, in the high noon of exploration, that some of the tin boxes unloaded at Mombasa contained spare, collapsible white men who could be shaken to life should extra authority be required.

Here was a vast and sultry land newly opened for the white man's profit. But Denys did not belong to any standard category of imperial pioneer. He did not share the mania for order and classification that had initially inspired Victorians to apply their prodigious energies to Africa. It was not commercial greed, either, that motivated him, or lust for power, or the impulse to "civilize" the African. He wanted only to carve a life out of open spaces and create sufficient personal freedom to live outside the frontiers of convention. He had capital to invest (though no information has survived as to how much), and on his initial visit planned to spend three weeks looking around with a view to acquiring land or a stake in a business—he had introductions from Geoffrey Buxton to help him, as well as a raft of school and family connections. If all went well, he would then return to England to tie up his affairs before sailing back to Kenya to settle.

IN NAIROBI, DENYS checked in to the Norfolk Hotel, an establishment to which neither Africans nor Indians were permitted entry. An imposing two-story building with a balcony that ran the length of the second floor, the Norfolk was the place where settlers congregated to exchange news, and sundowners on the terrace were de rigueur. Every train ferried in prospective new residents, many hoping to buy up what was now Crown land, especially in the highlands around the Aberdare Mountains. When Joss and Nellie Grant arrived in 1912, according to their daughter Elspeth Huxley, Joss bought a piece of land in the Norfolk bar from a man wearing an Old Etonian tie. The harvests that followed the drought had brought prosperity to Kenya, and the governor-general, the monocle-wearing French Canadian Percy Girouard, had successfully lobbied the authorities in London for funds to improve the infrastructure of Nairobi. Although the entire settlement was less than a decade old, blue gum trees had been laid out along the three main roads and there was an electricity supply that often worked. New arrivals found that most basic facilities were already in place—including a whorehouse known as the Japanese Legation, because its prostitutes were Japanese women who had come up from Zanzibar with the railway.

Of all the potential enemies queuing to sabotage immigrants, the sun was perceived as the most terrible. During the day, everyone buttoned on spine pads of quilted flannel, as it was believed that getting too close to the sun had a deleterious effect on the spine. Men wore cummerbunds under their revolvers to protect the spleen, an organ also at risk. People with metal-roofed houses at altitude wore hats indoors, as they thought the sun's rays penetrated iron. But the settlers did not indulge in sartorial pretensions for their own sake, and Kenya was not the brand of colonial outpost where dinner jackets were worn in the jungle. Even in Nairobi, it was not fashionable to be smart. This suited Denys, who usually looked as if he had just gotten out of bed. But he appreciated the company of his own kind. The Norfolk Hotel was known locally as the House of Lords, and the June 4 Old Etonian dinner was already a tradition in its high-ceilinged dining room, as it was in colonial hotels across India, where punkah wallahs fanned the old boys as they ladled on the custard—a substance that, like the empire itself, had advanced to the earth's farthest corners—and toasted the founder in claret that hadn't traveled as well as it should (a ritual more elaborately ridiculous than carrying a wheelbarrow on one's head). But in fact, although many aristocrats were attracted to Kenya in these early decades of immigration, they were not, among settlers, in the majority. Most new arrivals sweating up from the coast had little, if any, capital, and although earls and barons made news, far more settlers emerged from the middle classes. For them there was much hardship, and a crucifying reliance on the bank. When Henry Markham,* who moved to the Protectorate with his family in 1908, fell ill six years later, his farm was heavily mortgaged. He had an operation on his liver on the kitchen table and died, leaving his wife and sons with less than nothing.

When Denys first saw East Africa, scores of tribes and subtribes were still hunting and herding across the steppes and mountains, from the agricultural Bantu peoples of the Great Lakes to the tall and scarified cattlemen of the White Nile and the Congo Pygmies, who carried fire rather than made it. The land was trellised with their migration routes, both mythical and historical, and their past was rich with legends of lost cities and founding fathers who slid down to earth on the neck of a celestial giraffe. The majority were settled, including the most numerous, the Kikuyu, a central Bantu-speaking people who emerged as a single group in the fifteenth century and still lived in clusters of family-based villages, cleaving to many of the rituals of their ancient ways. Although most tribes in both Kenya and neighboring German East Africa had long before evolved some form of political superstructure over a kinship organization, and in some cases chiefs exacted tributes, there were no governments ruled by kings, as there were in southern Uganda. Governance in most cases lay in the hands of the heads of small clans, or of local councils composed of elders in an age-set system. But some tribes, such as the Hadza, secretive Bushmen who flitted around the crater highlands in the south firing arrows feathered with bustard vanes, had no chiefs or villages, and no concept of ownership. Hadza had little contact with other people, but most tribes had a hierarchical relationship with their neighbors. In the close papyrus marshes of the sudd—the dense, floating mass of vegetation that obstructs the White Nile—Nuer fought Dinka over cattle and land, and usually won; the Dinka took their revenge on the Bari, a small people who dwelled on the islands on the White Nile. But no tribe succeeded in intimidating the Maasai. For generations, they were invincible in East Africa.

According to their own mythology, the Maasai had migrated from an area north of Lake Turkana half a millennium earlier, reached the Ngong Hills in the seventeenth century, and continued south. Soon their land ex-

---

* No relation to Beryl.

tended hundreds of miles in every direction. They were not the murderous savages of legend, though that image had been heavily promoted by Arab traders in their bid to keep Europeans off their pitch. It was true, however, that young Maasai men in black ostrich plumes used to raid cattle from the lakes to the coast and were feared by Arab, Bantu, and European alike. But in the 1880s the Maasai were weakened by civil wars, and then by drought and disease. By 1900, they languished in decline, and clans of Samburu, the most northerly group of Maa-speakers, occupied swathes of their lands. Other tribes at a historical low point included the Kipsigi, the most numerous of the pastoral Kalenjin-speaking groups of the western highlands. Their less populous Nandi relations were the most formidable people on the western side of the Rift Valley at the turn of the century, raiding freely and attempting to fend off the white man. Bands of Rendille regularly fought Somalis over camels, on which both were reliant. A Cushitic-speaking Galla people from the eastern deserts, the Rendille, when they did not feel inclined to be disputatious, wandered the riverbeds of the Northern Frontier District chewing *mswaki* twigs and balancing on one leg, like herons.

Among these stood the mission African, the parody of the white man. Mission schools, of which there were forty in Kenya in 1911, were situated mainly on the coast. But secular colonists were already influencing the lives of coastal peoples more decisively than missionaries. The first large tribe to be deeply affected were the Giriama, cultivators who were compelled to pay tax to representatives of the Crown and send young men as laborers to government projects and plantations. Similarly, male Nyamwezi, who came from what was then central German East Africa, were working as porters for European farmers or pimply district officers straight out of Cambridge setting off to administer an area the size of England. A Nyamwezi could march with fifty pounds on his head as easily as with nothing, and his tribe, who had carried the chains of the slave caravans and the chop boxes of the first explorers, had naturally taken up the desks and ledgers of the next tribe of invaders.

EVERYONE AT THE NORFOLK was talking about the highlands, so, at the end of his first week, Denys returned to the railway station and set off through twenty-seven miles of juniper-wooded hills to the summit of the Kikuyu escarpment, the eastern wall of the Great Rift Valley, part of a 3,700-mile continental fault system that slashes Africa from Mozambique to the Red Sea (where it continues to northern Syria). Operating since ancient times as a natural frontier for both humans and animals, the Rift is Kenya's most outstanding topographical feature, a fold in the surface of the earth and a literal rift across the country, its escarpments dipping to a tawny floor of savanna teeming, then, with game. The Kenyan Rift varies in width, narrowing at Lake Elmenteita and flaring out again, like a skirt, at Lake Naivasha. Denys headed toward the thin middle section to stay with Lord Delamere, the most influential white man ever to settle in Kenya.

Hugh Cholmondeley, the third baron Delamere, always had the same meal for his tea: gazelle chops, blancmange, and tinned peaches consumed to the accompaniment of "All Aboard for Margate" on the windup gramophone. A gnomelike figure with red hair and a large nose, he was to become a firm friend of Denys's through the African years despite their differences. Besides his height and comic appearance, Delamere lacked Denys's charisma as well as his literary sensibility and musical gifts, but he could have taught Denys about ambition and achievement. Through focus, application, and monomania, he had kick-started East African agriculture.

Delamere had grown up on his family estate, Vale Royal in Cheshire, and acquired a taste for big-game hunting on a trip to Somaliland when he was twenty-one. In 1897, he trekked south from Somaliland and after a thousand miles on foot emerged on the northern levels of the Laikipia Plateau. There he looked out over the highlands—the fertile foothills, the temperate, cedar-forested slopes of the Aberdares, the rioting invasion of soundless life that followed the rains—and, after what he had been through, he thought he had found the promised land. He grew increasingly certain that the white man could develop these well-watered highlands, and it was a passionately held belief that determined the course of his life. Ever since he and his wife moved to Kenya in 1902, they had been experimenting with large-scale agriculture and battling to prove that white men could live permanently in the tropics (although they had left their infant son in Cheshire, just in case). Delamere had acquired land at Njoro, in the southwestern Rift—the equator ran through a corner of it, so he called it Equator Ranch—and sent voluminous orders home for stock and equipment. The difficulties facing the pioneering farmer, struggling to introduce British methods, were immense. The Maasai ewe was so shaggy that to the European eye it was not even recognizable as a sheep. Lambing, every white man knew, had to take place in spring: but when was spring? Horticulture was just as challenging, and, as most East African tribes were pastoral, nobody knew what might grow. When he got the idea of harnessing an abandoned railway steam engine to a plow, Delamere had to teach his workers how to use it. At least he had space on his side. When the plowhands asked how they should turn, he said, "Don't waste time turning. Just go straight on." Delamere worked through disasters and diseases (his own, and his animals'), and everything failed at first. In the inaugural lambing at Njoro, only six lambs survived from four thousand ewes. When he ran a herd of donkey mares with a zebra stallion in the belief that such a cross would be resistant even to the dreaded tsetse fly, and therefore make an ideal East African draft animal, one of only four foals was shot by a visiting hunter who thought he had discovered a new species. And yet Delamere persisted, a living symbol of the imperial belief that virtue belonged to the Briton who struggled to control his own environment. After further debacles with wheat, he negotiated more loans, brought a horticulturalist out to Njoro, and evolved the first successful East African wheat breed. When this was established, he moved forty miles down the Rift to Soysambu, where he had bought ten thousand waterless acres and established a stock farm—he was a herdsman at heart. He was already selling wool to London, and in 1910 formed a company that was to open a chain of butcher shops, importing machinery for the country's first cold store and bringing butchers over from England.

Delamere had already gone through well in excess of £80,000, though in his personal and domestic habits he was ascetic. He needed little sleep, often working from five one morning till two the next, and he had extraordinary stamina for one who suffered congenital poor health. When there was a labor shortage, he counted twenty-three thousand sheep by hand each week. He was also intimately involved in public affairs, and from the outset acted as the settlers' leader in their perennial disputes with the administrators, speaking with a distinctive hectoring confidence that invariably carried the day. Delamere was a looming and controversial presence in the small white community. He was inclined to Lear-like out-bursts of anger, though never with the Maasai, with whom he was as soft as butter. He laughed when they stole his cattle (Maasai, conveniently, be-lieved that all the cattle in the world belonged to them, the same feeling the Cheyenne in America had about horses), and had learned to speak several Maa dialects. Many Europeans indulged in a kind of romantic cult of Maasai adulation: the bravery of an enemy appealed to the element of chivalry bound up in the imperial ideal, and the athletic Maasai form re-minded a certain kind of settler of the classical hero. Others—all English-men—simply liked being despised. Yet there was no awareness of the complexities of tribal groupings, or of the multilayered threads of custom that bound Africans together in an elaborate sequence of delicate liga-tures, or of the intricate system of fines and penalties that covered every transgression big or small. Sir Charles Eliot, commissioner for the Protec-torate from 1900 to 1904 as well as a world authority on sea slugs, wrote that Europeans were not "destroying any old or interesting system but simply introducing order into blank, uninteresting, brutal barbarism."

Delamere and his wife, Florence, lived by the Mereroni River in Kikuyu rondavels, or thatched mud huts, and there was always space for travelers, especially those linked by the kinship of class. Early in the morning, cows woke the somnolent residents with hot gusts of fetid breath snorted through an opening. When the sun rose, skeins of flamin-gos returned from their nocturnal sortie and settled in a feathery clatter on the lakeshore. Herders clustered around fires in the greening mist, drink-ing a first gourd of hot milk laced with ginger. Later in the morning, gravid clouds tumbled ponderously in a never-ending procession, throw-ing shadows on the shoulder of the escarpment. Lake Elmenteita was too alkaline for fish, but it was all right for hippos, and their tuba voices or-chestrated the murmur of flamingos. In the bands of forest above the lake, behind gothic fronds, black rhinos lumbered from the salt licks like warm-blooded dinosaurs. When Denys arrived, rain had already cleansed the late-March air and a breeze wafted the smell of soda from the lake. The landscape had a numinous quality foreign to the Northern Hemisphere. Away from the sounds of the forest, out on a ridge, Denys, like Cortés, saw a new planet. The fears that traumatized twentieth-century England were not felt in Africa, and, looking out over the savanna of the Rift, he heard nothing but the stillness of the eternal beginning. Then the sun dipped below the escarpment and the flamingos took flight, and when the great digestive African darkness had swallowed everything up, Maasai smeared in sheep fat crouched by their fires and talked in low tones.

By the time he went home three weeks later, Denys had opened an account at the Nairobi branch of the Standard Bank of South Africa and, spurred on by his own private *Torschlusspanik,* committed himself to investments that included an interest in a chunk of bush in Dorobo and Nandi country, twenty-five miles north of the settlement on the Uasin Gishu Plateau. He had been in Kenya only a month, and he knew nothing about land. But he knew a lot about gambling and that, in effect, was what he was doing. At the beginning of April, the long rains in spate, he sailed home. As an acquaintance later wrote, "He had seen what men with imagination cannot help seeing in a dream country like Africa."

BACK IN ENGLAND, in the abnormally hot summer of 1911, Denys took his seat at Westminster Abbey for the coronation of George V. The ceremonies lasted a killing seven hours, every minute gilded in a mystic sheen of tradition. The abbey was banked with red tulips, white lilies, and blue delphiniums, and rows of ermined Lords, Indian princes in jeweled turbans, and scrubbed choristers in ruffled carmine soutanes watched the Prince of Wales kneel to offer his father allegiance under a gold canopy. Outside, the crowds in the streets stood ten-deep.

Toby had taken a job in the City selling stocks for a discount banking firm, a move that reflected the landed aristocrat's drift from patrician professions such as law, church, and army. His son, Christopher, was born on August 2, though his arrival did little to disrupt Toby's annual routine. He was obsessed with his car, an Italian Bianchi that featured in his diary more prominently than his offspring. Toby was a man of Solomonic deliberation—even as an undergraduate he had found fun an effort. When he appeared in a production staged by the university's dramatic society, he recorded after the first night, "Great success though personally bored to tears. Had to stand half an hour in an archway with a broken sword in tights." He was a rigorous socialite and rarely missed a ball, but he lacked Denys's glamour and spontaneity. He knew it, of course, but rather than resent his younger brother he nourished a painful devotion. Toby looked forward to Denys's return visits from Africa with what, for him, was fervid enthusiasm. That year, 1911, was the first of three consecutive summers that Denys spent in England, and on each occasion he alerted Toby of his ship's departure date, then wired from every port. Toby's diary reads like a countdown: Suez, Naples, Marseilles. . . . One year, he met every train from the continent at Charing Cross Station on a particular day, "hoping to find Denys's."

As adults, the brothers were emotionally close and mentally divided. An admirer of the visual arts, Denys cherished the old while embracing the new. Iconoclastic movements were springing up in every arena, from Sergey Diaghilev's Russian ballet to the theater of Shaw and Granville-Barker and the freestyle dance of the tunic-wearing Isadora Duncan. Denys had warmed to Roger Fry's groundbreaking exhibition "Manet and the Post-Impressionists" when it opened back in November 1908, despite the fact that the work was different from what had hitherto passed for art. The exhibition was, according to Virginia Woolf, a symbol of the way in which European ideas had invaded English conservatism. But the gap between conservatives and progressives was widening, not closing. Five years after Fry's show, Toby visited a second exhibition. "Went to see 'Post Impressionists'!!!!!?" was his only comment in his diary. Unlike his brother, Denys was equally at ease drinking port in the Tory stronghold of the Carlton as he was sipping hock-and-seltzer among the flashing mirrors and crimson velvet at the Café Royal.

In the December 1910 election, the second in eleven months, Liberals and Tories again came in neck and neck, and again the Liberals clung on. The following year was characterized by widespread social unrest, with almost a million workers involved in stoppages. More than fifty thousand armed troops were deployed to deal with riots; working men were shot dead; and in August, in the middle of the crisis caused by the arrival of the German gunboat *Panther* at Agadir in Morocco—a move Britain wrongly interpreted as evidence of German plans to establish a naval base on the Atlantic—four railway unions joined the seamen and dockers in the greatest transport strike the nation had ever seen. Nearing the end of his summer tour, Denys wondered if he was ever going to get out of the country. In the House of Commons, the Liberals had gotten as far as preparing the

Parliament Bill to abolish the power of the House of Lords, while their lordships themselves were still fighting to preserve the constitutional privileges of the aristocracy. In the first week of August, as Denys whirled around London arranging for the shipment of supplies to Africa, dancing at the Cavendish Hotel and dining off Gunter's suppers of langoustine and quail, the Lords perspired through passionate debates on the Parliament Bill. The vote took place the day Denys sailed from England. The government won, and the Parliament Bill became the Parliament Act. The next day the *Daily Mail* headline screamed THE FLOODGATES OF REVOLUTION ARE OPENED.

The revolution never came to pass, but the following summer the country was still churning with rebellion. Parliament was approaching a state of nervous breakdown over the question of home rule in Ireland. To imperialists like Henry, home rule was an abomination. There was talk of civil war. Denys was an outsider by nature; now events conspired to alienate him even from the familiarities of home. The suffragettes had that summer begun setting fire to the contents of mailboxes. The influence of their protests had seeped into the population at large, and pretty girls were no longer trussed up in fashions that thrust out their buttocks and breasts. London looked different in other ways, too. Motor taxis now outnumbered horsecabs, and the last horse-drawn bus had departed to the knacker's. Cinemas were springing up all over town, as movies continued to capture the public imagination. (During Denys's first three years in Kenya, the number of cinemas in London quadrupled.)

There were changes, too, on the domestic front. Topsy was married. Not only had there been no duchesses, ambassadors, or plutocrats this time; the Winchilseas had kept up their opposition to Ossie's Liberal antecedents, and they refused to attend the wedding. After a series of family summits failed, arrangements were made for Topsy's settlement, which was signed by her eldest brother one Monday morning. That afternoon, Toby gave her away. "Everything went very well, and Topsy looked very well," he wrote in his diary with characteristic élan. There was no reception, just a glacial honeymoon in Bude, Cornwall. Shortly afterward, the couple went to Vancouver, where Ossie worked as a ganger on the Canadian Pacific Railway.

In July of 1912, Alan Parsons married Viola Tree. Denys was best man, turning up at the church in an ancient shooting coat. The couple began their life together at what Viola called a "panelled slum" in Great Queen Street. Their finances were rickety and they ate spaghetti and parsnips, though at her father's insistence they soon moved to more salubrious premises on Welbeck Street, where they lived in "beautiful and happy chaos." The flighty Viola, who had gone into the family business, first as an actress then as an opera singer, was devoted to Denys. She named her firstborn after him, and he was honored by the role of godfather. Regulars at the semi-bohemian ménage included Charles Lister, now at the Foreign Office, Julian Grenfell and his brother Billy, Edward Horner, and Patrick Shaw Stewart, who had gone into the City and at twenty-five was the managing director of Baring Brothers. They all relished Denys's African stories. "He's such a tonic after all the dead-beats," wrote Julian Grenfell, who characteristically embellished his friend's exploits, reporting that Denys was based in a Nairobi palace, "entertaining the countryside on champagne and caviare." Grenfell planned to visit him in Kenya in the summer of 1914, but when the time came the war drums were beating and the trip was postponed—forever, as it turned out. In her old age, Viola looked back at "the Valhalla of Julian, Billy, Charles, Denys. . . ." It was already hard for them not to idealize the past. Denys himself was obsessively idealistic about Eton, returning to visit at every opportunity and once driving a girl over from a London party just to gaze at the school in the moonlight. It was part of a reluctance to grow up, and reflected a certain emotional immaturity. (His insistence on covering his baldness also bordered on the adolescent.) In later life, Denys had the gift of putting the past behind him, but Eton was the exception. When he was in England, it exerted a magnetic force. He remembered its simple joys even more clearly when mired in the conflicting demands of adulthood. Eton became a kind of Eden in his imagination, the setting of a golden period when he still had confidence in the future. Growing up was an expulsion. But his experience of a youthful paradise allowed him to believe in the African dream.

BETWEEN SUMMER SORTIES, meanwhile, Denys floundered on in Africa. He had pooled ideas and resources with John "Jack" Pixley, a Buckinghamshire friend who had followed him from school to Oxford ("another of those charmers," according to Elspeth Huxley). The pair sailed to and from Europe together between 1911 and 1913, plotting a range of business ventures that had little connection with the reality of East Africa. Vague ideas were aired about scouting for farmland or for mining opportunities: there had been much talk of minerals waiting to be discovered in Kenya. Like his father with his Australian goldmine, Cousin Artie with his railway couplers, and Uncle Murray with his horseless carriages, Denys was attracted to the get-rich-quick schemes that are native to the heart of the gambler.

On their first expedition, in the second half of 1911, Denys and Pixley trekked up to the Laikipia escarpment, seven thousand feet above sea level in the north of the Rift. The plateau there drops to a series of steplike foothills and the Lake Baringo basin, all of it drier than the central Rift, with fewer people and harsher colors. High up, the nights were bitter cold, and hyenas' eyes, red as embers, ringed the camp. In the morning, the two men dressed by lamplight and filled their pockets with cartridges. They walked through misty gulleys and up wooded hills, and when they climbed higher than the cedars they reached a belt of bamboos with feathery tops that met overhead and filtered the sunlight to a clear, pure green, like the windows of the great cathedrals. All white adventurers of the epoch engaged a team of boys,* and Denys and Pixley's crew now went off to barter with Kikuyu, returning with gourds of black honey crunchy with bee abdomens. This was the elemental life Denys sought. Steadily, as the little group journeyed south, his mind cast aside the clutter of Nairobi, of London, of four walls and all that went with them. At water holes he watched Maasai boys bleeding cattle. Twisting the head of a brindled bull to swell the jugular, a boy fired into the vein an arrow ringed with a small block of wood that prevented the tip from penetrating more than half an inch. When the boy plucked out the arrow, blood spurted into a calabash, and he closed the vein with his finger and thumb. Someone else would mix the blood with milk and cow's urine and let it ferment for a day until it was the consistency of soft cheese, and then it was eaten.

---

* *Boy* was used to refer to any African servant or porter. He was not necessarily young. The Swahili word *toto*, widely deployed in English, referred, on the other hand, to child servants.

In June 1911, the Colonial Office and its foot soldiers in Nairobi expelled the Maasai from their grazing for the second time in order to free up land for the settlers. Great bands of Maasai set out with 175,000 cattle and more than a million sheep, taking the names of hills, rivers, and plains with them, as toponyms embodied their past. From now on, the Maasai were doomed to live within fixed boundaries, and their system of pasture management based on unrestricted grazing was bound to break down. But they never rebelled. White historians have commented on the ease with which Kenya was subjugated, compared with the Congo and other territories on the continent. It is true that white heads did not bubble in pots, but in reality, the East African peoples were in no position to resist. They did not have the arms, the numbers, or the political will. The invaders, for their part, had no inkling of the cataclysm of social change they had unleashed. The imposition of random political boundaries, the destruction of the movement of the Maasai, the eradication of traditional agriculture—here were the roots of many tragedies of twenty-first-century Africa. In the middle of October, Denys and Pixley reached Uasin Gishu, a fabled plateau in the Rift initially settled by Boers, who hacked their way up the densely wooded slopes by lighting fires under their oxen's noses to make them continue. There was only one proper settlement on the plateau, and the land in which Denys had an interest lay to the north. Flax had been planted, and the brown cone-shaped stacks were already stretching out toward the Cherangani Dorobo Mountains. Denys remained there for several months. He visited the other farmers and learned to pour boiling water over black ants before they ate the puppies' eyes, to build sun shelters for pigs in the dry season, and to bait a leopard with a dead goat in a gun trap. When they skinned a leopard one morning, the pelt, according to one settler, "smelt of the sweat of a thousand jungle nights." Denys went porcupine hunting using spears. The beasts, a menace in the vegetable patches, would dash off at high speed and then suddenly go into reverse, causing the pursuer to tumble into a thicket of sharp quills. At lambing time, he sat with the others to eat fried sheep's tails for breakfast after heavy sessions at the Rat Pit, the "bar" at the back of the general store of the Uasin Gishu settlement, and when the short rains began in October the yards turned to liquid and water streamed down the metal walls of the cowsheds. When the rain stopped in the early evening, the sky was an immensity of unstained light, and the last trickles of water rounded into pearls on the sills.

On January 1, 1912, the cluster of buildings that made up the plateau settlement was officially named Eldoret. That same season, a branch of the Standard Bank opened on the main street. The safe, once unloaded from its wagon, was too heavy to move, so the bank was built around it. If customers arrived early they found the manager, Mr. Shaw, soaping himself in a hip bath behind the counter. There were now 250 farms on Uasin Gishu. The High Court was preparing to sit there, and a farmers' association had been formed; Denys was appointed to the committee charged with organizing its agricultural show. During the course of his first three years in Africa, he continued to buy up land. He acquired a substantial estate at Naivasha on which to ranch cattle and grow pyrethrum, a chrysanthemum flower used in the production of crop insecticide. At one stage, he was also considering cotton farming. But as a full-time occupation farming bored him, at least after the intellectual and physical novelty had worn off. Denys had never aspired to be a farmer in the Delamere mold; his restless spirit needed physical expression. He was still searching for something to give his life purpose, to engage his ample gifts and to make money. For a short period in his endless quest for another horse to back, he turned his attention to trading.

In 1912, Denys and Jack formed Finch Hatton and Pixley, Ltd., and bought up a chain of *dukas,* the small stores that sprouted all over Africa where the white man turned the earth. One was at Lemek, a high valley not far from the Loita Plains and Narok. All Kenyan townships began as a string of *dukas,* the shopkeepers almost exclusively Indian. Once a settlement had a dozen or more, a man would appear with a Singer sewing machine at which he would treadle furiously day and night, and another would set up as a tinsmith, hungry for cigarette and paraffin tins. But the stores more or less ran themselves, and Denys was still looking for other ways to earn money. With his father and the Avunculus in mind, he now joined the board of the newly formed East African Exploration Development and Mining Company, a consortium led by Fred Marquodt, a prospector who had discovered rubies in adjoining German East Africa. Rumors of coal were circulating at the Norfolk (none had yet been found in the Protectorate), and even of a diamond seam. The public was invited to buy shares in the company. But the venture flopped, and when Marquodt died, in May of 1913, the consortium expired with him.

Denys quickly lost interest in mining. He could not decide what he wanted to do; he had no vision or goal, no dream-fevered idea of an achievable destiny. Singled out as a star throughout his life, he had no compulsion to prove that he could do anything in particular—not until he was middle-aged, anyway. His comings and goings in Africa in his mid-twenties reflected his equivocating character. It was the approach of a dilettante. Unable to commit to anything, he carried nothing through to conclusion.

His friend Bertie Cranworth commented on his lack of ambition. Ten years Denys's senior, Cranworth was an impoverished peer who had settled in Kenya in 1907 and striven gamely to make a success of a variety of schemes from transport to newspaper publishing. Like most successful settlers, he had immense physical stamina and a resourceful imagination. Like Denys, he was averse to formality, but as a proud Old Etonian he enjoyed cracking a bottle to celebrate the fourth of June. Over the course of two decades, the pair were to spend many days and nights together—some of them in hostile circumstances—and Cranworth came to look on Denys with admiration and affection. "With his vast talents, he might doubtless have made a success of public life, but it just bored him," Cranworth wrote much later. "Once I remonstrated with him in later years on his apparent lack of ambition and the more than partial burial of his great talents, but he was quite unrepentant and pointed out that one had but one life and that he reckoned that few people had had more out of it than he had." Cranworth believed that had Denys lived longer he would "finally have yielded to pressure in this respect." I wonder. If Denys failed to achieve, it was not because he was ultimately weak. He loved to win—he hated being beaten at chess, for example—but all his talents were subsumed in seeming indifference. It was true that in middle age he told Karen Blixen that he had not lived up to expectations. But he did not mean the professional status of which Cranworth thought him so capable. It was a more ethereal sense of the lack of any spiritual code that would make sense of it all. When at last he did begin to discern a place for himself in the world, there was no time left.

—

WHATEVER HE WAS GOING to do, Denys needed a base in Nairobi. In May of 1913, he paid £4,000 for a house in the salubrious Parklands district. The vendor was the three-hundred-pound William Northrup McMillan (he did not use the William), a wealthy American of Canadian parentage who was knighted in 1918 for war services. He had a goatee, and those of his African employees who were able to grow goatees themselves immediately did so. Pixley shared the house, and it served as a staging post for numerous settlers and travelers. At that time, Nairobi was expanding exponentially. Fifty-nine motorcars and a hundred motor bicycles had been registered, a stock exchange was planned, and the first permanent doctor had opened consulting rooms. Roland Burkitt, a son of the vicar from County Wexford, believed that nervous exhaustion caused by the climate was responsible for almost every ailment. He therefore counseled maximum protection. Houses should be kept as shady as possible, people with blue eyes should wear dark glasses, and everything should be lined with red—a color that was believed to act as a barrier against solar rays. The seat of a hardworking settler's worn-out trousers often revealed its scarlet lining like a traffic light, and this, in Nairobi, was a badge of honor. As a medical practitioner, the doctor's record was patchy, and he was known as "Kill or Cure" Burkitt. But he and his spectral Goanese assistant, Assumption, were working against stiff odds. Malaria was endemic, plague often erupted in Nairobi, and smallpox, yaws, bilharzia, tick typhus, typhoid, and paratyphoid were all occupational hazards, as were anthrax, tetanus, amoebic and bacillary dysentery, and tropical ulcers. Many of the settlers' babies died, their lonely little graves choked with blackjack from the shores of Lake Victoria to the ports of the Indian Ocean.

Relations between the settlers and the administration were always poor. Settlers considered that officials sheltered behind a salary and pension prospects and did little to understand the risks faced by the pioneers. They also resented the fact that the only club in town was run by civil servants. The Nairobi Club had a bar and a large billiard room, the walls festooned with the usual array of horns and dented with the imprint of errant balls. It was ramshackle enough, and in what one of his business partners called "an unusual outburst of respectability," Berkeley Cole, a prominent farmer, announced that he was "sick of being treated like a pig and yearned for a club of a refined nature where you rang a bell and a drink was brought to you on a spotless tray." A backer came forward, a site was designated three miles from town, and architects, surveyors, and builders were imported. The result was a low, unobtrusive edifice with modest Doric columns at the entrance and a pinkish pebbledash finish, the interior designed around parquet floors, a peristyle that was initially not roofed, and a fleet of sofas with loose chintz covers. The Muthaiga Club was generally considered to be ahead of its time, as well as too far out of Nairobi, and at first membership was low, but a coterie of aristocrats—including Berkeley, Delamere, and Denys—remained enthusiastic. Although only fourteen of them sat down to the inaugural New Year's Eve dinner at the close of 1913, the event was staged *comme il faut*, with multiple courses prepared by a top chef shipped in from the Bombay Yacht Club and music played by the band of the King's African Rifles. Muthaiga had the best cellar in Africa, with a range of clarets from Châteaux Pauillac, Lafite, and Latour downward, and a shop selling Charbonnel and Walker chocolates and freshly baked croissants. Delamere was the first president, and over the years he and his cronies nurtured that peculiar sense of deliberate enclavity that marked out the colonial club from Bombay to Calgary. Muthaiga was Denys's home away from home in East Africa for two decades. Lounging in his characteristic slouchy pose on the terrace with its modern blue screens, surveying the tennis courts and the trailing bougainvillea, he found the companionship he needed after the solitary life of the bush. "The very best of company," said Cranworth, "he was the life and soul of any convivial gathering at which he was present."

The settlers were also suspicious of the administration's intentions toward Africans. In 1911, the year Denys arrived, a passionate editorial on "the economic conquest of Africa" in the *Leader* (effectively the settlers' mouthpiece) warned the governor of the perils of handing "natives" too much power. When Galbraith Cole, Berkeley's younger brother and, like him, a well-known settler, killed an African stock thief, he was acquitted of murder even though he admitted the crime. But outrage in England led to his deportation, and the other settlers didn't like it at all. It was, according to the *Leader*, "a sop to the negrophile Cerberus" at home. "I believe," Delamere thundered, "that even an isolated case of local injustice is better than interference by the central government in the liberties of a colony."

Berkeley Cole, the fourth son of the Earl of Enniskillen, had followed his brother Galbraith to East Africa in 1906 and established a cattle farm at Naro Moru (Black Stone), between Nyeri and Nanyuki on the lower slopes of the twin-nippled Mount Kenya. He was an energetic, forceful man who lived at Naro Moru with his African staff, sheep that roamed the dining room, and a Russian bearhound that ate off his plate. Berkeley was deeply involved in settlers' affairs and for five years sat as an elected member of the legislative council representing West Kenya. Like Delamere, his brother-in-law (Delamere married a Cole sister), he was a Maasai worshipper, and he also nurtured a profound admiration for the Somali people. He was never seen without his personal Somali servant, Jama, and he kept a Somali mistress in Nairobi. Denys, too, admired the stoic and sensitive Somalis and had acquired a servant of his own, the inscrutable Billea Issa, who accompanied him to war and on visits to England like a medieval retainer. Berkeley was to become Denys's closest friend in Kenya, and it was through him that Denys met another man who played an important role in his life. Arthur "Tich" Miles was a debonair farmer-settler in his early twenties, and in him Denys recognized his own brand of cheerful nonchalance, humor, and reckless adventuring. Tich's father had been a captain in the Eighteenth Hussars, but died under chloroform on his sofa while being operated on for piles. Although they were not related, both Tich and Berkeley were slight, with elongated Modigliani faces, Roman noses, and piercing eyes, and each wore a toothbrush mustache. Tich weighed barely seven stone (half Denys's size), but he was a powerhouse when it came to energy. Enthusiasm and detestation both foamed up in him like geysers. "Nature had endowed him with a physique about ten times too small for the great heart it sheltered," Cranworth wrote. Sir Edward Grigg, the governor of Kenya in the twenties, commented, "At all times, however bad, he saw life through a haze of knightly romance, and tackled every new physical trial that came his way like a fresh dragon to be met and slain." Tich and Denys once sang the whole of *Carmen* as toreadors, with a third man as the bull.

—

IN 1913, DENYS RETURNED to England for almost four months. His parents had sold the Harlech estate: the Plas, shops, cottages, farms—in all, 347 acres had come under the auctioneer's hammer. Like many landowners, the Winchilseas had reduced their holdings partly out of economic necessity and partly as a response to the long assault on "landlordism" most forcefully expressed and enacted by the Liberal chancellor of the exchequer David Lloyd George. (The Harlech area happened to be his home turf.) Many English proprietors got out of Wales both before and after the war, or at least pared down their estates. But in England Henry had clung to his eight thousand acres around Haverholme, for the time being at least, and now that he and Nan had moved back there Denys was able to shoot pigeons again in Evedon Wood and row down the unruffled Slea to fish for pike. Snails still stuck to the locks of the water buttercups; the red willows near the brickworks still flexed their long limbs over the pond; and late-blooming roses continued to rear from the pitted brick of the kitchen garden wall. The park came alive with the scents and colors of an English summer, and early in the morning mist hung like radiant gauzy fabric over the fens, draping the woods in diaphanous folds. Denys's earliest memories were imprinted on that flat landscape, and it embodied something deeply loved. But he had begun to see how small it was.

On the other side of the park, Aunt Edith was still ruling all she surveyed at the Cedars. For years, she had been obese. Then she met Dr. Valentine Knaggs, an advocate of a vegetarian diet that also eschewed sugar and salt. Edith threw herself into the regimen and was swiftly transformed, keeping the faith, and the diet, even after she discovered Knaggs gnawing mutton chops in the summerhouse. Now she drank stewed peas in tomato juice and took meals on the veranda even when it snowed. She kept up with the Season and was a fixture in the court and social columns of *The Times* as she powered around the country attending weddings, balls, and funerals. Toby and Margaretta, meanwhile, had rented a house near Byfleet, in Surrey, and on July 12 that year their daughter Daphne was born there. Denys found Toby fretting about money, as usual. The stock market was performing poorly, in response to the uncertain political climate. "Things very flat," Toby noted in his diary. "Russia being rather rude to Austria." But he had seen Nijinsky dance, and was so moved that he judged it "very good." Byfleet was conveniently close to Brooklands airfield, and while Denys was staying they all went to watch the French pilot Adolphe Pégoud loop the loop (or "fly upside down," as Toby put it—"wonderful") above a herd of butter-yellow Guernseys. That summer, Denys took to the air himself. He went up with Victor Barrington-Kennett, a huge athlete and joker from a military family and a friend from both Eton and Oxford. Over the years, Denys had enjoyed many days with Victor and his three brothers at the Barrington-Kennett London home in South Kensington. Victor had recently joined the Royal Flying Corps Special Reserves and learned to fly, and in August 1913 he took Denys to the airfield. The first time they went up their motor lights failed, but it was enough to keep Denys enthralled.

IN NOVEMBER 1913, DENYS set about his most ambitious scheme to date: a six-month odyssey to buy cattle from Italian Somaliland. Cattle were in permanent demand in the Protectorate, but only the richest settlers could ship in Australian or South African breeds: the rest were dependent on the bony Somali herds intermittently driven south by nomadic tribesmen. Few ranchers were prepared to hazard the journey themselves. Denys saw his chance. Galbraith Cole invested half the capital and would initially keep the cattle on his farm at Gilgil, near Lake Elmenteita. Denys was to go up himself with a small team of Africans and a mysterious colleague who called himself Baron Blanc. He planned to buy stock from the Somalis, who raised their herds in Jubaland, the northeastern corner of Kenya, and across Italian Somaliland. It was a nine-hundred-mile round-trip, and it was to be one of the greatest adventures of his life.

With Blanc, six African staff, and his Somali servant, Billea, Denys headed for the oceans of scrub and shale that began at Isiolo, the northernmost limit of the Protectorate's cultivable zone. The single *duka* where they bought final supplies smelled of frankincense and dust. Beyond it lay the whole Northern Frontier District—a blanched landscape of sandstorms and flies, of burning winds, narrow valleys, and settlements stunned by the sun. Everything was thinner and more enervating than in the fat grasslands to the south. Little was known of the NFD, despite the fact that it stretched hundreds of miles, up to the Sudan and Abyssinia (Ethiopia) to the north and across to Jubaland and Italian Somaliland to the east. It is still largely unsettled even now. Crisscrossed by ancient migration routes, it was an area infamous for lawlessness. That year, Abyssinian *shiftas* (bandits) had been raiding Rendille and Samburu herders, and a detachment of the King's African Rifles had been dispatched from Nairobi to restore order. Farther north, in British Somaliland, the dervish resistance to colonial occupation was in full spate under the leadership of Mohamed Abdullah, whom the British dismissed as the Mad Mullah. As the wind blew with its desert persistence, Denys and his crew headed past the tiny settlement of Archer's Post through pink hills and broad alkaline plains. Kapok plants with mauve and white flowers grew among the doum palms; the anthills, which had been red and brown, turned white (some were twenty-five feet high); and gradually the other colors, too, drained from the land. It was a journey of exotic exhilaration. In constant movement through the desert north, Denys found a resting place for the spirit.

They followed the wells east to Gurre country, where myrrh trees grew alongside stagnant pools, their bitter perfume infusing the air with gloom. Under the tyranny of the sun, the white men and the *totos* crossed the Juba River into Italian Somaliland, to straggling settlements where wild dogs loped, men sweltered and dozed, and remorseless flies described circles in the heavy air. Although the Italians administered the territory directly, and settlers cultivated bananas and sugarcane in the extreme south, there was little evidence of the civilizing Roman mission to the Somalis. In practice, the land still belonged to Abyssinian "Tigre" bandits and Somali tribes that included the Aulihan and Marehan, both subclans of the Ogaden—tall, silent men with large black eyes, dusty hair, and lean faces that expressed a certain tense readiness. They existed in a state of perpetual hunger, and blood feuds were handed down the generations like batons, forgotten origins honored in eviscerations. The self-reliance of the nomad resonated with Denys, as did the contempt for discipline and order. ("By Allah, I will not be a slave to the Government," the northern Aulihan headman and rebel Abdurrahman Mursaal said in 1917.) The Somalis were unyielding and flinty, like their wilderness. They considered themselves superior to the chunky men of the south.*

Somewhere in that desert, in some scorched and gritty temporary camp, Denys bought his angular, sand-colored cattle from a group of Aulihan. The bulls wore bells carved from desert acacia, and a quiet tinkling orchestrated the homeward march like a lonely percussionist marking time. They trekked for weeks and weeks, alone except for occasional herders, who leaned carelessly on their spears, ankles crossed in the stance of pastoralists from the Sudan to Maasailand. Sometimes Denys went on ahead with some of the boys, leaving Blanc to follow with the cattle. At night, the wind mounted into wild fits, ballooning the tents. Occasionally rain whipped down in short, sharp bursts, and when the torrent subsided and the shale cooked in steam, the herders' camels, even more bad-tempered than usual, showed their bladdered tongues. Denys was off the map, where he liked to be. Simple pleasures took on a heightened intensity: the smell of camel milk in a smoke-cleansed gourd, the thin yelling of Somali singing on five sad notes, the purple hieroglyphs of shadow on the sand below a thorn tree. When the evening breeze whistled in the ant-hollowed bulbs on the branches, the boys built a fence while the sentry tugged his cloak-blanket and fed the fire, a pinprick of light in the granular black. Later, the chalk-faced master emerged to sit by the fire and read the Bible. Denys had left his faith in the nursery, but unlike many of his generation he did not replace it with a guilty conscience. He accepted religion without belief and carried a Bible on all his trips, reveling in the sonorous poetry of the Old Testament. It appealed to his longing for the elemental, and, just as his spiritual self was alert to the intimations of Schubert, he found in the verses of Job or the Song of Solomon a kind of rhapsodic melancholy, an elegiac sense of autumnal transience that set all to rights. He knew chunks of the Bible by heart, and his Muslim companions were impressed by what they perceived to be piety. Few white men would have had the mental furniture to cope with the sparsity of desert life. But Denys recognized something in the wilderness that was more authentic than anything in the overengined material world. Some years later,

---

* During the Second World War, Somali troops resented being considered Africans at all, and demanded to be treated differently from the Bantu regiments.

the Irish soldier-writer Gerald Hanley lived in the Somali desert, similarly stripped down to what he could carry. Like Denys, he appreciated a life close to the bedrock of existence. Death was close, as every nomad knew; just as it was close under the thin crust of civilization that tried so hard to conceal it. "True solitude," Hanley wrote, "is when the most restless part of a human being, his longing to forget where he is, born on earth in order to die, comes to rest and listens in a kind of agreed peace."

GALBRAITH HAD BEEN loafing around the world since being deported, desperate to get back to his thirty-thousand-acre stock farm overlooking Lake Elmenteita in the highlands shouldering the Rift. At the beginning of August 1914, he was on a ship returning to Britain from South Africa, where he had been visiting one of his sisters. When news that war had broken out was signaled to the ship, the captain turned it around and proceeded back to the Cape. Spotting his chance, Galbraith chartered a dhow and smuggled himself back into Kenya during the confusion of the first days of war, hoping that he would be able to serve. He got himself undetected up to Naro Moru, his brother's farm on Mount Kenya, and there was joined by a weathered Denys, nearing the end of his trading trip. He had left the cattle in quarantine at Rumuruti, on the Laikipia Plateau. Now he set off with Galbraith to collect them, and after a week's delay to comply with quarantine regulations they drove the herd south to Gilgil, Galbraith traveling under a pseudonym. It was a joyful safari, despite the looming presence of war.

Known in the family as Bim, Galbraith was reputed to be the finest stockman in the country. He was an acerbic figure with lively intellectual interests. "I have never in my life had to deal with so strong a character," one of his English farm managers wrote. "He reminds me of those stately gentlemen we used to read about in *Westward Ho!*" He behaved "like a vicious highbred horse or some fucking aristocratic snake," flooring recalcitrant Africans with a punch in the face if he wasn't actually killing them. According to the manager, he was hard as flint and cold as ice, "but by Jove he has a brain and one can say anything to him, and he will switch his brain on to it and ferret it out. He has more intelligence than anyone else in East Africa and more distinction of mind." Galbraith was not confident in company, and said that when he met new people he felt as though he had an ostrich egg in his throat. Notwithstanding his brutality, he had a streak of sensitivity, a characteristic that appealed to Denys. Both men, according to observers, were unsuited to the age in which they lived. Cole's obituary in *The Times* concluded, "It seemed that Galbraith Cole belonged by rightful heritage to a different age than ours. His haughty, dangerous nature would perhaps have been more suited to the 'spacious days' of Queen Elizabeth. . . . His aristocratic nature held the secret of a singular grace. . . . He was as unregenerate as a hawk or leopard, and combined with his wilfulness a winning delicacy that was impossible to withstand."

It took seven days to get the cattle down to the farm. "You will imagine the immense pleasure it was for me to see Gilgil again," Galbraith wrote to a friend. As for Denys, he had brought off a great coup, and his adventure was the talk of Nairobi. At last he had begun to use his gifts, and it seemed that he was finally getting somewhere in his attempts to establish a life in Africa. Later, he told Cranworth that he had never enjoyed six months more.

Finch Hatton could best be likened to a sinuous-
limbed dog-puma indolently sunning himself under
the swaying palm trees of the Amazon till such a
time as vigorous action is imperative.

—LLEWELYN POWYS,
Black Laughter, 1925

WHEN BRITAIN DECLARED WAR ON THE CENTRAL POWERS, THE SET-
tlers were immediately involved because Kenya and German East Africa
shared a long border. Once news spread, white men poured into Nairobi
from the farms to look for the war. They came on foot, on horseback, by
train, or in ox wagons, dressed in torn shorts and pith helmets and brandishing elephant guns, revolvers, and bamboo canes with knives strapped
to one end and pennants to the other. But the lights that were going out in
Europe had not yet been lit in Africa, and there was no War Office machine to churn out uniforms and instructions. "Men are requested to parade in whatever kit they possess," the *Leader* advised. Some settlers
voiced the opinion that the real fighting was going on in Europe and that
they should be there. "This is their country!" thundered Galbraith, paw-
ing the ground up at Gilgil. "Supposing everyone went home. . . ." The
existing military force in Kenya consisted of three battalions of the King's
African Rifles (KAR) and two machine guns, one of which was broken.
Colonial defense policy was geared primarily to the suppression of native

uprisings, not to attack by contiguous Europeans. The heterogeneous new force included Swedes, Australians, and Swiss settlers; a Turk also signed up, until it was discovered that Turkey was on the other side. Many had long licked their lips over the fertile plains of German East Africa—land that was obviously too good for the Germans. "Yes!" Galbraith had confirmed when traveling there before the war. "The Squareheads have entirely spoilt Kilimanjaro, so much so that the disgusted visitor almost sees it cubiform in shape."*

On August 5, martial law was declared throughout the Protectorate. Imaginary enemy aircraft were sighted, and in many cases shot at. "There is not the slightest doubt in my mind that an aeroplane was manoeuvring in the vicinity of the KAR lines on Sunday evening," one man wrote feverishly to the *Leader* on August 15. In reality, the East African Luftwaffe consisted of one biplane that had been sent out for an exhibition in Dar es Salaam before the war and crashed on its first flight. Reports of unmarked ships circulated in Mombasa. "Neither I nor anyone else who lived through them will ever forget the first days of August 1914," one settler wrote twenty years later.

GERMAN EAST AFRICA was larger than France and Germany combined (as well as what is now Tanzania, it included the regions of Urundi, later Burundi, and Rwanda). It shared a border with six countries, all of them hostile to Germany except Portuguese East Africa (now Mozambique), and when Portugal joined the war in 1916 it, too, sided with the Allies. The aim of the Allied campaign was to overpower enemy forces and occupy their colony. The Germans had a vast territory to defend on many fronts and over terrain ranging from deserts and volcanoes to river deltas and fertile uplands where colonists grew coffee. There were hardly any roads or maps, but there was enough "ready cover to conceal all the armies of the world," according to one officer. Active operations were impossible during the long rains between April and June and the short ones between

* Queen Victoria allegedly gave the flat-topped Kilimanjaro to her grandson the kaiser as a birthday present, as he had no snowcapped mountains in all German East Africa, whereas she, in Kenya and Uganda, had some to spare. Cartographers had only to draw a kink in the frontier, and Kilimanjaro was German. Like many good stories, this one is probably apocryphal.

October and December, and, in between, troops were dependent on water holes that often ran dry. Few commanders in the history of warfare could have maintained an effective fighting force under those circumstances. But the army of Wilhelmine Germany had its man. When war was declared, the *Schütztruppe* ("Protective Force") was under the command of a one-eyed Pomeranian lieutenant colonel named Paul von Lettow-Vorbeck. The son of a general, he had attended the best military schools and had served during the Boxer Rebellion in China and the Herrero revolt in German South-West Africa (now Namibia). Spare and square-shouldered, with short bristly hair, he was forty-four at the outbreak, an intelligent and urbane man who, according to Karen Blixen, who met him on the ship to Dar in 1913, gave "a strong impression of what Imperial Germany was and stood for." His troops at first consisted of two-hundred-odd Europeans and twenty-five hundred Africans armed with obsolete pattern rifles firing cartridges that exploded in a cumulonimbus of black powder. But von Lettow was an outstanding soldier—tactically innovative, adaptable, imaginative—and when he surrendered after the armistice the commanders who had fought against him wanted to shake his hand.

AT THE AGE OF twenty-seven, Denys had just begun to use his gifts in a meaningful way. There were signs that a more mature figure was emerging from the eternal schoolboy. But the war tore him up by the roots, as it did so many. He viewed the prospects now stretching ahead with gloomy skepticism. Denys considered men in uniform "not human beings," and he had no interest in the concepts of service and sacrifice that were vital components of the imperial idea. His friend and fellow settler Cranworth, who was to serve alongside him, remembered that he "made no secret of the fact that warfare bored him to distraction." However, while he didn't thank God for giving him the chance to fight, like his contemporary Rupert Brooke, Denys threw himself into what he called "sodjering." War presented itself as an extension of Eton, or as a sport against which to pit one's wits. ("I can remember thinking that we were the home team and the Austrians were the visiting team," Ernest Hemingway wrote about driving a Red Cross ambulance in Europe in 1918.)

At the end of August, Denys hurried back to Nairobi, leaving the cattle at Gilgil with the fulminating Galbraith. He had decided to join an auxiliary unit of a hundred untrained Somalis that Berkeley Cole was raising in the Punjab tradition; its proposed semi-independence appealed to him. Once a captain in the Ninth Lancers, Berkeley was a natural leader, and when the Somalis marched into Nairobi to volunteer he judged that they would make able bush soldiers. He and Denys were joined by Tich Miles and two other white officers, and the five of them set about procuring mules—all the racehorses were already spoken for. Many semi-autonomous units sprang out of the crowds of eager settlers eddying around the yard of the makeshift Nairobi recruiting station, among them Arnoldi's Scouts, Monica's Own (after the governor's daughter), and Bowker's Horse, though the latter was renamed Bowker's Foot after the Germans rustled its horses.

Berkeley's unit was sent to patrol Kenya's most vulnerable target, a 150-mile section of railway close to the frontier in the Kilimanjaro region. Small parties of Germans were already making bombing raids, and within a fortnight von Lettow had captured Taveta, a strategically crucial British border post. While invading German soldiers set Belgium alight in the Northern Hemisphere, their colleagues hoisted the imperial flag on British soil in Africa. Meanwhile Berkeley, Denys, and the Somalis marched between the railway and the border northwest of Taveta, fending off more raids and preventing the Germans from advancing. It was a unique and curiously compelling landscape, the plains on the German side broken by isolated hills that seemed to leap from the earth out of nowhere, as if a couple of unimportant tectonic plates had collided at high speed. Where there were tracks, they were through nine-foot-high elephant grass or nine-inch-deep sand. But the Somalis turned out to be brilliant trackers, as Berkeley had surmised. They also loved drill and ceremonial, and in action they went wild. "Once they began to shoot, their eyes lit up and they became almost unrestrainable," Cranworth noted with trepidation. Dust got into everything, including guns and food, and once the short rains began in November the ground liquefied. Night reliably left the men marooned and vulnerable: if each slow dusk was a drawing down of blinds on the western front, its speedy equatorial cousin crashed shut like a steel trap. The troops contended with marauding lions and leopards, and one colonel said it was like fighting in a zoo. In the first eighteen months, thirty Allied men were killed by animals, and one battle was interrupted by a rhino that charged one side and then the other. A private wrote home, after complaining about the bully-beef rations, "On guard on a dark night it's very trying on your nerves listening to the roars these different animals make, and you fancy every black object is coming towards you." If the large animals sometimes left them alone, the smaller ones never did. "Every known type of pestilential creeping animal seems to think he can take up abode in one's tent as an 'Honorary Member,' from the fat black millipede about 6 in long to that occasional and very unpleasant visitor, the puff adder, whose bite is practically certain death," one officer wrote. "White ants, black ants, red ants, all thoroughly imbued with military ardour, spend their days and nights 'digging themselves in.'" Besides malaria and dysentery, tick fever rampaged through the camps. There was no field hospital for miles. "In all this campaign, our most deadly enemy was not the human foe . . . but . . . fever," wrote an English doctor who followed the Second Rhodesian Battalion throughout the war in East Africa. Supply oxen were killed by the tsetse fly, which increased its range during the rains. "It has not always been too pleasant," Denys commented in a note home to his former girlfriend Pussy—the only one of his wartime letters from Africa to have survived. But there was none of the routine of the western front, or the formalized system of trenches. There was no parapet or wire, no Field Service postcards or Fortnum & Mason hampers, and no official brothels with blue lights for officers and red for other ranks. It was guerrilla warfare, African-style. But, like the soldiers in Flanders, Denys and his colleagues thought it would be over by Christmas. As December 25 approached, he lobbed plum puddings over enemy lines and staved off boredom in the company of Tich and Berkeley. They were known in the mess as the Three Musketeers. Tich, a lionhearted midget, ended the war a major with a DSO and an MC (Military Cross). The *askaris* (black soldiers), whom he ordered around in inaccurate but effective Swahili delivered tempestuously, respected him beyond all other officers. Around the campfire he told "resplendently coloured stories," sprinkling his speech with French expressions and savoring each dramatic incident. In the quiet hours, his talk occasionally lost its exuberance and he became sad, regretting the passage of time, but like Denys he kept horror at bay by relentless adventuring.

Von Lettow was focusing on the British railway. He remained close to the border at Taveta, the Allied post near Kilimanjaro, his contact with the outside world effectively severed. Occasionally, he was able to pick up wireless messages from Togo, or even direct from Germany, but otherwise he had to depend, for all his news, on intercepted wireless messages or captured mail. Not until February 1915, when he sat down for dinner in the railway station at New Moshi, did von Lettow receive a letter from his sister telling him that their brother had been killed at Libramont, on the western front, on August 22, 1914. As for the Africans, they were bemused at the spectacle of white men shooting one another's brains out. But they served in the thousands on both sides, either as *askaris* or as porters. Germans and British alike were permanently dependent on porterage. The dearth of roads meant that, away from the railway, supplies had to be carried through the bush. At the peak of the campaign, von Lettow needed 7,700 men just to ferry food to his *askaris*. On the Allied side alone, 44,500 East African porters died in service.* The unleashing of European-style war on the continent was, in the century that followed the campaign, to have a yet more dire impact on Africans. Along with unnatural borders, mechanized warfare was among the most cataclysmic of colonial legacies.

ON SEPTEMBER 20, 1914, the light cruiser *Königsberg* destroyed the HMS *Pegasus* off Zanzibar. Back in London, the affronted Admiralty now made capturing the *Königsberg* its highest priority. British vessels, hurriedly repainted from civilian white to wartime gray, tracked her to the Rufiji Delta south of Dar. The dreadnoughts were unable to enter the shallow waters, and the *Königsberg* remained concealed within mazy miles of mangrove swamp. While Denys and the Somalis patrolled the border three hundred miles to the north, the *Königsberg* was blockaded in the Rufiji for 255 days in one of the most protracted naval engagements in history—

---

* Both sides viewed the indigenous people as expendable parts of the country they were fighting over. As one historian has said, "Lettow-Vorbeck's brilliant campaign was the climax of Africa's exploitation: its use as a mere battlefield."

one that occupied twenty-seven British ships and burned 38,000 tons of coal. The ship and her company literally decayed in the pestilential palm groves, but when she was eventually sunk, 120 survivors were able to join the land campaign, and even the ten guns that had been thrown overboard were salvaged. Six weeks later, an even greater disaster unfolded when a four-thousand-strong Indian expeditionary force consisting of British officers and their sepoys made an amphibious assault on Tanga, the ocean terminus of one of the German railways and the country's second port. It was a pretty town laid out with the neat, whitewashed houses of German settlers, but horribly humid in November. The Indian troops were poorly trained and equipped, and the story of the battle reads like one of the infamous cock-ups of the Light Brigade kind that litter British military history. Secrecy was overlooked to the extent that Nairobi newspapers reported the attack before it took place, and, unknown to army commanders, the Royal Navy had already signed an unratified truce with the German authorities in Tanga. When the fighting finally began, hundreds of thousands of bees joined in when machine-gun fire shattered their hives. The battle plan, conceived in London, was ill-suited to the terrain. The Indian divisions were visibly terrified. British casualties reached 817; the day after the failed invasion, hundreds of corpses lay in heaps, putrefying in the sun. The Germans had been outnumbered eight to one, but besides winning outright they also captured enough weapons, telephone equipment, and clothing to last a year. German settlers mobilized behind von Lettow. "The success at Tanga called forth and revived the determination to resist all over the Colony," he recalled. It would not, after all, be over by Christmas. The settlers realized they might lose all they had built up. Sitting it out up in Gilgil, Galbraith noted, "This reverse will increase the difficulty of our taking GEA a hundredfold." In Europe the western front, locked into the trench system, settled into self-destructive stalemate.

THE YEAR 1915 was a bad one for the Allies in East Africa. There were no major land battles, just a slow guerrilla war of attrition. The Germans had been cut off from supplies and reinforcements by a naval blockade, and von Lettow realized that he could not win a conventional war. Instead, he had to husband his ammunition and equip his forces for the long haul. He decided to encourage the enemy to attack, and thereby tie up as many Allied troops as possible for as long as possible. To this end, he quickly developed a small, flexible field force with units capable of waging guerrilla warfare for as long as it took. Every month, the *Schütztruppe* became more efficient. Von Lettow was a brilliant guerrilla strategist, and his *askaris* were to enter military folklore. Resourceful German colonists applied themselves to producing supplies, even extracting their own quinine to combat malaria. Up in Nairobi, the papers had little to report except casualties until June 26, when, after months of waiting, news came through that a combined military and naval force had captured Bukoba, a German settlement on the eastern shore of Lake Victoria. This was the first real good news for the settlers. "Now the scene should change, and the thermometer of our spirits and hopes rise rapidly," the *Leader* reported. But the mercury continued to fall.

The sulfurous British intelligence chief Colonel Richard Meinertzhagen was consistently critical of Allied commanders. He was present at Tanga, and later stated in print that it was "the best example I know of how a battle should not be fought." A pipe-smoking ornithologist with a small mustache and dark hair that he wore slicked over his head, before the war Meinertzhagen had served in Kenya with the Third Battalion of the King's African Rifles. In a famous incident in 1905, he met the Nandi *Laibon* (chief) to negotiate a truce. As the pair were shaking hands, Meinertzhagen shot the man dead. He was recommended for a Victoria Cross. "On the whole," he confided in his diary that evening, "I am feeling rather pleased with myself." His Teutonic name, it was now said, was regrettable.

Meinertzhagen ranted about the Allied commanders who strutted around their cars dressed in tight knee-high boots, thigh-baggy trousers, pith helmets, and belted bush jackets slung with field glasses, and he judged that none were of the caliber of von Lettow.* Whether they were as bad as he suggested or not, they were certainly handicapped by lack of

---

* Meinertzhagen took a few potshots while he was gathering intelligence at Tanga. One of the figures at whom he aimed, and missed, turned out to be von Lettow himself. After the war the pair became friends, and von Lettow recalled the incident in his autobiography. "This was my first social contact with my friend Meinertzhagen," he wrote of the shooting. During the Second World War, Meinertzhagen sent the general food parcels.

manpower, despite the arrival of the Loyal North Lancashires (the only regular British unit to serve in the campaign). In the war rooms of Europe, the invasion of South-West Africa was considered the only significant action on the continent, and East Africa remained a low priority. Politicians had plenty to occupy them elsewhere: as the bees were stinging at Tanga, bombs had already fallen on England and twenty-four thousand Tommies on a shilling a day had been slaughtered at Ypres. Throughout 1915, Lord Kitchener, Secretary of State for War, considered that as East Africa was strategically worthless, it needed only to be defended, and he sent his manpower to other fronts, especially as the losses in France mounted. But Rhodesian forces landed at Mombasa in 1915, and so did the Legion of Frontiersmen, officially gazetted as the Twenty-fifth Battalion of Royal Fusiliers. Personnel included Arctic seal poachers, a Buckingham Palace valet, and Northrup McMillan, the twenty-two-stone Canadian American.

Still camped north of Kilimanjaro, Denys and his unit were experiencing difficulties of their own. The Somalis may have enjoyed drilling, but they found aspects of army discipline unacceptable and eventually mutinied. For three days, Berkeley reported to his brother, "it was touch and go," and the officers believed their throats would be slit at any moment. But disaster was averted, and most of the Somalis were deported. Berkeley was put in charge of a hundred mounted infantrymen from the Loyal North Lancashires and a company of Gurkhas with a Maxim gun, Cranworth took over the remaining Somalis, and they amalgamated in a new unit called Cole's Scouts. Denys and Tich joined them, along with Denys's Somaliland companion Baron Blanc, now employed as an intelligence officer. They were using Somali horses and transport donkeys; Cranworth got hold of iodine to paint his mounts black-and-white so they looked like zebras. Under orders to patrol the border along the southern game reserve, the Scouts found themselves in scrubby country that gently rose and fell around the water holes. There was little action. "We spent long hours mounted and dismounted, and especially at machine-gun work, surely the dullest of all human occupations," Cranworth wrote. One evening, the lions beyond camp seemed especially numerous—and to be closing in. When the roaring (actually somewhere between a grunt and a growl) shook the glasses on the officers' table, Denys grabbed a torch and went out, taking Cranworth with him, though the latter at least picked up a loaded rifle. "Steadily the roars approached till they seemed all around us and I broke into a cold sweat," Cranworth recalled. "There came a minute's pause and then the awe-inspiring sound boomed off right against us and the hair rose on my head. Denys switched on his torch and focused it full on a great tawny brute, certainly not ten yards away. 'You can stay and be eaten if you like. I'm off to the mess,' I said. Denys laughed and came with me only with the utmost reluctance." For Denys, there was always one more roll of the dice.

By July, the Scouts had moved southwest to join the main advance camp at Maktau on the Voi-Taveta Road. The Germans had been driven back across the border and were camped fifteen miles away at their advance base on Mbyuni, a low hill in one of the corridors between the colonies. The Allies were about to attack under the command of Brigadier General Wilfrid Malleson. Everybody except him was baffled by the decision to attack Mbyuni; even if the Allies had won the position, they would have been obliged to retreat to Maktau, whence they had come. "Presumably there was some reason for the enterprise, but it was never disclosed to us before or after," Cranworth noted. He had been obliged to ride a mule all the way from Maktau; his black-and-white-striped horses had died, presumably of iodine poisoning. Cole's Scouts led the flanking column and approached the German position in darkness. Machine-gun and rifle fire from rock and sand emplacements foiled the main attack, and no one among the Allies knew what they were supposed to be doing. At one stage the Scouts lay in the bush for hours, awaiting orders and under fire from a concealed sniper. Denys went to sleep under a thorn tree. But it was a costly muddle. A junior officer grappling with a heliograph in long grass remembered the endless moaning column of wounded streaming past him. "The damaged, dusty gory men reminded me of broken tools," he said. When the command came to retire, British casualties numbered two hundred, German twenty-seven, and whorls of vultures hovered over the abandoned dead. "We have lost the initiative," Meinertzhagen commented sourly. "If only they [the Germans] would capture Malleson it might be an advantage."*

---

* Meinertzhagen was eloquent in his condemnation. "Jollie [a colonel in the Allied forces] is a decrepit old woman," he wrote of one officer, "without the courage of a hedgehog or the energy of a guinea pig, and in saying that I am libelling two charming little creatures."

"If the initial attempt of the expeditionary forces had been successful," Denys wrote home to Pussy in the surviving note, "the Germans would have probably given in very soon, but unfortunately, as you know, it was a fiasco owing to over-confidence. As it is now, they are rather pleased with themselves and are giving as good as they get. They have the advantage that most of their troops are African and know the country, whereas the bulk of our forces are Indian, are unused to this country, and go sick very easily." Cole's Scouts was now disbanded—perhaps inevitably, the blustering commando units of the early days had been subsumed into the large and strictly conventional East African Mounted Rifles (EAMR). Denys went back to Nairobi to arrange a scouting job in a different area. While he was there, he saw the photographs and films of Belgium that were being shown on the bioscope at the Theatre Royal. Denys was sick of war, but did not want it to end "before the Germans have had a taste of what they have given Belgium and France."

He collected his letters from the main post office, among them a long one from Pussy. She had married and had three children in rapid succession; when a fourth appeared in January 1915 she called him Denys, and now wrote to ask the other Denys to be godfather—his second namesake. He replied with a gracious acceptance, declaring that he wanted to present his godson with a German scalp to commemorate his birth. But his light-hearted letters from Pussy were anomalous. Most of his mail was unfathomable in its horror, a raid on the inarticulate. His friends were all being killed. ("Jesus, make it stop," the poet Siegfried Sassoon wrote from the trenches.) Charles Lister, the trade-union-supporting son of Lord Ribblesdale, had perished on a hospital ship off Cape Helles in August 1915 after being wounded three times at Gallipoli. Julian Grenfell had won a DSO at Ypres. He went home on leave, returned to the front with his three greyhounds, and was killed in May 1915. His brother Billy died two months later, within a mile of where Julian was hit. The marmalade-headed Patrick Shaw Stewart wrote to his lover, their mother, Ettie Grenfell, on the loss of her boys: "Darling, if I could only give up my life to you and be a thousandth part of what you have lost." But the war hadn't finished with Ettie. Shaw Stewart, who had distinguished himself at Gallipoli, was to die at Cambrai in 1917 while temporarily commanding a battalion. Going around his line at dawn, he was hit in the face by shrapnel and killed instantly. He was twenty-nine. Among his papers they found a poem in his hand:

> *I saw a man this morning*
> *Who did not wish to die:*
> *I ask, and cannot answer*
> *If otherwise wish I . . .*

Before the year was through, Denys learned that Topsy's husband, Ossie Williams, had died at Loos, commanding a company of Welsh Guards. He was shot going to the aid of a wounded soldier. After so many years of waiting, Topsy was alone again, this time forever. She and Ossie had a son, Michael, who was not yet two, and a month-old daughter, Anne, whom her father had never seen. Denys remembered swimming across the Dwyryd estuary with Ossie at night, carrying their clothes on their heads; walking together into the bosomy hills behind Harlech in the westering light; and playing Ping-Pong in the timbered games room at the Plas. It was hard for the living to stay sane.

IN EAST AFRICA, the imperial eagle remained aloft from the mangrove swamps of the Rufiji to the rarefied air of Kilimanjaro and from the shores of Lake Tanganyika to the red-tiled planters' villas overlooking the Indian Ocean in Dar. Von Lettow had been promoted to full colonel. He was immensely popular. "I doubt whether any army, in any country, has ever looked up to its supreme commander with such confidence and admiration as did the German troops in East Africa, all through that long campaign," wrote Nis Kock, a Danish-speaking Jutlander who served as an ordnance specialist. German East Africa was now the enemy's sole overseas territory. The Allies desperately needed reinforcements in order to invade through one of the Kilimanjaro funnels. Salvation came from South Africa. In November, it was announced that between ten and twenty thousand South African troops were on their way. The replenished East African Force deployed at the beginning of 1916 under the command of Jan Smuts, the Union's forty-five-year-old minister of defense and one of Britain's most elusive opponents during the Boer War. Now he was leading his old adversary in fresh battles, and at last the Allies had a leader Meinertzhagen admired. He always said that Smuts was the only commander who listened to the intelligence reports he gave. Denys and his colleagues felt a surge of optimism—the first for many months. Frustrated by a year and a half of bitty and inconclusive warfare, and cut off from the main theaters, they had become demoralized. The news they did get of the outside world offered a poor prognosis: every month the war seemed to spread farther, spilling outward from Europe like a poisonous tide. In Europe, people were beginning to call it the Great War. Now the Allies in East Africa had Smuts and new troops, as well as armored cars that had been shipped in to support them on the ground and even their first airplanes. After an unsatisfactory year of deadlock, preparations were under way for a major offensive.

After six more months of bush scouting, Denys returned to Nairobi on leave before the end of 1915 and found the remaining settlers complaining that the generals and captains from India were strutting around "full of their own importance." They filled the clubs, wrote the indignant Doctor "Kill or Cure" Burkitt, "where they groused about the absence of pukka sahibs, pukka golf, pukka polo, pukka bearers, pukka clubs, and all the other pukkas they had left behind in India." Soldiers arrived by train in the middle of the night and, finding no billets, dossed in front of the New Stanley Hotel, where the manager served them breakfast in the morning. Denys raced off to inspect his rural properties. Almost every farm in the country was struggling, and many had been abandoned. The export of coffee, sisal, and flax were essential to Kenya's well-being, but the war had cut the settlers off from their markets. (In 1917, coffee was actually declared a prohibited import in Britain.) Nobody was able to renew equipment. And although the wives were managing, there was no reserve of women and older men to keep things going as there was in the more established colonies, or in Britain itself. "One hopes that the war will soon be over, as everybody's affairs are going to rack and ruin," Denys wrote.

His observation adumbrated the more universal collapse of the decade to follow. Three years after he inspected his derelict farmland, the war was over. Even then he recognized, as many did, that the armistice was no harbinger of peaceful return. By 1918, few could still believe in the social and political solutions that had led to the war in the first place, and into the void flowed a deep tide of cynicism. In the presence of overwhelming "rack and ruin"—physical, economic, spiritual, intellectual—the futility of accomplishment was apparent to all, and Denys, despite himself, was to become the perfect antihero for an age.

Jack Pixley, Denys's friend and business partner, was serving with the Grenadier Guards on the western front. There was nothing Denys could do alone on his properties, and the Parklands house had been converted into a military convalescent home, so when he had leave he started going instead to Galbraith's farm between Gilgil and Lake Elmenteita. Before breakfast, when the air was fresh with the smell of dew and cedar, he walked among the six-hundred-year-old trees and the new green shoots of spring and looked out across the plain at the hammocking stomachs of the zebras, all as it had always been, untroubled by the unfolding catastrophe. He taught himself to play the guitar, and got to know Galbraith's fleshy-lipped farm manager Llewelyn "Lulu" Powys, whose ten siblings included the writers John Cowper and Theodore Francis. (Llewelyn went on to achieve success as a novelist himself.) He had sailed out to the job in East Africa in the hope that the altitude of Gilgil might cure his consumption. Formerly a teacher, Llewelyn was ignorant of farming, and never took to it; he said that burning off ten thousand lambs' tails with hot irons was "as frustrating as teaching French at Broadstairs," and that the mephitic process of dipping sheep to prevent scab was even worse. He had come to hate the sheep individually. For six days a week he drudged from dawn to dusk, lying in bed for an extra hour on Sundays to drink China tea and smoke Egyptian cigarettes. He never really shook off his consumption, and could not go home as there was no one to replace him. His fiancée wrote to break off their engagement. He was so lonely that he befriended local girls; he claimed it was only fear that restrained him from congress ("The Pox is so extraordinarily prevalent that I am scared"). His sensitive temperament was unsuited to life in the African bush, which every day brought death close.

Galbraith, whose presence in the Protectorate had now been legalized, had hoped to be able to do intelligence work, but he was suffering chronic rheumatism and arthritis and was permanently reliant on two sticks. He bought a car in 1915, though some days he was too ill to do anything but sit on the veranda with a rook rifle "and plug at anything I don't like the look of." He hated being cut off from news, often speaking of his fear of opening the papers to read the casualty lists. Rumor, a staple of war, drifted even to Gilgil; the most outlandish concerned *askaris* who ate their victims. In the first weeks of 1916, a story spread through the Protectorate about an Allied attack on Lake Tanganyika in a ship that had been carried out from England. When the truth emerged, it was more spectacular than even the most inventive rumors.

Both sides had known from the outset that control of the Great Lakes was critical. Innocent blue ponds on the map, in reality these were uncharted inland oceans that formed unbreachable frontiers. Lake Nyasa, the southernmost, fell gently into British hands in August 1914. Lake Victoria, the northernmost, was trickier, though by March 1915 it, too, was under Allied control. But in between the two the Germans controlled twelve thousand square miles of Lake Tanganyika, and throughout 1915 a new twelve-hundred-ton German warship was shifting large detachments of *Schütztruppen* across the lake to raid weakly held British and Belgian posts on the southern and western shores. In the early months of that interminable year, a white hunter named John R. Lee approached the saturnine first sea lord, Sir Henry Jackson, with a plan. A small, armed motorboat could conceivably overpower the German Tanganyika fleet if its potential for surprise, speed, and mobility was judiciously deployed. To get to the lake, this unfortunate motorboat faced a three-thousand-mile overland journey that included five hundred miles of unexplored bush, as well as forests, deserts, and the odd mountain range. Jackson did not flinch. "It is both the duty and the tradition of the Royal Navy to engage the enemy wherever there is water to float a ship," he decreed. He decided to order two boats, not just one. The officer chosen to lead the Lake Tanganyika Naval Expedition was Lieutenant Commander Geoffrey B. Spicer-Simson, known as Spicer, a man with a torso densely populated with tattoos of snakes, birds, and butterflies. He had spent most of his career behind a desk, but had once carried out a survey on the Gambia River, so he had volunteered to go back to Africa. Oaths of secrecy were sworn all around. The Admiralty commandeered two mahogany tenders from the Thorneycroft shipyard. They were forty feet long, with twin screws and two one-hundred-horsepower engines each, and they were converted for combat with steel plating, a three-pound gun mounted forward, and a Maxim aft. The firm also built special rubber-tired trailers and furnished a lorry with supplies. On June 8, 1915, Spicer took the improbably named *Mimi* and *Toutou* on a rushed and inauspicious shakedown cruise on the Thames, and shortly thereafter the boats were loaded onto a ship and the whole cavalcade set out for Cape Town, the officers parading in full uniform (including swords) for the send-off. At the Cape, boats, trailers, and lorries were hoisted on a special train to Elisabethville, the capital of Belgian Congo's Katanga Province, more than two thousand miles away, then on to the village of Fungurume, forty-two hundred feet above sea level in the malarial heart of Africa. Four hundred African laborers with several dozen teams of oxen began hacking paths and building bridges.

On August 6, the boats were craned onto the trailers, which were in turn shackled to two ten-ton traction engines, each with its own wood-burning locomotive. The ponderous three-mile caravan then set off through the Congolese swamps. Exuding clouds of viscous smoke, snorting and hawking, the machines quivered frequently to a stop, clanks yielding to irritable commands barked across the savanna in kitchen Bantu. The smell of lubricating oil snaked through the bush. In total, Africans built 150 wooden bridges to get *Mimi* and *Toutou* to the Great Lake. Much of the territory was tinder-dry, which meant that the traction engines had no purchase either in the dust of the desert or on the soft sand of the valley floor. Grass fires frequently cut off the route, which rose to sixty-two hundred feet at the highest point. The trailers failed and were replaced by the carts that were supposed to be carrying fuel. Toward the end, the men poled everything down the Lualaba River, the uppermost waters of the Congo, and discovered a new enemy: the tsetse fly. After so much labor and hardship, it looked as if they were to fail so close to their goal. Instead, they traveled the final two hundred miles on a narrow-gauge railway, and then, four and a half months after leaving England, Spicer saw the matte-blue waters of Lake Tanganyika. They had dragged a pair of fighting ships across Africa.

Toward the end of December, while half a million Turks and Allies were being killed or wounded at Gallipoli, the boats were launched. On Boxing Day 1915, a Sunday, a German ship emerged out of mist that the sun had not yet burned off the water. In their camp near the newly constructed Allied harbor, as all hands fell out after Divine Service, Spicer peered from the top of a lookout post with a cigarette holder in one hand and a pair of binoculars in the other, ordered his chief petty officer to dismiss, and added, almost as an afterthought, "and man the launches for immediate action." Crowds of Holo-Holo tribespeople lined the shore and cheered. The fighting was interrupted for six weeks by typhoons that careered off the mountains. In the end, Spicer sank the smaller two of the three enemy vessels on the lake and obliged the Germans to scuttle the warship. A telegram arrived bearing "His Majesty's congratulations to his remotest expedition," and another announced a DSO for Spicer. Back at home, one headline read NELSON TOUCH ON AFRICAN LAKE. To the lakeside tribespeople, Spicer was a demigod. Squat clay figurines with tattooed torsos began appearing under the borrasus palms. But the real feet, it turned out, were also made of clay. Spicer had gone marginally bonkers and taken to wearing a skirt. He was sent home.*

MEANWHILE, OVER ON the Indian Ocean, the first batch of South Africans disembarked at Mombasa followed by another contingent of Indians. Meinertzhagen interviewed many of the South African officers and noted that "they all seem quite confident that they will finish the campaign in a couple of months." He knew better. And so did von Lettow. Smuts himself arrived on February 19, 1916, a dapper little man with steel-blue eyes who toured Allied positions in an open gray Vauxhall and immaculate khaki drill. He was determined to start his convergent offensive as soon as possible, before the long rains began in April. Within a month his troops had finally breached the Taveta Gap and marched through the funnel into German East Africa. Capturing the German headquarters at Moschi on March 16, a Loyal Lancastrian trooper reported to a staff official, "When we arrived at the place it resembled Blackpool Winter Gardens more than anything else as far as tropical scenery went."

Denys had been transferred to the General Staff of the First East Africa Division, the latter at this stage consisting of Indian, Rhodesian,

---

* Twenty years later, the battle for Lake Tanganyika inspired C. S. Forester to write a novel called *The African Queen*.

and British troops spread over two brigades and an artillery group, with KAR and EAMR detachments. Smuts now sent them farther south. The bulk were to march through the slender forest belt that marked the course of the Pangani River, which itself more or less followed the northern railway from the southern slopes of Kilimanjaro to the coast at Tanga. As they started out, a Reuters cable reached their camp with news that the battle of Verdun had begun.

The march down the Pangani was among the most murderous maneuvers in the whole of the Allies' endless push south in pursuit of von Lettow. Entire battalions hacked through shoulder-high razor grass while the temperature hovered at a sluggish 100 degrees. Europeans were prone to collapse with heatstroke in the still furnace of midday, even as their colleagues were freezing in the silvered Flanders trenches. On March 14, the first rain fell. The mules, which carried most of the supplies, began to sicken. Denys, moving with general headquarters behind the main columns, camped at a rubber plantation. "It is hot, and the camp is infested with every manner of noxious insect, but one cannot help enjoying the pleasure of camping on enemy territory after so many weary months on our own," wrote Meinertzhagen, who was with them. Smuts had ordered his commanders to surround the Germans at the railway and therefore block their retreat. But troops failed to reach the railway in time. They had succeeded in pushing von Lettow south, but they had not captured him. Brigadier General Sir James Stewart, a balding figure with a toothbrush mustache, was held responsible. (He was "a hopeless, rotten soldier," according to Meinertzhagen.) "If General Smuts considers that I am responsible for unnecessary delay, I wish to resign my command," Stewart wired from Taveta. Smuts did blame him, and Stewart did resign. Denys had a different perspective from Meinertzhagen. He had seen decency in Stewart and did not judge him only as a soldier. He regretted Stewart's departure and was bitter at the injustice of the military machine that destroyed the reputations of honorable men while inflating those of arrogant fools such as Brigadier General Sheppard—known as Ha Ha Splendid, the phrase he yelled whenever a fight was imminent. A month later, Denys wrote warmly to Stewart at his new post in Aden ("I still have those six bottles of Muthaiga Club champagne with me here!" the general replied cheerfully). Denys did not have the stomach for the political maneuvering that was inseparable from military command. But he now began serving under a remarkable soldier who was to play a decisive role in his army career.

Smuts had summoned Lieutenant General Reginald Hoskins from France to command the First Division. The forty-five-year-old Hoskins knew East Africa—he had been inspector general of the KAR before the war. According to Cranworth, he was "perhaps the most gifted soldier of the campaign, and certainly the most popular." He wore a sweater rather than his regulation tunic, which Denys liked. The regard was evidently mutual: Hoskins chose him as one of his aides-de-camp, an appointment that led to Denys's promotion to temporary lieutenant. From then on, he accompanied Hoskins and the other chiefs wherever they went, shuttling about with a map in one hand and field glasses in the other, sleeping four or five hours a night if he was lucky. He sat around tables cluttered with candles, black-boxed field telephones, soda bottles, revolvers, and papers, relaying news flashed in by heliograph and leaning back against stacked cases of rations to deliver his own strategic advice. "Never in my experience did anyone in this comparatively lowly position achieve such influence, more perhaps than that of any other member of the staff," Cranworth wrote. Charisma is mesmerizing. People wanted to absorb themselves in Denys. "Such was his charm that I never heard a grumble at his ascendancy," Cranworth concluded.

Much of the First Division had moved north back up the Pangani to wait out the long rains in a relatively dry camp. Hummocked bunches of blue and green bananas arrived on porters' heads, and pyramids of hay pursued lines of ammunition crates deep into the bush. At night, cooking fires glimmered in the crowded porters' camp that stretched behind rows of tents, where turbaned *naiks* from the Twenty-ninth Punjabis, black-fez-wearing *askaris* from the Northern Rhodesia police, and sepoys from the Second Jammu and Kashmir Rifles polished their *kukris* and cleaned their barrels, and waited. Smuts, they knew, was planning simultaneous attacks on other fronts: a British Ugandan column was coming south from Lake Victoria, another British force was moving up from Northern Rhodesia, troops were landing on the coast, and Belgians were to march into Rwanda and Urundi and on to Tabora, an important settlement in the western heartlands of German East Africa. Many figures were bandied around, but the truth was that by April the Allies were far superior in numbers: about forty-five thousand against the German sixteen thousand. The Allies were encouraged by the Portuguese declaration of war on Germany the previous month. Meinertzhagen, however, reported the first Portuguese attack as follows: "Their boats ran aground, they forgot to bring with them any food, they landed at a spot where there was no fresh water, they commenced the operation in the evening, having spent the whole day in full view of the enemy trying to make up their minds, and finally they were decimated by enemy machine guns of which I warned them and the whole force was killed or captured." Von Lettow was more mobile than the Allies, as he had far fewer men and was operating in his own country. Smuts's plan to surround the retreating enemy was consistently foiled as the Germans refused to stay still and allow themselves to be enveloped, time and again slipping away before the outflanking force could work around to their rear. "It is like looking for a needle in a haystack to try finding Huns in the jungle if they don't want to be found," one officer wrote.

While the Allies kept pushing south in pursuit of their German needles, in the middle of May Denys was still camped with Hoskins behind the lines at Kahe, west of Lake Jipe and close to the border. The rains had stopped, and the country sang. Lizards ran in peace, sap rose in the crop-headed willows, and each morning arrived amiably, as if there were no war. But the men resting at Kahe soon had to rejoin the big southern attack. On May 21, Smuts ordered Hoskins to command his division down the Pangani in three columns. Lumbering lines of men, oxen, horses, cycles, heavy guns, and wagons crawled through clouds of red dust kicked up by the animals. They had insufficient water and inadequate rations, and supply vehicles could not follow until trees were felled to form a makeshift road. Men marched for fifteen hours without food, then lay on the ground to sleep without blankets. Many contracted amoebic or bacillary dysentery, or both; others had blackwater fever, which turned their urine black and almost always ended in death. Fleas and jiggers accompanied everyone everywhere, and on the long march down the Pangani thousands of toes were amputated. Jungle sores as big as fists suppurated unchecked. The knee-length shorts and short sleeves worn by British forces left them vulnerable to mosquitoes bearing malaria (*Schütztruppen*

had long sleeves and puttees), which often caused cardiac failure and in-
sanity, as well as the better-known symptoms. The rivers they crossed
were infested with crocodiles, and on the banks they all sank to their
waists in mud. The crisis in the supply system worsened as they moved
farther from headquarters. The exhaustion was bone-deep. It wasn't the
troglodyte world of the trenches, but it was another kind of hell. The war
in East Africa—virtually unknown to the outside world—was, in its safari
through purgatory, a negative metaphor for the Kenyan paradise of the
epoch handed down in literature and myth. And the campaign remains
buried under the weight of history, whereas Karen Blixen's luminously famous first line—"I had a farm in Africa, at the foot of the Ngong Hills"—
has irreversibly enshrined the lyrical romance of the same landscape.

DENYS AND MOST of the division stopped for a week at Buiko, a dusty railway village where the Pare Mountains ended and the Usambara chain
began. They were now fifty miles inside enemy territory, but the goal of
capturing von Lettow, forcing his troops to surrender, and occupying the
country seemed as elusive as ever. The retreating Germans had destroyed
most of the Buiko station, blowing up the offices, the points system, and
the water tower, and they had driven away all the inhabitants except one
Indian trader, who, in a shed with a little square window that served as a
counter, sold soap, cigarettes, and Sanatogen. The soap, which was blue,
cost a rupee and did not lather. But lather or not, it was wonderful to rest
in the Buiko dusk after so many dismal marches. In the mornings the men
swam in pools, hard soldiers' bodies breaking the dark surface and carving
through the water as the dawning sun gilded their indolent guns on the
bank. A woundless tranquillity settled on Buiko. On June 4, 1916, Denys,
Cranworth, Sir John Willoughby, who was commanding a unit of armored cars, and Colonel Robert Lyall, in charge of the Second Kashmir
Rifles, all Old Etonians, gathered to celebrate the school's foundation.
Each brought a tin of food, and Denys, typically, managed to get hold of
a bottle of champagne. "Never did *floreat etona* go down better," Cranworth remarked.

The division followed the railway down to Mombo, a small German
settlement fifty-five miles west of Tanga and the coast. The air was dark

with tsetse. An officer rode into camp from the signal station carrying a Reuters dispatch about the battle of Jutland. It was difficult, in the tropical radiance of East Africa, to picture rows of gray battleships disgorging black smoke over the North Sea. "When we had read it," one officer wrote, "our minds were filled with a torturing uncertainty which shadowed the whole of that day. . . . It made us anxious to be done with this sideshow, to have it finished once and for all, so that we might help to get to the root of the whole tragedy, at home in Europe." Shortly afterward, they learned about the sinking of the *Hampshire* and the loss of Kitchener. Up on the plains outside Nairobi, a group of white farmworkers sat hunched over a wireless. "Suddenly, the news came through, 'Kitchener is dead,'" one of them recalled. "There was a hush. Everyone spoke in whispers, 'Surely this is the end of all things?'" But nothing had ended in the East African jungle. The Germans were retreating south toward Handeni, the terminus of the narrow-gauge tramway that connected with the northern railway at Mombo. This was about a hundred miles from the Kenyan border. On June 30, Denys was driving along a stony track not far from the main German column with Hoskins and his other aide-de-camp, Lieutenant E. R. Macmullan. They were traveling without an escort. Suddenly shots crackled over the thorn trees. Snipers had ambushed the car with rifle fire. Macmullan died instantly, a spurt of dark blood arcing from his neck over the top of the filthy windshield and landing with an innocent patter on the dry rocks. The shots went on. Denys almost took a hit; there was nowhere to drive. It seemed a pointless way for a general to die. But Denys faced off the attackers with gunfire and they disappeared back into the bush. He had saved the life of Hoskins, his hero. Later, the general recommended him for a Military Cross, which he was duly awarded. It was a comparatively rare honor in 1916.

By June 20, the Allies had occupied Handeni. Smuts had other troops moving in from the east and south; it seemed he finally had the enemy on the run. On the twenty-third, Hoskins himself led a picked column to attack a German encampment on the Lukigura River. Denys marched through the night. The track was impassable by wheeled transport, so they loaded the guns onto the mules. After twenty hours on foot, they opened fire on Germans positioned on the opposite ridge of the valley. The boom of the old German rifles gradually faded. It was Hoskins's first notable achievement and, according to the official history, "one of the few engagements of the campaign in which the British troops enjoyed the elation of victory in battle. . . . The whole force gained new confidence in itself and its commander." Soon the central railway, too, was under British control, isolating its terminus, Dar es Salaam (also the seat of government). In July, Tanga fell. "One can only think with pain of the South African mob, with their cowboy habits, in well kept and clean Tanga, but this will only be a passing episode," wrote the *Hamburg Nachricten* when the news reached the motherland.

Smuts's army was winning the war, and decomposing on its feet. "Mere superiority in numbers, without full ability not only to move them rapidly but to maintain them adequately, was an embarrassment, not an advantage," the official history acknowledged with hindsight. The supply chain, lengthening daily as the troops pressed southward, now virtually collapsed. Ha Ha Sheppard, the commander Denys most despised, wired the War Office, "Many men are almost naked." They were also malnourished. Since May, the First Division, the effective fighting force in the vital northern sector, had lost fifteen hundred of its fifty-five hundred men. It took seven hours for lorries to transport the worst casualties back to the temporary field hospital at Handeni. The ruts were so deep, and the lorries so hot, that many of the wounded were jolted or cooked to death. Half the division had had malaria. Sixty thousand Allied horses and mules had already perished, and twice as many oxen. But the men carried on. By the third week of August 1916, the division was well on the way to Morogoro, the old German capital and an important depot immediately north of the Uluguru Mountains. After two days of marching, they heard bombs falling from their own aircraft. They entered the undefended town on August 26 and commandeered a sausage-making machine in the Bahnhof Hotel. Cranworth inspected the hastily evacuated government house. "On every piece of furniture was laid an exhibit of human excreta," he wrote. "This example of frightfulness apparently pleased them and certainly didn't hurt us, but struck me as a curious example of *Kultur*."

Von Lettow's units withdrew south of the railway, and Denys's division was ordered out in pursuit, marching around the eastern edge of the Ulugurus with both infantry brigades pushing to cut off enemy routes south. It was one of the most difficult operational zones of the campaign;

Smuts wrote later that they were waging "a campaign against nature." The eight-thousand-foot Ulugurus rose abruptly behind Morogoro, slashed by gorges and swampy valleys, slopes jungly with ancient trees woven together by creepers. "Picture the difficulty of keeping in touch with your own people in such a jungle, which, the moment you enter it, swallows you up in its depth of undergrowth as if you were a rabbit taking cover in a field of ripe corn," a frontiersman wrote. In repose, it was a tranquil landscape. The mountains maintained, in their dignity, that war was nothing to do with the Ulugurus. At the end of the day, the cliffs cooled and eastward shafts of sun filtered through the clouds to flood the dry grass in amber light. Close to camp, butterflies lay folded along the reeds, and when the sun began to warm their brittle Prussian-blue wings they quivered in the still valley air. But the enemy had destroyed the bridges as they retreated, and Denys spent the first days of September supervising the construction of new ones, to the crashing accompaniment of the howitzer battery shelling forward units. ("Colonel furious, I furious, all of us wet and filthy," a KAR subaltern wrote.) Vehicles were again unusable, and the division was dependent on the files of Kavirondo porters threading up and down the valleys with gourds at their waists and chop boxes on their heads. Hoskins reached Tulo on September 9. Nine hundred Germans were fighting hard. At camp, stretcher bearers greaved in mud ferried in the wounded and bloodied bodies that lay heaped and steaming on the ambulance carts as if conjured by Goya. But by the morning of September 13 the Germans had slipped away.

OVER THE NEXT MONTH and a half, as rain halted the advance south, Denys's debilitated division was reconstituted. Twelve thousand spent South Africans went home. The bulk of those who remained moved to make their base at Kilwa Kisiwani, a former Arab slave port 120 miles south of Dar and 300 miles from Kenya. The first to arrive either took up defensive positions or began building piers. On November 13, Hoskins and Denys established headquarters in a villa near the whitewashed German church. West African regiments had come to beef up Hoskins's protean field force—barefoot Nigerians and Gold Coasters in conical pith helmets. But in an offensive fifty miles northwest, tsetse flies killed off 660 newly arrived mules and ponies in five weeks and a lion ate thirteen men. The rains were unusually heavy, and the waterlogged black cotton soil swallowed a wagon and its six mules. "Rations were so green with rottenness and so full of weevils and maggots that they could only be eaten with the eyes closed," said a Baluchi officer. Besides fending off mosquitoes and rats that gnawed on wounds, men had to use razors to extract burrowing grubs from their flesh. (Cranworth had one in his penis.) They camped among pools of yellow water spiraled with blood, T. S. Eliot's "rats' alley / Where the dead men lost their bones." Many enemy camps had already been evacuated. A Baluchi detachment approached one with bayonets fixed, but found only gramophones continually playing German military marches. The battle of Kibata, at the beginning of December, unfurled in a miasma of orders and counterorders, runners and telegraph wires, midnight footsteps on gravel paths, and the whine of the solitary mosquito that always succeeded in penetrating the net. Both sides spent Christmas trying to bury their dead before the hyenas got to them.

The casualty lists lengthened. Still, Hoskins was confident. "I feel with one big effort the end is in sight," he wired the War Office. Smuts sent von Lettow a Christmas letter congratulating him on receiving Germany's highest military honor, the *Pour le Mérite*. Von Lettow replied politely, saying that he approved of what he called "the mutual personal esteem and chivalry which existed throughout." Talk of chivalry at this stage of the war revealed the isolation of the East Africa campaign. It was a throwback to another age of warfare, one in which men still believed in the mystical value of patriotism. By the end of 1916, after the apocalypse on the Somme, in which almost twenty thousand British men were killed by German machine guns in a single day, the expiatory magic of the Grail was perceived at home as the lie it was.

ON JANUARY 20, 1917, Denys and Hoskins were eating breakfast at temporary headquarters near Kibata, discussing what to do next. Suddenly a runner appeared with the electrifying news that Smuts was relinquishing his command. He was going to the imperial conference in London and had selected Hoskins to replace him as commander in chief. This was perfect for Denys, as it would mean high-octane adventuring without the brake of high command—effectively, he had become high command, since Hoskins treated him as an equal. Hastily organizing their servants to pack and their *syces* (grooms) to saddle their mounts, he and Hoskins rode twenty miles to a waiting Ford, which conveyed them to a landing strip cleared from the bush at Kilwa. A Royal Flying Corps BE2C biplane was waiting. It was a patched-up reject from the western front with a seventy-horsepower engine, and it looked more like a metal butterfly than a plane, but it lofted them over the emerald delta of the Rufiji basin and landed in a typhoon of dust at the British army's forward command post.

Hoskins was a popular appointment. First, he was British. Second, he was known to be an effective administrator. He took command at an auspicious moment—by the beginning of 1917, Smuts had occupied three-quarters of German East Africa and was in control of all ports as well as both railways. But although von Lettow was in retreat, he was still determined to tie up as many Allied servicemen as he could. And the situation on the ground was appalling. Men were sick, half-starved, and facing crippling transport and communication difficulties over a four-hundred-mile front the supply routes of which groped back a hundred miles. Wounded men could be three hundred miles from a field hospital. The country south of Rufiji, where they were headed, was little known and covered in low-lying tropical forest. The rain had begun again with undue violence (it was one of the wettest seasons ever), drowning Hoskins's hopes of striking a decisive blow to end the campaign. In the middle of February, he was forced to end his offensive till the land dried out in May—to all intents and purposes a three-month cease-fire. But it gave him the opportunity to reorganize. Choosing the southern port of Lindi as his operational headquarters, and working under a battalion of thunderous clouds, he bombarded the War Office with telegrams pleading for guns, medical supplies, bayonets, and, above all, reinforcements.

The Germans, too, were up against it in the first months of 1917, though now they were almost self-sufficient. They vulcanized their own rubber, distilled salt from plants, and made bread from sweet potatoes, bandages from bark, and benzine for von Lettow's car from copra, the dried flesh of the coconut. They learned how to extract fat from elephants and hippos (a well-fed hippo provided more than two bucketfuls of appetizing white fat), ripen maize artificially, and make shoes from antelope hide and captured saddles. Officers traveled in small units, each with a cook, servants, and chickens—though the latter tended to reveal their position to the enemy. ("An order issued in one force that the crowing of cocks before 9 am was forbidden brought no relief," von Lettow recorded in his memoirs. When food supplies dwindled, a directive came down that no officer was allowed more than five servants. In fact, despite their resourcefulness they had far too little nourishment. Nis Kock, the Jutlander, was struggling to manufacture mines in the Rufiji jungle. "The German army was so weak during these months," he wrote, "that a puff of wind could have tumbled it over," though he added, "but the puff of wind did not come." He kept trying with the mines until he blew himself up.

Throughout February, Denys and Hoskins continued to deluge the War Office with requests. They also asked Uganda and Nigeria for porters and set about the recruitment of new KAR battalions. Hoskins calculated that, as the majority of the transport animals had died, he needed 160,000 porters. Meanwhile, Denys dealt with reports of broken roads and broken-down transport as well as ox wagons loaded with diseased corpses, limping columns of emaciated prisoners, and hundreds of German East Africa Indian civilians whom nobody wanted. "The enemy is evidently systematically handing over all useless mouths to us," Hoskins wired the War Office in exasperation in one of his nightly telegrams. Failing supplies had devastating consequences. People tried stewed hippo sweetbreads and bush rat pie, as well as poisonous roots and herbs, which killed some of them. They dug up horse carcasses and ate them. One company consumed the rawhide spars of a bridge. Into these strained camps came the news that six hundred Germans had cut through the British cordon and were marching on Tabora. (This splinter group was kept on the run for eight months and finally forced to surrender near the British border in October.) But then more armored cars arrived and were fitted up in Dar, exhausts cracking as loudly as their machine guns. Extensive repairs were completed on the railways. Hoskins and Denys began to zoom around the country in open-topped staff cars and on small planes, inspecting troops, meeting field commanders, and liaising with their allies. They drove through the coconut groves edging the coastal plains to meet with Portuguese commanders in Dar, where base wallahs shifted paper from one pile to the next in borrowed headquarters, and in the hotels exhausted white officers paid exorbitant prices for adulterated whiskey and stolen army supplies. On April 18, 1917, Denys and Hoskins flew up to Lake Victoria for a meeting with Belgian commander Colonel Huyghé at his Ujiji headquarters. Denys managed to get a few days at Gilgil. "He had done awfully well throughout the war," wrote Galbraith, who was now too crippled by arthritis even to drive. "He's not a soldier, and hates soldiering. He seems to think this campaign will be over about August." By the third week of April, it looked as if Hoskins's elaborate transport plans were beginning to pay off, as almost five hundred lorries were on their way. He had increased the KAR from thirteen to twenty-two battalions and had one hundred thousand Africans in the field. (It was far fewer than he needed, but never mind.) In the end, the War Office fulfilled the majority of his requests. "He had managed to get things done by urgent representations and hard work," wrote an officer who was there.

Hoskins now issued his plan for a May offensive. But on the third, without warning, the War Office dismissed him. "In view of the trying climate of the East African theater of operations," read the telegram, "and the consequent strain of prolonged service in such conditions . . . You will return to England by the most convenient route." It was the week after Denys turned thirty, and a bitter gift. Hoskins had taken over a spent force and renewed it; his three-month command had all been in the rainy season, and now he was denied the chance to see his carefully prepared plans in action, as his superiors far away judged that he had "lost grip of the operations and perhaps become tired." The decision was met with outrage on the ground. "All the military folk are very disappointed and surprised at Hoskins being taken away," Galbraith said. Denys certainly was. "If they had left Hoskins there," he wrote later, "I firmly believe he would have finished off the show by the end of 1917 in spite of being handicapped with Sheppard." As his aide-de-camp, Denys would automatically accompany Hoskins back to England and on to his next posting.

At noon on May 30, in Dar, Hoskins handed campaign command to General Jacobus "Jappie" van Deventer, a mountain man of a Boer. The rain had stopped. The deposed general and Denys returned briefly to Nairobi before sailing back to London to await orders. There was little time for Denys to do much except visit Berkeley, who was suffering so badly from dysentery that Galbraith, who had struggled down from Gilgil to nurse him, was convinced that he was going to die. "We are all depressed beyond words at the prospect of the change [of command]," Galbraith wrote. "Hoskins has done so much to make his men enthusiastic under the most trying circumstances and with his personality appears to have won the goodwill of everyone who came into contact with him. Things were I believe in a state bordering on chaos when he took over and he has made prodigious efforts to prepare for a final effort and now on the eve of his advance he is superseded." Hoskins and Denys had a lugubrious passage home.

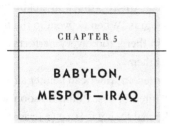
> When I think of Denys, the noun "personality"
> springs to mind.
>
> —LORD CRANWORTH, *Kenya Chronicles,* 1939

NEWSPAPERS AT HOME WERE STILL GLOATING OVER A SMASHING VICtory near Messines, southwest of Ypres, on June 7. British miners had spent a year tunneling under enemy lines in order to lay a trail of explosives. When nineteen mines went up at once, ten thousand sleeping Germans were killed, and Lloyd George felt the tremors on Downing Street. But by the last week of July, gloom had again settled over England. Denys, still in full-time employment as Hoskins's aide-de-camp, waited on home leave until another posting came through. They found everyone talking about food shortages, rising costs, and servant problems. The war had come to London when a bomb killed a hundred civilians, and as there were no air-raid sirens yet, fresh attacks were presaged by a bicycling policeman with a placard around his neck that urged TAKE COVER. The streetlights had acquired masks, and murky evenings contributed to a general sense of cheerlessness. It seemed, to Londoners, as if the war had always been there, and since the end of 1916 they had faced the possibility that it might go on forever. Each year they had less food than the year before, as well as less heat, less light, and less hope. So this, Denys reflected, was the "world grown old and cold and weary" that Rupert Brooke had suggested he would be glad to leave. He found some small consolation in the swirling cigarette smoke of the Café Royal or at a marble-topped table at the Four Hundred Club on Bond Street, where women in cloche hats danced the tango in the glow of colored lights. When he went to the theater, he found that the war had seeped in there, too: every performance was now parenthesized by the national anthem.

Among his friends, Iris Tree had married an American painter against her father's wishes and settled in the United States. Philip Sassoon was working as private secretary to Field Marshal Douglas Haig (a Brasenose man), and had the testing job of putting a gloss on the Somme debacle. Alan and Viola Parsons, née Tree, had moved to Mulberry Walk in Chelsea. Their son, Denys, had that year acquired a sister, christened Virginia in honor of America's entry into the war. Alan, who had joined the civil service, was medically unfit to serve, and worked his way through the war as private secretary first to the home secretary and then to the secretary of state for India. But most of Denys's male friends had been killed. Diana Manners, who was nursing at Guy's hospital, said that every young man she had ever danced with was dead. When Denys went up to Haverholme to join his parents, his reappearance was the first ray of light to illuminate those dark ground-floor rooms after years of waiting for news that, when it came, was usually bad. Sections of the park had been parceled out into allotments in the relentless quest for food, but the feathery bend of the Slea was untroubled, as were the electric-blue mayflies that somersaulted into the water in the setting sunlight. Toby was serving in France with the Royal East Kent Yeomanry, and the bereaved Topsy was living in Herstmonceux, in Sussex, with three-year-old Michael and two-year-old Anne. From her house near the rectory she could hear the artillery at night, reminding her over and over of what she had lost. Cousin Muriel had unexpectedly metamorphosed into a philanthropist. She had founded an Anglo-Russian hospital in Petrograd, and on the night of the first Bolshevik rising was dining with Prince Yusupov when his palace was attacked, though they continued the meal in the basement. (Yusupov was among the young men at Oxford with whom Denys had gambled all night at No. 117. He had since returned to his homeland and murdered Rasputin in the same basement.) That summer, Muriel traveled from Petrograd to her field hospital and found wounded men arriving in railway vans "stacked like straw" and mixed up with corpses. In August, more than three hundred Russian soldiers there shot off their left hands so they would not have to return to the front.

Back in Ewerby, Muriel's mother, Edith, was also running a hospital: a small convalescent home for wounded soldiers, where she spent her days bossing a team of village nurses. On Sundays, Denys sat with her and his parents in their seignorial pew at St. Andrew's, watching the gray walls stained crimson and purple by the light shining through the colored glass as the organ rolled through another rendition of Cowper's "God Moves in a Mysterious Way," now practically an anthem on the home front. Talking to Ewerby boys on leave from France, and to Edith's convalescents, Denys learned about another kind of war. They spoke of the pallor of German flares that illuminated undrainable villages through the brown fog of dawn; of the wet bulk of sandbags heaped up in reserve trenches; and of the short-ened cough of antiaircraft guns coming down from the morning sky. They spoke, too, of the onions drying under eaves at Westoutre; of the unex-pected glare of many-windowed châteaux; and of sullen columns of Kitch-ener's army marching under the trees that canopied the road from Béthune to Neuve-Chapelle, calf-deep in mud. The gray French rain was unpre-dictable and unfeasibly damp, not like the African rain: it was so miserable, and confounding, that the Tommies said Fritz could make it rain when he wanted it to. But nobody knew anything of Denys's war. Mock trenches had been constructed outside his old house in Kensington Square to show civilians what the western front was like, but there were no models of the razor grass around Kilimanjaro or the tsetse-infested forest that followed the banks of the Pangani. On November 12, 1914, a bereaved mother had written to *The Times:* "As one who has lost a dearly loved son in his coun-try's service in East Africa, I cannot forbear writing in approval of your article alluding to the complete absence of news from East Africa in partic-ular. Day after day we scanned the papers . . . but all was silence. Then on Sunday last came the fateful telegram. . . ."

All soldiers returning on leave spoke of their isolation, and of the wall that stood between them and those who had stayed at home—in some cases, a barrier that remained inviolate long into the Peace. But for Denys, who had fought on a minor front a long way off, the alienation was acute. His news from Africa was also dispiriting. The cattle he had led hundreds of miles through the desert had been decimated by rinderpest, an acute viral disease—so he had backed a loser even on that venture—and his inability to do anything about it made him feel alienated from that part of his life, too. On August 8, he wrote to Pussy from Haverholme, addressing the letter to his two-year-old godson, Denys. Pussy had forgotten to give him her new address. "Will you convey to her [your mother] as delicately as possible," wrote Denys senior, "that it always makes it easier for her correspondent to answer her letters if she gives him her address? Your dear mother, Denys, is not altogether free from a hereditary weakness of her sex—namely of expecting a little more than it is possible to give. I have found it to be so in most countries I have visited including Africa, the great Keep-it-Dark continent. However, I have with my accustomed resource—your godfather has no modesty—already discovered a means of getting a letter to your mother in spite of her reticence as to her whereabouts. . . ." He then went on to describe his ingenious method of making sure his letter was forwarded. "I have not complied," he continued, "with your rather thoughtless invitation to send you a telegram. Economy Denys! Wartime economy! I am saving up all the money I normally spend on telegrams to buy you a tin mug as some sort of Godfathering present. I had meant to try for a handsomely chased, heavily embossed solid gold George III punch bowl. . . ." And he explained that the loss of his cattle rendered such extravagance impossible, labeling smudges on the pale gray Priory writing paper "tears."

In reality, Denys was beginning to doubt the viability of a future in Kenya. So many of his investments had failed to yield a return, and now war had shattered the economy. In short, all was uncertainty, and the sunny days of August 1917 were a bleak time to be in England. The assault on Passchendaele to the northeast of Ypres began at the end of July and continued, like a slow amputation, for three and a half months. Heavy air bombardment and torrential rain wrecked the network of streams and dykes, turning the battlefield to mud, and soldiers dodged German bullets only to slip from a duckboard and be sucked to their death. It was, wrote Edmund Blunden, who was there, "murder, not only to the troops but to their singing faiths and hopes." Denys was not sorry when a telegram arrived at Haverholme ordering him to London to join Hoskins and prepare for immediate departure. But their destination was not entirely a welcome one. It was Mesopotamia (now Iraq), a theater with a reputation so grisly that it intimidated even veterans of East Africa. When Edward Temple Harris, an English doctor serving in German East Africa, was faced with the prospect of his third "Christmas feed in this only-fit-for-the-lions country," he told his brother that if the campaign came to an end he hoped to be posted to a hospital in France. "Our great dread is Mesopotamia if this is over first," he wrote. "That would put the lid on it."

Denys rushed around London, restocking his medical case with morphia at Savory & Moore, and his traveling humidor with cigars at Alfred Dunhill. The Trench Requisites section of the department stores offered periscopes, wire cutters with rubber-covered handles, and Mortleman's Patent Sound Absorbers, further reminders that the war was different in Europe. Then, as August came to a close in a sad England, he and Hoskins journeyed by rail through France and down to the southern Italian port of Taranto. There they waited among dreary rows of tents and boardwalks, killing time until the *Saxon*, an old Union-Castle liner, arrived under the escort of two Japanese destroyers. From Taranto they traveled only after sunset, as enemy submarines were prowling the Adriatic. But it was one of the escorting destroyers that one night accidentally rammed them amidships. Although the breach was above the waterline, the destroyer was badly damaged, and the *Saxon* was obliged to lie up off the Albanian coast and wait for a replacement escort. For two days Denys swam and sailed in warm waters, and at night, under a spray of stars, he played cards on deck with the other officers. He had found a kindred spirit in an American captain traveling to Mesopotamia with the Middlesex Regiment. The pair quickly established the basis of a friendship that was to last through many years of separation.

The blond-haired Kermit Roosevelt was Teddy's second son. Two years Denys's junior, after graduating from Harvard he had worked for a railroad company in Brazil, but he lacked his father's ambition and, unlike his elder brother, he was not a corporate man. Although slightly built, Kermit, like Denys, had immense physical stamina. He was by far the most literary of his six siblings and one half sister, and he and Denys exchanged books while marooned in the Adriatic, both eager to beef up their acquaintance with Babylonian history before arriving in Mesopotamia. Kermit had chosen to serve, at least initially, with the British Expeditionary Force. Apart from a penchant for gambling, he was a solitary figure. "Very few outsiders care for him," his mother, Edith, once commented. "But if they like him at all they like him very much." Introspective like her and adventurous like his father, Kermit was both a man of action and a sensitive, imaginative thinker. So was Denys, but he had the character to reconcile the two. Kermit, in the end, did not; it was his personal tragedy. There was alcoholism on both sides of the family, and in the 1920s and 1930s Kermit drank himself almost to death, eventually finishing the job by shooting himself while serving in Alaska in the Second World War. He was his mother's favorite; among her children, she wrote, he was "the one with the white head and the black heart."

When the escort arrived, they sailed south into the Ionian Sea, anchoring at Pylos Bay in the southwest of the Peloponnese, known historically as Navarino, where the little harbor was crowded with white hospital ships, small black cargo boats, and gaunt dreadnoughts. The *Saxon* had no fans or ventilating system, and when a batch of stokers deserted at Port Said in protest, the captain called for volunteers. "Finch Hatton and I felt that our years in the tropics should qualify us, and that the exercise would improve our dispositions," Kermit said. "We got the exercise. Never have I felt anything as hot . . . the shovels and the handles of the wheelbarrows blistered our hands. We had a number of cases of heatstroke and the hospital facilities on a crowded transport can never be all that might be desired." Many of the troops were ill. When someone died, the others stood with rifles reversed and heads bowed while the body, swathed in a Union Jack, was lowered into the Red Sea as a bugler sounded the last post.

THE OTTOMAN PROVINCE of Mesopotamia, Land of the Two Rivers, was a region of yearning plains traced by the sinuous writhings of the Tigris and the Euphrates. It was also strategically vital. First, it was on the all-important route to India. Second, its gulf port, Basra, lay close to the refinery that processed British oil supplies pumped from South Persia, and, then as now, government policy was directed by hunger for oil. In fact, much of the territory consisted of inhospitable desert where bands of Arab robbers marauded unchecked in temperatures in excess of 120 degrees. But oil was oil. Once Turkey entered the war on the side of the Germans in October 1914, it was only a matter of time before the Allies invaded Mesopotamia in an attempt to seal off the Persian Gulf. The Germans, for their part, were fixated on the idea of establishing an eastern empire and had been stoking local support. Their agents had even spread rumors, widely repeated in the bazaars, that the kaiser had converted to Islam.

Until February 1916, the Mesopotamia campaign had been directed from India. But Indian high command had never handled a major overseas expedition before, and its army was already buckling under the commitments war had imposed. Communication between London and Delhi was poor, British policy was inconsistent, and military planners catastrophically underestimated the problems of a 550-mile riverine supply line. (There were no roads to speak of in the whole of Mesopotamia.) The river system, difficult in the dry season, turned into a lake by mid-May, when ten thousand square miles of land lay underwater—the flood, perhaps, described in Genesis. The first eighteen months of the campaign had been fought by inadequately trained troops and an eclectic fleet of requisitioned Calcutta-built river steamers, Royal Navy shallow-draft gunboats, and ambulance paddle steamers. The climate did nothing to improve rations that were second-rate when they started their journey. When the soldiers pierced their tins of bully beef, the contents shot out in a liquid jet. Their ammunition was labeled MADE IN THE USA. FOR PRACTICE ONLY.

Medical facilities were deplorable at best, and, in addition to the usual roster of tropical diseases, the swollen sick list now included cases of sandfly fever and smallpox. Despite all this, the Anglo-Indian force beat the Turks back when they met on and around the delta, and their successes led British newspapers to refer to "the Mesopotamian picnic." The victories were little short of miraculous, and it was almost inevitable that they would culminate in one of the most spectacular failures in British military history. In December 1915, close to thirteen thousand British and Indian soldiers were besieged at Kut al-Amara, in the curve of a loop in the Tigris south of Baghdad. Of all the infernos of the First World War, of all the crucifying battlefields, entrenchments, and prisons, the former licorice factory at Kut was among the worst.* In April 1916, the starving survivors

---

* In the terrible months of January–March 1916, when hundreds of men lost their lives in the abortive efforts to relieve Kut, the usual incomprehension manifested itself in communications between base wallahs in Basra and soldiers on the ground. One officer, when asked during an artillery bombardment to report on the attitude of the enemy, dodged a volley of bullets to signal "Hostile." When he was asked by return to elaborate, he wrote, "Very hostile."

surrendered, only to be force-marched through the desert and horse-whipped in prison camps in Asia Minor. Between January and April, the Tigris Corps lost twenty-three thousand men.

Hoskins, who was to command the Third (Lahore) Division, had served in the Egyptian army for four years and had experience of the Arab world. But Mespot, as it was known, was by now an unpopular posting, and there was no more talk of picnics. The fall of Kut had shocked the British public. Ugly rumors circulated about the plight of the wounded and the scandalous absence of medical facilities. A commission of public inquiry was established, and in the ensuing hurricane of righteous indignation Secretary of State for India Austen Chamberlain, who had correctly come in for censure, resigned his post.

THE TROOPS TRANSSHIPPED at the Gulf. An entire Bengali regiment squeezed into the barges lashed to the sides of Denys's steamer before it proceeded through the Shatt-al-Arab, a series of muddy channels in which men maneuvered gondola-like *mashoof* while women ran along the banks carrying baskets of eggs and chickens, robes flying. Everyone disembarked at Basra, where hundreds of uniformed Indians thronged the vaulted passageways of the bazaars. Continuing north by paddle steamer, Kermit and Denys went ashore at Amara and met an armed sentry. "I slipped behind my companion to give him a chance to explain us," Kermit wrote. At Sunnaiyat, on the old Babylonian plain near Kut, they inspected the remains of looters who had been tampering with unexploded grenades abandoned in 1915. "The trenches were a veritable Golgotha with skulls everywhere and dismembered legs still clad with puttees and boots," Kermit concluded.

They finally disembarked at Kut, covering the remaining hundred miles to Baghdad by train. The railway followed the old caravan route past the remaining arch of the great hall of Ctesiphon, the ancient city buried under mountains of sand. The scattered settlements in the drab tableland were shabby after years of neglect, the minarets decaying and the people dulled to a stupor by heat and hunger. It had been an exceptionally punishing summer; fetid smells seemed to emanate from the sand itself. Some said Mesopotamia was the original Garden of Eden, but it didn't look like it.*

In the major post-Kut reorganization, the War Office had taken control of the campaign. The whole enterprise had begun as an effort to protect oil supplies, but as it unfolded, the prize of Baghdad—and the Berlin-to-Baghdad railway—became an end in itself. By the end of 1916, nearly two hundred thousand fresh British and Indian troops had arrived to launch an offensive under Major General Stanley Maude. The new force was supported by a flotilla of modified paddle steamers, thousands of horses, mules and carts, a fleet of Ford vans, and twenty-four specially adapted planes with aerial cameras and the latest bombing equipment. High command was gradually waking up to the fact that mechanical transport was more suitable than the four-legged kind in Arabia, because oil was produced locally whereas fodder had to be imported from India. Sappers beefed up the primitive port facilities and built a series of narrow-gauge railways as well as ordnance depots and clinics. When the offensive began, it went almost without a hitch. Baghdad fell in March 1917. It was a devastating setback for the Ottoman Empire, which was still reeling from the Arab Revolt, and certainly marked the end of the German dream of a new India in Arabia. But the campaign was not over. Intelligence sources reported that there was a new Turko-German force assembling at Aleppo, and Enver Pasha, the Turkish war minister, was obsessed with the idea of recapturing Baghdad. The Germans had invested heavily in a new force, *Yilderim* ("Thunderbolt"), and preparations were under way to deploy it in Mesopotamia, though in fact it never was. Whitehall decided that the army in Palestine was better placed than Maude and his troops to go into Upper Mesopotamia. Maude was therefore ordered not to move but, instead, to consolidate his position and tighten his grip on the region.

Baghdad itself had changed little in appearance since the days of the caliphs, except for the pontoon bridge that Maude had thrown across the

---

* A typical bit of forces' doggerel went:

> *Is this the land of dear old Adam,*
> *And beautiful Mother Eve?*
> *If so, dear reader, small blame to them*
> *For sinning and having to leave!*

Tigris. The milky waters below teemed with the cauldron-shaped *gufahs* that Herodotus describes carrying merchandise from Nineveh to Babylon. Armenian refugees, red-fezzed Muslims, and Persians in silk coats streamed through the Southern Gate to mill around the peacock-blue mosques and mud-brick slums, unperturbed by the presence of another invading army. Denys sat in coffeehouses drinking clear, bitter coffee, smoking a narghile, and watching Kurdish porters with sacks of dates on their backs and women haggling for bracelets with babies on theirs. The smell of unleavened bread and lamb spitting over charcoal pervaded the bazaar, but back at headquarters rations were monotonous, the only treats an occasional consignment of condensed milk or tinned salmon. Dust storms plagued everyone everywhere, and the south wind left a thick sandy deposit in teacups and canteens. Denys focused on playing bridge, and saw a lot of Kermit. "Dear K," he wrote in a note attached to a check for seven pounds ten shillings to pay off a gambling debt. "Your tie herewith, and your ill-gotten gains. I may be station-wards about ten—if so I'll bring a pack and rubi you properly in the break—you perfectly priceless old thing. DFH." When they grew tired of bridge, they ate salted watermelon seeds in the riparian garden of the Persian consul, or climbed down the banks of the Tigris and dug out bricks eighteen inches square on which they could make out the seal of Nebuchadnezzar.

News from the north was good. British forces closed in on the Turks throughout the autumn and into the spring, as did Russians advancing from the north and east. Meinertzhagen was partially responsible. He had been shipped out of East Africa after a funny turn in November 1916 and subsequently resurfaced as the intelligence chief of the Egyptian Expeditionary Force, in which capacity he was busy tricking Turks in Palestine—at one point dropping them cigarettes laced with opium grains. Then, on November 18, after a run of British victories, Maude died of cholera. He had acquired the status of Kitchener to the army in Mesopotamia and his death was a disaster. But early in December reports came in that British troops had entered Jerusalem, and church bells were ringing there for the first time since the war began. This was the end of Turkish hopes of recapturing Baghdad, and it foreshadowed the close of a campaign that had cost thirty thousand British and Indian lives. Elsewhere, however, the censors could not disguise the fact that news was not encouraging. Reports came in of the catastrophe at Caporetto, where the Italian army had collapsed at the end of October, and of a Bolshevik coup in Petrograd, the latter creating anxiety among the Allies that the new leaders might pull Russia out of the war, allowing the Germans to shift large numbers of men to the western front. By December, the Russian army had more or less disintegrated, and on the twenty-second the Treaty of Brest-Litovsk did bring Russia out of the war. General Sir W. R. Marshall, who had taken over from Maude, was asked to reduce numbers in Mesopotamia. This was excellent news for Denys. He wanted to get out— the campaign had shifted to Upper Mesopotamia before he even arrived, and down south there wasn't enough to do. He had accompanied Hoskins on motor sorties up the Tigris to the bitumen wells around Hit and through the pretty villages along the Euphrates, where wooden wheels looped through the sky to irrigate gardens buzzing with arsenic-green birds. But he was frustrated, and so was Kermit, who was about to request a transfer from the British Expeditionary Force to the American army in France.

Denys had been thinking of learning to fly. Military airplanes had been deployed in substantial numbers for the first time around Ypres in August 1917, and the potential of airpower in battle had suddenly burst on the consciousness of War Office mandarins. "Ministers are quite off their heads as to the future possibilities of aeronautics for ending the war," announced Lord Trenchard, the new chief of air staff. (In recognition of the importance of planes in war, on April 1, 1918, the Royal Flying Corps and the Royal Navy Air Service were to be merged into a new institution called the Royal Air Force.) The life expectancy of a British pilot at the front was eleven days, and the War Office was now desperate for pilots. It was the perfect moment for a man addicted to risk to begin his flying career. Training courses were hastily being established where military units were already embedded, among them one at a base near Cairo, which appealed to Denys, as he did not want to spend the winter in Europe. He hated cold weather, and it was bad for his heart, so he had the idea that, once qualified, he would fly on a European front in the summer months and then get moved out East for the winter. A short time into his Mesopotamian tour he therefore applied, with Hoskins's approval, to train as a pilot with the Royal Flying Corps. When he learned that he had been accepted, he found Hoskins a replacement aide-de-camp and, after the first rains had softened the plains into brackish pools, traveled by train down to Basra. He had been ordered to proceed at once for Egypt. But before he could start his flying course he heard that Pixley, the old charmer with whom he had first trekked over the Laikipia escarpment, had been killed at Houthulst Forest in France.

Denys's business relationship with Pixley was at the center of his complex network of Kenyan projects. The pair jointly owned the Naivasha farm, the chain of *dukas,* and other property. It was therefore essential for Denys to return to Kenya to untangle arrangements, and he was due a long leave anyway. He applied for permission to return, and deferred the start of his flying course until June. Back in Nairobi, he rented a bachelor room at Muthaiga; the Parklands house had been converted into a military convalescent home. The club had itself been taken over as a hospital for most of 1916, but was now operational once more, selling Virginia cigarettes and holding dances at which Goan stewards served sandwiches and fruit. It was usually a convivial place to stay, as members dined at one long table, but now most male settlers were away fighting, or dead.

Denys soon found that it was almost impossible to achieve anything in Nairobi. After a brief and unsuccessful attempt to deal with the business of Finch Hatton and Pixley, he therefore turned his attention to his ambitious plan to travel to Cairo for his flying course via Uganda and the White Nile. He wanted Billea to accompany him. Denys had left his servant behind when he sailed home to England with Hoskins, as it seemed unlikely that the Somali would be allowed to accompany him on whatever posting was in store. After "frantic wiring to all the heads in GEA and PEA [Portuguese East Africa]," Denys located him, and the loyal Billea returned to service. Denys then set about enjoying his leave. Berkeley, at least, was in evidence. In early May, he and Denys went to the Nairobi station to greet Galbraith and his new bride, Nell, née Balfour (she was the niece of the foreign secretary and former prime minister, Arthur), on their return from their wedding in England. Nell had been profoundly touched by the war: her first fiancé had died at Kut. She took to Denys straightaway and invited him down to Kekopey, the new house that Galbraith had built on his farm at Gilgil. "A very attractive person with a delightfully wide range of interests," Nell reported to her mother. "We went 'pigging' with him several times but the pigs were very wild and he was not shooting well so we got none. We got three buck one day—meat for the boys who badly wanted maize meal or posho as it is called and is very expensive owing to the shortage in this country. . . ." It was a difficult year on the farm, with sheep and cattle dying off, and porcupine were eating the beans to boot. Galbraith was debilitated by the long journey out from England. But the roses were in bloom, and it was difficult to be sad with Denys in the house. He had bought an old Ford, which he referred to as a *sufuria*, the Swahili word for a tin cooking pot. "It was nice to be in the country again, and I covered wonderful distances," he wrote to Kermit.

There was a dinner at Muthaiga. It was two weeks before Denys left for Cairo. His friend Algy Cartwright, who had been posted to another front, invited him to a valedictory meal. Two women made up the numbers. One was a daughter of the previous governor. The other was Karen Blixen. April 1918 was a bone-weary time to be in Nairobi. In the weak electric light of the dining room, Denys talked at length of his expedition to Somaliland, of elephant-stalking through wet mimosas, and of nights spangled with stars. Karen Blixen found him "an unusually charming person." The following week, Denys joined a hunting party on the Blixens' farm and stayed the night. The next day he drove back to Nairobi with Karen, and they had lunch. "It is seldom that one meets someone one is immediately in sympathy with and gets along so well with, and what a marvellous thing talent and intelligence is," she wrote to her mother. But her words failed to convey the *coup de foudre* that had taken place. In November, she wrote to her brother, expressing the hope that he might one day meet Denys, "for I have been so fortunate in my old age to meet my ideal realised in him. . . ."

ON MAY 14, DENYS and Billea started on their long inland journey to Cairo and the flying course. As most of the trip was on the Nile and its various tributaries, Denys sold the cooking pot (he got £50 more than he had paid for it)—though at Nimule, on the Ugandan-Sudanese border, he discovered "quite a nice piece of country which one walks." This hundred-mile trek ended at Rejaf, near Juba at the southern end of the sudd, the floating mass of reed and weed that clogs the White Nile. It was lush, tropical country shadowed by the Imatong Mountains, the sparse villages more African than settlements in the dry, Arab-flavored north. "I heard elephant all one night, but I had to leave them without a visit to push on and catch the boat at Rejaf," Denys wrote to Kermit. They traveled by steamer through 250 miles of swampy lowland drained by the headstreams of the White Nile. The sudd was a prehistoric crucible of slime, a return to an earlier stage of evolution. Dense aquatic vegetation dispersed river water over the saucerlike clay plain into a labyrinth of steamy channels inhabited by dark and menacing forms and fringed with fifteen-foot papyrus. In some places weeds had built up into islands, necessitating artful navigation and motionless hours in temperatures in excess of a hundred degrees. Late in the evening, semi-amphibious sitatunga marsh antelope emerged from the papyrus to feed, their elongated, flexible hooves springing off the decayed green matter. It was a relief to reach Khartoum. Still run as a military administration (the hundred officers of the Sudan Political Service ruled a million square miles of territory in nominal partnership with Egypt), it was more or less a white man's town. The Sudanese lived in mud huts across the Nile at Omdurman, which Denys visited to inspect the Mahdi's tomb. Overgrown with vegetation, it had not yet been repaired, and there was still a hole in the roof marking the entrance of a shell fired by one of Kitchener's gunboats.

Stewards plundered the mean little stores of Khartoum to replenish supplies of tinned sausages, Eno's Fruit Salts, and Reckitt's Blue (a washing powder that dealt with stains largely by dyeing them blue), and then they left. The steamer continued through the deserts of northern Sudan, entering Egypt while the Bolsheviks were busy murdering the tsar and his family in Ekaterinburg. When Denys reached Cairo, on June 21, he checked in to Shepheard's Hotel. But he had been mistaken about the date of the flying course and had missed the beginning. If he had known, he would have stayed in Sudan longer. He was furious; the journey had been a glorious break from the tension of the previous four years. In the weeks in the sudd, Denys had wandered in an interior no-man's-land, allowing his thoughts to drift downward, through layers and layers of consciousness, until they reached something solid, and he touched again the sense of self dislodged by the meaningless horror of war. Wilderness offered him a glimpse of the inner world. It was incoherent, as inner worlds always are, but it was preferable to no glimpse at all.

Now, stuck in Cairo, he was instructed to wait at the Abouktir depot until the next course started, but he didn't like that idea at all ("About eight in a tent I suppose and *such* an eight probably"), so he made a successful attempt to prolong his leave. He was concerned that he might not be able to have Billea with him on the course: other officers weren't used to the African colonial's habit of surrounding himself with servants. "I may have to part with him, as I'm going to school and it seems a shock to them that anyone can want a servant of his own," Denys explained to Kermit. "However I shall make a pretty determined attempt to retain him." And he did. Meanwhile, there was Cairo to enjoy, once he had shaken off a touch of fever. Shepheard's was the nexus of European life and a venerable institution in its own right, its Italianate façades overlooking the noisy streets of Ezbekieh in one direction and the hotel's own gardens, filled with tufty date groves and crows, in the other. It was one of the palatial hotels built along the great trade routes of the empire, subsequently colonized, in peacetime, by rich Europeans and Americans seeking winter sun. Denys knew many people in Cairo that summer, and breakfasted in company on the broad terrace at Shepheard's before visiting Coptic churches and inspecting gold workshops in the Khal Khaleel, where the rutted alleys were too narrow to walk two abreast and the merchants wore long vests of sea-green Syrian silk. At night, he had dinner under Shepheard's rigid-tentacled chandeliers before vanishing into the honeycombs of Cairo. He got leave to go up to Alexandria while waiting for his course to begin, and there, too, he "had rather fun meeting a lot of fellows I knew." Decanting from the Mohamed Ali Club into the afternoon sunlight, he found the unpaved streets thronged with dervishes in patchwork cloaks, veiled beauties filling their water jars, and white-skinned pickets doing their rounds to keep the troops in order. While he was there, he got a wire from Hoskins. Denys had been trying to establish his whereabouts; he knew that his former commander had moved up to the front in Mesopotamia and was now somewhere in Palestine, where Allenby was pushing north through the Turkish garrison. It turned out that Hoskins was on the line near Jaffa, three hundred miles away. Denys rushed up and found him. "He was in good form," Denys wrote to Kermit. "I had a great time with him for two days and visited J'lem and B'hem."

THE THIRTY-EIGHTH TRAINING WING of the Royal Air Force had commenced functions at Heliopolis in the environs of Cairo toward the end of 1917. Besides basic flight training, it ran aerial bombing, navigation, and gunnery schools, the students billeted, as Denys feared, in a cluster of yurtlike tents surrounded by barbed wire and blasted five times a day by calls from the adjacent minaret. Denys's course began with nine weeks in the classroom. This didn't suit him at all. "So far it is like being back at Oxford except that one's companions are rather different and one has to attend the lectures," he wrote. It was hard ("They work us morn to morn"), and the classrooms were crowded. But, as usual, Denys found a means of escape. "We keep going by slipping in to Cairo to have a meal and wine at the Turf and Sporting Club fairly frequently," he told Kermit, who was now fighting in France. But on account of his heart the medics passed Denys fit to fly only in warm climates. He was disappointed that he would not be able to serve on a European front even in summer. Once qualified, he had planned to return to England for a spell, but it was now clear that this would be at the coldest time of year, and he admitted to Kermit that he was not sure his health could stand it ("Am a little doubtful about how I should winter there these days"). "Good luck, and don't get killed," he ended the letter.

The nine weeks ground on, but in September, before the course was over, Denys injured his right foot when a piece of barbed wire jammed under the nail of his big toe. The Cairo doctors, "after chopping and burning it about for some time, eventually reduced the unfortunate limb to such a condition that they hastily rushed me into hospital and tore off the nail." He was sent to Helonaus, where the Grand Hotel had been converted into a convalescent hospital, and his toe immediately turned septic again. One might have been relieved that one was not about to be dispatched to be burned alive or smashed to dust in France. But Denys was disappointed. He was missing an opportunity to take the greatest risk so far. "It begins to look as though the war will be over now before I am fledged," he wrote morosely. Kermit sent him a book of short stories by the American writer H. G. Dwight, which he enjoyed, and he was mightily cheered up by

Hoskins, who came down to visit "in wonderful form." (Already a major general, Hoskins was knighted in 1919 and awarded the Order of the Nile by the sultan of Egypt.) The "show" in the north was over. Allenby had continued north through Palestine and met the Turks at Megiddo, where they finally collapsed. The Allies had also cleaned up in Mesopotamia. "I am very glad that Marshall rounded off the Mespots show so neatly," Denys commented, "and that we walked into Nineveh, that great city."* But he was sour about the progress of the war elsewhere. He felt that the Germans were refusing to lie down and die nobly. After a decisive French victory on July 18, the Allies had been making steady daily advances in France against a hungry and demoralized enemy. By the end of September, they had swept along the whole western front, though the Germans fought a dogged rearguard action virtually all the way through France and Belgium. "The Boche in defeat," Denys wrote, "is making it plainer than ever that he possesses neither a sense of humour nor of dignity, eg he has just announced through the Swiss government that he wishes to make an arrangement by which both sides shall cease to bomb behind the lines: that *he* intends to cease this ill-advised practice forthwith. And then his delightful note to the Tscecko-Jugo Slavs reorganising them as a nation and saying that Berlin will be delighted to welcome their Ambassador! Boche humour is another name for horseplay and Boche dignity is another name for bombastic pride." As for his own news, Denys was cross about that, too, especially as the weather was perfect for flying. "If my toe had not let me down I should by now be well on my way through towards completing," he told Kermit. "As it is the next few days may see a German collapse and with it the end of any point in my remaining a sodjer."

Was there any point in continuing to invest in Kenya, either? In December 1917, Allied forces in East Africa had finally pushed the Germans out of their own territory. It was therefore demoralizing to hear that the wily von Lettow had sneaked back in and was fighting his way north. The Rovuma River marked the boundary between German and Portuguese territory. "Von Lettow has now recrossed the Rovuma and is again in GEA!" Denys wrote angrily to Kermit. "If van Deventer [the commander

---

* British involvement in the region was not over. Between the armistice and 1922, the cost of Iraq to the taxpayer was in the region of £100 million. One wonders if the cycle of war and massive expenditure to protect the god of oil will ever end.

in chief appointed to replace Hoskins] was not a Boer this would certainly procure him the very choicest raspberry; but I suppose he will be allowed to blunder on, ably assisted by Sheppard, his Chief of Staff, until Lettow takes Nairobi, unless the defeat of Germany in Europe puts an end to hostilities in BEA [Kenya]. As Smuts gave van Deventer a KCMG [Knight Commander of St. Michael and St. George] for allowing Lettow to escape south of the Rovuma the least he can do now is to procure him a Grand Cross of the British Empire for letting him escape north of that river again." Denys's contempt for politicians had yielded to bitterness. What had been the point of that endless movement down the hellish, hallucinatory banks of the Pangani? He continued to excoriate Allied leaders by comparing them unfavorably with Woodrow Wilson, the American president, whom he deemed to have been "very satisfactory lately—opinion about the Germans has hardened very much in America for which we ought to be most thankful, as it will serve to brace up what Maxse [Leopold Maxse, the editor of the *National Review*] describes as the Westminster Invertebrates." Denys viewed politicians with the same contempt that he had for military leaders. There had been talk of a general election in Britain before the end of 1918 and Denys didn't like the sound of it, especially as hordes of newly enfranchised women voters were to be unleashed at the polls: "What in the name of the Kaiser Lloyd George is plunging England into a general election [for] with 7 million women voters, just at the end of the war is more than I can fathom. Why not get the war over first: but perhaps we shall! Keep well: it must have been nice having your family with you in France. Denys."

Nine days later, the war ended.

DENYS REMAINED IN CAIRO until he qualified. He abandoned his plan to return to Europe, perceiving that the weather would be atrocious and the country stupefied, as if awakened from a deep sleep. He needed to assess his affairs in Kenya in order to decide if he was going to stay the course. Recent reports had been bad. In October his friend Lady Colville, a Frenchwoman who had set up a military hospital in her Gilgil hotel, had written with news that Denys's *duka* at Lemek had been incinerated by Maasai rebels. It was part of a widespread Maasai rebellion. After years of peremptory treatment by Nairobi civil servants, the Maasai had refused to accept an attempt to conscript their *moran*.* Their objection was met with machine-gun fire. Parties of Maasai proceeded to pillage European and Indian-owned stores in their reserve, cut telegraph lines, and generally spread terror. People were killed on both sides, settlers along the boundary applied for police protection, and their Kikuyu laborers started to desert. The *moran* had again greased their spears when the panicky administration dispatched Delamere to negotiate peace. Denys had lost stock, including hides and skins, to the value of over £5,000. He blamed the administration, which had, he reported to Kermit, "again shown itself in typical colours by stirring up trouble with the Maasai in the most senseless manner. . . . I trust that we shall be able to obtain compensation eventually . . . but you may be certain that the Maasai will not be keen to pay up; and Government having now probably got the wind right up will try to shirk responsibility in their usual manner." He continued to wonder if there was any future for him in Africa. "As things are pretty messed up in BEA I shall probably settle to get out as soon as possible," he said.

In this spirit, Denys and Billea returned to Kenya, retracing the route they had taken seven months earlier. "The Nile played up quite according to the guide books as regards game," Denys recorded. "I saw four lots of elephant at different times, one very big herd: and one morning we came across a lot crossing the river, about 20, and one young bull had got swept down below a proper landing place and could not get out, and as we passed by he drowned and sank before our eyes." He recovered his strength, which had been sapped by the long series of infections, and felt much better in the warmth of southern Sudan, which he had always found to be a "comfortable climate." At Rejaf he hired a cook, "a real Swahili ruffian of the old safari type with a huge black beard; his name he gave as Hamisi, but I notice his associates call him Simba, on account of his mane no doubt. He devils chicken *à merveille* and is an expert baker, so I intend to retain him if he will bear with me." Hamisi stayed with Denys for eleven years, and in the end gave his life for him.

At Rejaf, Denys was also joined by his old friend Chevallier Kitch-

---

* In the Maasai age-set system, *moran* were young males between adolescence and marriage. *Moran* are usually described in English as "warriors."

ener, elder brother of the more famous Herbert and now the second earl.*
Kitchener senior had served in Manipur and Burma in the 1890s and was
sent to East Africa in 1915, "though in what capacity nobody knows,"
Meinertzhagen had remarked. Denys had soldiered with him, as had
Cranworth, who admired him. Even Meinertzhagen was intrigued by him,
despite complaints that the colonel "emits hot air by the cubic yard."
Denys referred to him as "Old Kitchener," and he was indeed seventy-
two, which was old enough to be tackling the hundred-mile trek through
dangerous bush to Nimule. But he was game, arriving at Rejaf equipped
with a camp bed, blankets, a shotgun, two tins of *petit beurre* biscuits, and
a set of false teeth. "It was just as well that I had a certain amount of stuff
and a couple of chairs with me," Denys told Kermit. Having reached
Nimule, dentures intact, the party proceeded to the eastern shore of Lake
Albert, whence the next leg, to Masindi Port at one end of Lake Kyoga, en-
tailed "furious wiring, relays of porters and an old motor lorry which took
us the last 30 miles on the iron rim of one back wheel." At Masindi they
boarded the *Speke,* an old rust bucket that barged her way through the
reeds obstructing the shallow waters of Lake Kyoga, depositing the party
at the mouth of the Victoria Nile, where they transferred to the *Stanley*
and voyaged south to the railhead at Namasagali. There, on January 26,
1919, they picked up the Nairobi newspapers and read about the death of
Teddy Roosevelt. "I am very sorry," Denys wrote immediately to Kermit.
"It is a great loss for the right cause just now when the next three or four
years will demand much clear thinking of the leaders of civilisation, and I
know how much it must mean for you." The papers were full of the government's Soldier Settler scheme, which, in order to stimulate closer settlement, was offering land grants in the Protectorate to men who had
served. "You ought to take up some and come out and settle here," Denys
finished his condolence letter to Kermit. ". . . I feel that your wife would
like BEA, but I am never quite sure of it as a country for white women and

---

* By special provision of succession made when Field Marshal (Horatio) Herbert Kitchener was
granted a peerage for his performance in the Sudan, his elder brother (Henry Elliott) Chevallier
Kitchener succeeded to the earldom when the former drowned in 1916. When Chevallier first arrived in Nairobi, a woman he met at a Government House reception asked him if he was any relation to "the" Kitchener. "Young lady," he replied, "in my family I am 'the' Kitchener."

children."* Denys's attitude to women was typical of his generation. But it was a generalized view. In his personal relations, he was never attracted to submissive women.

DENYS ARRIVED BACK in Kenya three months after the war ended. Von Lettow had learned of his defeat when one of his *askaris* ambushed a British motorcyclist carrying dispatches with details of the armistice. A special clause had been written into the armistice giving von Lettow a month from November 11 to surrender, as the architects of the Peace knew that it might take that long to find him. The Germans had received no information from the outside world for a year, and von Lettow assumed that his side had won the war. It was inconceivable to him that both the eastern and the western fronts had collapsed. "All our troops, native as well as Europeans, had always held the conviction that Germany could not be beaten in this war," he wrote later. But on November 25, with the remnants of a brimless sun hat on his head and a long beard touching his chest, he stood under a limp Union Jack at Abercorn, near the toe of Lake Tanganyika, and ordered his 155 officers and 1,168 *askaris* to lay down their arms in the sheeting African rain. They were Germany's only undefeated army.

* The idea that white women were constitutionally weaker than men, and therefore unable to withstand the tropics, persisted for decades. Well into the thirties, white female teachers were obliged to spend one year out of every three "resting."

CHAPTER 6

MY WIFE'S
LOVER

As for charm, I suspect Denys invented it.

—BERYL MARKHAM,
West with the Night, 1942

IN THE LAST YEAR OF WAR, THE WEATHER HAD COLLUDED IN THE MISERY of the Protectorate when drought and famine overtook the land. The waters sank, a flaky mold settled over the Rift, and at night a burning wind blew the sulfuric exhalations of Lake Elmenteita across the plains. Many Africans died, and the living followed old caravan routes to the next fouled water hole. Monkeys came down from the trees, antelope trekked along the horizon in sad lines, and muddy tongues lolled from carcasses on every hillside. Rinderpest killed most of the cattle, and those that survived were gobbled up by ravenous game. Only the vultures grew fat. "The sun rose and sank in a blinding heaven, and under its hideous presence all sensitive life trembled and shrank," Llewelyn Powys wrote. In October 1918, Spanish flu, a calamitous pandemic, swept through East Africa, destroying those the drought had spared.

LIKE MANY, DENYS RETURNED to heavy financial losses. But, even as he was counting his own personal cost of war, Africa won him back. Although he was drawn home to England by family ties and an appetite for culture until the end of his life, the feral energy of the tropics was an antidote to the postwar twilight of the West. Denys emerged from the war with an

MC (Military Cross), as well as a Pip (the 1914–15 Star medal), a Squeak (the 1913–18 Campaign medal), and a Wilfred (the 1914–18 Victory medal). But he found little to celebrate, and no solace in the sentimental pronouncements of British newspapers. "They are at peace," went Laurence Binyon's poem "For the Fallen," now quoted ceaselessly; "it is only for ourselves that we have to be sorry." Denys had never believed in the romance of war, even before eight and a half million died. As for the Treaty of Versailles—supposedly drawn up to ensure the end of all wars—he considered it the Peace that passeth all understanding. This was prescient, as the peace was phony.

Before the rains, Denys went up-country to inspect his land. Most farms had fallen into dilapidation, forcing owners to start again. The managers of the three main banks cooperated with generous loans, nobody paying much attention to petty details such as interest rates. Everyone on the Uasin Gishu Plateau in the Rift Valley, including Denys, invested in flax. With the resourcefulness of true pioneers, the settlers never tired in their pursuit of new crops or industries. Sweet potatoes, pawpaw, beekeeping, trout farming, the manufacture of chemical pulp for paper production—all featured in their laborious roster of experiments. They were determined to get ahead on their own terms. "Among the white community of the Protectorate, a unanimous opinion prevails that the psychological moment is near for cutting the umbilical cord that still connects us with India," an editorial in the *Leader* announced. (In particular, they wanted to abandon the rupee in favor of the pound.) For the majority, life in the bush was as physically grueling as it had always been. Many women spent their evenings dosing the children with paraffin and digging jiggers out of their toes with safety pins. Some lived in squalor. Nellie Grant described a visit to her neighbors the Harrieses, a Welsh couple, in about 1921: "When you sat down to a meal, you had to push Muscovy ducks off the Chippendale chairs. A hatch was opened between kitchen and living room and an indescribable, utterly horrible stench belched forth, followed by the food. The Harrieses' bedroom, a large rondavel, was shared between the marital bed and a large, probably five-hundred-egg, incubator. The roof above was lined with a tarpaulin to keep the incubator, not the Harrieses, dry." Nellie herself started at Kitimuru, her farm at Chania Bridge (now Thika), with nothing, fetching her groceries from Nairobi in an oxcart. And she, the niece of the first Duke of Westminster, had been brought up in mansions in which a man was employed just to clean the oil lamps and Nellie tobogganed down oak staircases on tea trays.

Back in Nairobi, Denys sold the Parklands house and rented a cottage on the grounds of Muthaiga; as Delamere was looking for a pied-à-terre, they took it on a joint tenancy. A neat stucco building with its own small garden, it overlooked the golf course, the newly acquired ox-drawn lawn mower, and the women strolling the grounds under their parasols. Denys rarely went unnoticed. "Lots of women were in love with him . . . at least eight . . . absolutely adored him," Cranworth wrote. He created around him a sea of excitement in which he floated with loglike calm. But one admirer was about to disperse the competition, at least temporarily.

KAREN BLIXEN WAS TWO years older than Denys. Her family nickname was Tanne, and in Africa she was Tania to her English friends. Both her grandfathers were Jutland landowners; her mother came from a family of Unitarian bourgeois traders, while her father was an aristocrat. Disjunction is fertile ground for snobbery. Tania and her four siblings grew up in Rungsted, a fishing village on the coastal road between Copenhagen and Elsinore, in North Zeeland. On one side the family home nestled into the beech woods, and on the other it overlooked the waters of Øresund and, on a clear day, the Swedish coast. In the winter, fishermen walked over the ice to Sweden. Tania's father had lived as a trapper with Native Americans. He went home to a career as an army officer and a member of Parliament, sitting as an Independent with leftish inclinations. Then he hanged himself in a Copenhagen boardinghouse. Nobody knew why. Tania was nine.

When Denys met Tania, she was thirty-three. She had deep-set dark eyes, a beak nose, and abundant chestnut hair, and her face was sometimes beautiful and at other times all wrong. In old age she said, "One of the things in my life I have been unhappy about is that I was not better looking than I actually was. On the other hand, one of the things I have been pleased about is that at least I was as good looking as I actually was." One settler noted her "strange beauty"; another, Ferdinand Cavendish-Bentinck, said "she was no great shakes to look at." All her life, Tania struggled to be thinner. At times she seemed almost weightless, incorporeal as an El Greco figure. She loved clothes, and stopped off in Paris on her way to Africa to stock up on couture gowns. In the twenties, she kept a mannequin at Pacquin's and later, when she became a writer, she dressed her characters in finery, like peacocks. Elspeth Huxley described her as a person "full of magnetism and restless energy, like a benign witch," and also noticed that her makeup was usually "all awry." Tania was the kind of woman who lied about her age (Denys thought she was five years his junior); not a crime, just silly. She received no formal education until she was seventeen, and that was at art school. But she spoke several languages.

As a young woman, she had fallen in love with Baron Hans Blixen-Finecke, one of her hard-living Swedish second cousins. He wasn't interested, and Tania ended up with his twin, Bror. She never tried to hide the fact that she was not in love with Bror. A feckless charmer, he was muscular and moonfaced, with fair hair and pale blue eyes. After graduating from agricultural school, he managed a dairy farm on the family estate, but it was not his métier. He was hopelessly irresponsible with money and had the constitution of a cart horse: well into middle age, he could drink a bottle of gin at night, rise at dawn, and hunt all day. Beryl Markham, who traveled with him, said that he went about for years with enough malaria in his system to kill ten men. Known to his friends in Africa as Blix, he was an immensely respected hunter, and although Beryl said he was "never significantly silent," he was modest to the extent that he made molehills out of mountains. He is often cited as the model for Hemingway's white hunter Robert Wilson in "The Short Happy Life of Francis Macomber." In all likelihood that honor went to Philip Percival, a sportsman with whom Blix later went into partnership in a safari firm; but the point is, Wilson could have been Blix, and Blix could have been Wilson. He and Hemingway were friends. When Hemingway won the Nobel Prize in 1954, a year in which Karen Blixen had been tipped to get it, he said in an interview on the day of the announcement, "I would have been happy—happier—today if the prize had gone to that beautiful writer Isak Dinesen [Tania's pen name]," elaborating privately to a friend later that "Blickie is in hell and he would be pleased if I spoke well of his wife."

When Tania and Blix announced their engagement, in 1912, her family viewed the union with misgivings. Tania, however, a victim of the Scandinavian claustrophobia so remorselessly described by Ibsen, yearned to escape provincial Denmark. "How desperately she longed for wings to carry her away!" her brother Thomas wrote of her teenage years. She and Blix decided to farm rubber in Malaya. But when an uncle returned from a safari in Kenya enthusing over that country's potential, they switched continents. Her family put up the money for a seven-hundred-acre dairy farm, and Blix went ahead to get started. Their plans were laid, according to Thomas, "without any petty attention to detail." In September 1913, Blix sent his fiancée a thirty-page blood-spattered safari journal in which he revealed that he had sold the dairy farm and bought a forty-five-hundred-acre coffee plantation at the foot of the Ngong Hills, twelve miles from Nairobi and, at six thousand feet, a little higher. The settlers had decided that coffee was a crop with unlimited potential. ("Gold meant coffee," Blix wrote home.) Africans were not allowed to queer the pitch. When a group of enterprising Chaga planted coffee in the foothills of Kilimanjaro, European farmers were furious. British settlers rushed to support their German neighbors, the matter was debated in the House of Commons, and the hapless Chaga were ostracized from their markets. Blix, meanwhile, had acquired one of the largest coffee plantations in the country, and the deal he cut also included land of about the same size near Eldoret. It was impossible for him to know that his farm at Ngong was too high, the soil too acidic and the microclimate too dry, and, above all, that the cold winds sweeping down from the hills at night meant it was no place for a coffee farm. As the crop takes four or five years to bear, it was to be a painfully protracted lesson. But at the beginning of 1914 Tania packed crystal, a French clock, an exercise machine, and a pair of Scottish deerhounds called Dawn and Dusk, and sailed to Africa. In her short story "The Dreamers," written years later when her African dream had been shattered, the narrator describes a journey of his own. "I was on my way from the North, where things were cold and dead, to the blue and voluptuous South," he said.

Blix rowed out to meet his fiancée's ship wearing a *terai* hat* as limp as a wilted frond, and they spent their first night at the Mombasa Club in the company of von Lettow, who had made friends with Tania on the voyage.

---

* The *terai* was a felt hat, usually double-brimmed and usually worn by women. Men generally favored the sola topi, made from the Indian sola plant.

The next morning, the Blixens were married. Their witness was Prince Wilhelm of Sweden, a friend of Blix's, who had come out on safari. When the proud husband took his bride to their home, a modest brick bungalow among wild figs and lilac-flowering Cape chestnuts, twelve hundred field hands lined up to welcome her. Karen Blixen's love affair with Africa began. She felt, she wrote later, like "a person who had come from a rushed and noisy world, into a still country."

Before she met Denys, Tania spoke scathingly of the English ("I find that nation quite, quite unbearable"), favoring everything French on the unarguable grounds that the French were more stylish than their Anglo-Saxon neighbors. The settlers were a poor lot, she thought, especially the wives, and apparently there were not more than ten "decent" women in the country. Her empathy with the Kikuyu and the Somalis, on the other hand, was so strong that she felt they were "like brothers," though in reality she did not perceive Africans as equals so much as human extensions of the landscape. In general, she liked ordinary working people, and she liked aristocrats. She wasn't at all keen on the ones in between. "If I cannot be with the aristocracy or the intelligentsia, I must go down among the proletariat," she wrote. Her fiction is crowded with nineteenth-century noblemen and their ancient retainers. The feudal setup of the African farm appealed to her imagination, and she once remarked that her life at Ngong was very much as it would have been in Denmark in 1700. In her allegiance to the romance of myth, she was, in a way, fatally addicted to the past. But her affection for Africa was genuine. Through the vicissitudes of her life at Ngong, her voluminous letters sing with the joy she found in the pure highland air. It was a metaphorical purity as well as a literal one, as Africa, to Tania, was unpolluted by the norms of Danish society. "The Danish character," she wrote, "is like dough without leavening." Africa supplied the yeast. It was untrammeled, dangerous, and closer to nature. When Blix took her on safari, he taught her to use her own Mannlicher Schoenauer .256 magazine rifle fitted with a scope, and she spoke of the "ecstasy" of hunting. She liked sweep and grandeur, and later imbued her tales with it (often with little substance beneath the glittering surface). And she loved the theater of Africa, as exemplified in the drama of a lion kill or the spectacle of a row of Kikuyu warriors erect in front of her house, oiled torsos hung with ornaments, spears ready.

Blix was not an intellectual. "My fingers itched to hold a weapon rather than a book," he said. Tania remarked privately that he didn't know if the Renaissance came before or after the Crusades. But neither was he the boor often portrayed. His own letters reveal how deeply he responded to the African landscape. A hunter to his bones, he wandered for months through the forests of Uganda and the Congo, as well as Kenya and Tanganyika. In many ways, he conveys the beauties of Africa on the page more persuasively than Tania. He was grateful to have seen the continent in its pristine state. "So far," he wrote as he set off for Lake Kivu, "the tourist has not discovered it, and I would like to see it in its undisturbed glory, before railways and air routes have arrived, before luxury hotels and nightclubs have grown up like poisonous fungi—before it's been tarnished and made ugly by a civilisation which is unable to let things well enough alone." He developed farsighted ideas about the role of education in Africa, and his opinions of the rights of indigenous peoples indicate a refined sensibility—refined, at least, relative to his peers. He was also a connoisseur of the female assets of each tribe. He wrote admiringly of the softly rounded bodies of the Marua, the chiseled features of the Somalis, and the oblong skulls of the Wamba, which, being bent slightly backward, meant they could "sleep on one's shoulder without causing cramp." Blix loved life, and lived it hard; it is difficult to dislike people who put fun above prudence, as something in all of us wants to hang the school fees and the opinions of the neighbors. But there is often a dark side that admiration conveniently discards. In Blix's case, it was syphilis. Early in the marriage, he infected Tania. It was endemic among the Maasai, and everyone knew that he was sleeping with Maasai women. Like most sexually transmitted diseases, syphilis can make some individuals infectious despite an absence of outward symptoms, and Blix was apparently never ill, at least not at this stage. But Tania was sick. In the summer of 1915, she went home to consult a venereologist—not the most auspicious moment to travel overland through France and Belgium. She had already been treated with mercury tablets in Nairobi, and now was subjected to Salvarsan, an unpleasant arsenic-based medication. By the time Tania returned to Africa, she believed that she was no longer infectious, and the evidence indicates that she was right, though it was not a result of her medication, as she supposed. The primary symptoms of syphilis normally arrest themselves, and patients frequently develop enough of an immune response to be noninfectious. Her later clinical history makes it clear that she continued to harbor viable spirochetes somewhere in her body—that she still had syphilis, in other words, and was simultaneously infected but not infectious. The mercury tablets had poisoned her system and introduced health problems that never left her. But she made a good psychological recovery from the onslaught, and was still hoping for a child. She felt "extraordinarily sure" that she would have one. Despite everything, she was astonishingly loyal to her husband—it is one of the most likable things about her—and she was emotionally loyal to him till the end. "If I should wish anything back of my life," she said in old age, "it would be to go on safari once again with Bror Blixen." He had the same effect on other women. His second wife said, after his death, that he had been a wonderful, unfaithful husband and the best lover she had ever had (and she had a few), and that she deeply regretted leaving him. "If it did not sound so awful," Tania wrote home from the farm some years later, "I might say— that to me, the world being what it is—it was worth having syphilis to become a baroness." In fact, she was more human than this preposterous remark suggests. When she was dying, she told a sister-in-law that fame as a writer was no match for the normal female life she had renounced.

Tania returned to the Protectorate early in 1917. Heavy rains fell that season, and the coffee flowered like a cloud of chalk. The blossom smelled bitter. Then a drought came and the berries withered. But she kept going. It was a lean landscape at Ngong. "It was Africa distilled up through six thousand feet, like the strong and refined essence of a continent," she said. In March, the Blixens moved to a stone bungalow called Mbogani ("house in the woods"). It had been built by a Swede in 1912, and came with several handsome pieces of Scandinavian furniture. The dining room and the study were paneled in mahogany and the floor was mahogany parquet, except in the hall, where it was covered in protective linoleum. It was a dark house, but it was cool and the rooms were still and silent save for the rustle of the wind in the frangipani. Tania was happy to be back, despite the fact that she had been accused of harboring German sympathies. It was an unfair charge, as she had undertaken valuable supply work for the Allies, traveling many miles on foot with a team of oxen. The Dinesens were anything but pro-German. Tania's father and grandfather had both fought the Prussians over North Schleswig, and her brother Thomas had been quick to abandon his country's neutrality and join up for the latest war, serving at Amiens as a private in the Quebec Rifles. All suspicion vanished on December 21, 1918, when it was announced in the *Leader* that Thomas had been awarded the Victoria Cross.*

In February 1919, the Blixens gave a shoot, and Denys was among the twenty guests. He had not seen Tania for ten months. It had recently rained, and the Ngong Hills, previously burned like a doormat, had turned emerald. Denys developed a fever and stayed on to recover. Tania was delighted. "I don't think I have ever met such an intelligent person before," she told her mother. She was in awe of Denys's learning and the guileless charm with which he deployed it. He began to teach her Latin as he got better, and they sat on the stone bench outside her house talking about painting and music until the hills turned black. Although she sometimes went with Blix on safari, she was more often alone at the farm, and Denys walked in on her solitude. His personality was like a light that flooded her life. Tania wrote home describing him as "one of the old settlers," a group in which she considered one found "a much better type" than one did among the later arrivals. She was especially impressed by the fact that his father was an earl. "I think it is great good fortune for a country to have a class of people who have nothing other to do than follow their own bent," she said. If she had a son, she decided, she would send him to Eton. This would be preferable to the boringly egalitarian system in Denmark, where everyone grew up "in the same restricted conditions." In her vision of the world, the aristocracy exemplified freedom from the stifling moral code of the "bourgeois" society represented by her mother's family.

TWO OR THREE WEEKS after renewing their acquaintance, Denys invited Tania on safari. For ten days it was to be just the two of them (with the usual squadron of servants). There was no need for subterfuge. Blix was

---

* Neither British nor American forces would have Thomas, because he was a foreign national, so he made his way to Canada to enlist. At the recruiting station, he was asked if he was a homosexual, the evidence being that he was wearing a wristwatch. He said he was not. There were no further questions.

happy for his wife to experience the freedom he enjoyed, and delighted that she had chosen such an agreeable partner. He had often drunk with Denys at the Norfolk and now started introducing him as "my good friend, and my wife's lover." They had a certain amount in common, temperamentally, but whatever it was that they shared, Blix had more of it. If Denys was a free spirit who believed in living for the moment, Blix was the same thing taken to its logical conclusion. Denys tempered his behavior with concern for the well-being of others. Blix had little time for such niceties. The dilemma between going and staying did not trouble him. If he felt like going, he went. It was an attractive option, but the cost fell to others. As for Tania, she had no moral qualms, and had already had an intimate friendship with another Swedish baron, Eric von Otter, an ascetic individual who was a student of Islam. (Blix didn't mind Otter at all, but he was bored to tears by all the Islamic talk. In the end, he banned any mention of Mohammed between the hours of twelve and four.) Tania's position in the settler community was awkward. Denys accepted her for what she was. Through all the years they were together, she usually remembered that she had to accept him for what he was.

They went to the hunting grounds of Mount Kenya and followed the whirr of green parrots to the edge of the camphor forest that lay between the timber and the bamboo. At night, after the pink sifting clouds had passed over the camp, a boy filled paraffin tins at the water hole and prepared the canvas bath while Hamisi marinated impala fillet in the oven he had sunk and boiled spur fowl bones for the thin, peppery bouillon that Denys liked. After dinner they talked of books, returning to the parables of the spiritual journey at the heart of all great literature. Tania's conception of God was interchangeable with the notion of destiny—a kind of universal force that directed one's life. God puts in an appearance in most of her stories, and one of her collections is called *Anecdotes of Destiny*. Before they found each other, neither she nor Denys had a companion in Kenya with whom they could discuss such matters. In addition, they shared a passion for Africa. Tania was part of Denys's deepening contact with Kenya, and her lyrical response to the landscape and the people attracted him. They sat for many hours as the shadows of the porters moved silently between tents and thorn trees stood sharp against the sky. The tropical night, she wrote, was like a Catholic cathedral compared with the

Protestant skies of northern latitudes—not a bad setting for the heady, in-filling euphoria of nascent love. After all she had been through, she was alone with a man she adored. Five years later, she said that she had fallen deeply in love with Denys when they first met, and that it was not the yielding tenderness so often described—it was like being struck with a blacksmith's hammer. As for him, he relished the company of an attractive woman as well as the opportunity to talk about books and philosophy. Denys was half sportsman and half poet, and Tania brought the poetic to the fore. And when she was passionate she rose like a wild spirit.

A few weeks after the safari, Denys was guest of honor at Billea's wedding, and Tania accompanied him. The groom, magnificent in a gold Somali robe, bowed down to the ground in welcome and performed a ceremonial sword dance, "all wild with the desperado spirit of the desert." Tania was ushered into the bridal chamber, where the walls and bed were hung with ancestral embroidery and the dark-eyed bride sat stiff with silks, amber, and fear. Afterward, Denys and Tania made plans: they would go down the Nile from Cairo. Tania was blissful. To consummate her happiness that year, the harvest on the farm was good. The big coffee drier lumbered through its rotations and the beans were taken out in the middle of the night, the cobwebs of the great dark hangar illuminated by lines of hurricane lamps. Later the coffee was hulled, graded, sorted, and packed in sacks, twelve to the ton, that were sewn up with a saddler's needle before being loaded onto wagons and drawn by oxen to Nairobi. Once the harvest was in, the Blixens left for Europe. In September 1919, Denys also sailed home. He wanted to buy into a London-based firm that was setting up trading schemes in Abyssinia. It was a risky idea, but none of his other ventures were yielding revenue. Flax had collapsed, he had got out of coffee, and nothing had come of the cotton proposals. Crops refused to grow on a farm he had acquired between Rongai and the Mau summit, and his cattle were dead. Something had to be done. Unlike Delamere, who succeeded in Kenya through hard work, Denys had so far treated his schemes as gambles. Now he was thinking ahead. He decided to return to London to raise capital. There was no more talk of selling up. A more mature emotional outlook led him to seek longer-term projects requiring viable finance and sustained work, rather than merely putting his money on red or black. He was still dabbling in commercial projects, but the

Henry Finch Hatton, thirteenth Earl of Winchilsea

Nan Finch Hatton with (left to right) Toby, Denys, and Topsy, photographed in Sleaford in 1889

*Denys and
his mother*

*Toby and Denys at
Haverholme*

Denys went on to captain the
Oxford University golf team.

Topsy and Denys

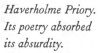

Haverholme Priory.
Its poetry absorbed
its absurdity.

Julian Grenfell and Denys, puppeteering in the Pop club at Eton, 1904

Denys as a teenager, photographed by his mother

Toby with the Haverholme gamekeeper

Denys at Eton:
"Autocrat and
democrat, an
adored tyrant"

Nan, Henry, and Margaretta
at the Priory in 1919

Denys, Nan, and Henry in
Haverholme Park in 1922

Toby, Ossie and Denys. Denys always dressed in a hurry.

Toby and Denys

*"As for charm,
I suspect Denys
invented it."*

*Nine hundred
fifty-three elephants*

The Mara Triangle. "He had seen what men with imagination cannot help seeing in a dream country like Africa."

Denys (second from left) with Rose and Algy Cartwright at Lake Naivasha

Nairobi in the 1920s

Denys, Jack Pixley, and Tich Miles with Lady Colville in 1914

Denys with buffalo, on safari near Lake Jipe with a client, 1927

Cole's Scouts watering close to the border between British and German East Africa, January 1915

Denys, serving in Cole's Scouts in the First World War. He is interrogating an askari suspected of spying for the Germans.

Two of the Three Musketeers: Berkeley Cole and Tich Miles, serving in Cole's Scouts in 1915

*Tania (Karen Blixen)
with Dawn and Dusk*

*Tania and Blix
on the farm*

*Tania,
photographed in
Denmark before
departing for
Africa—and
marriage*

Kikuyu moran outside the farm in 1922

Tania, breakfasting with Minerva

Tania and staff.
Farah is second from left
in the front row.

The farm at the foot of the
Ngong Hills, with Tania in
the foreground

Denys (below, center) on safari with his client Frederick Patterson, an American manufacturing tycoon. Denys was rarely photographed without a hat, as he didn't want people to know he was bald.

The beach house (above) at Takaungu

Denys gets himself out of trouble.

Denys (left) and Edward, Prince of Wales, take a tea break during the 1928 royal safari

Beryl Markham: not your run-of-the-mill Circe

Three thousand people gathered at the farm for the ngoma in honor of the Prince of Wales during his 1928 safari.

One of Denys's own photographs. By the time he turned forty, he was more interested in shooting with a camera than a gun.

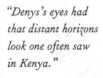

"Denys's eyes had that distant horizons look one often saw in Kenya."

Denys and the custard-yellow Gypsy Moth

Abyssinian scheme, besides having a future, allowed him to explore a new area of Africa, and to expand and enhance his relationship with the continent. As for his romance with Tania: they met briefly in London that autumn, then they were to be parted for two and a half years.

DENYS HAD NOT BEEN in England since 1917. Based alternately at Haverholme and at the Conservative Club in London, he toured the country, visiting everyone he knew who had not died. Although there were still parties, the Edwardian carnival was a distant memory. Housemaids no longer came upstairs to hook frocks before dinner, and the persistence of rationing ruled out lavish entertaining. Four years of fighting had thrown shadows over so many lives, and to its bones the nation felt what Churchill called "the ache for those who will never come home." Denys visited the recently widowed Mrs. Barrington-Kennett at the house in Onslow Gardens where he had spent so many happy days with his huge flying partner, Victor, and his brothers. Three of the four boys had died: one a year for the first three years. Victor's plane had been shot down over the Somme. As Viola Parsons said, "The war did not end with a shout of joy, but with the bleak outlook of a world without young men. Everyone felt a dull feckless feeling, as after a funeral."

Besides scything the population, the war had smashed the social and moral foundations on which Denys's world had been built, and since the armistice, unemployment, sour industrial relations, and inflation had set the tone for a generalized disillusion that had seeped over Britain. It was a malaise that led to the collapse of the political middle ground and induced a pervasive sense that only personal values mattered, and that the point of life lay in the experience and understanding of the self. Denys, who had never been concerned either with politics or with conventional achieving or doing, was suddenly in tune with the mood of the era. "Everything I had known before the war seemed to be withering away and falling to pieces," wrote Siegfried Sassoon, who was born the year before Denys. In addition, it was Denys's first European winter for almost a decade, and cold, damp weather always precipitated a slump in his spirits. Up in Lincolnshire, he shivered in the familiar corridors as dark feathers of smoke drifted across the park, a bitter wind blew off the fens, and winter shouldered in from the north. The pale October leaves were already falling fast, and early in the morning a sable-blue cold hung over the fields. By December, the herbs in the hedgerows were snowy with rime. The cook made him poached fish in parsley sauce, and he hugged the fire.

Toby had remained with the East Kents until the end of the war. He was mentioned in dispatches and awarded a Distinguished Service Cross. (His batman lived so far behind the lines that Toby, the viscount, had to learn to mend his own socks.) Now almost as bald as Denys and more rotund, he had returned to his career as a discount banker and settled in London with Margaretta and their three children. He remained as close as ever to Denys, despite their different personalities. Popular culture would have been an oxymoron to Toby, whereas Denys had the common touch. Denys was a good organizer, but he was not fastidious, nor was he a worrier. Toby kept an obsessive track of the number of cigars remaining in his store at Benson and Hedges, noted the time of every train he ever took, and fretted about money all his life. In the early twenties, he had something new to worry about: Margaretta was furious about his relationship with another woman in their circle, and a succession of private scenes and late-night arguments were duly documented in Toby's diary. As for Denys's romantic life, his most regular companion on this eleven-month visit home was Geoffrey Buxton's sister Rose, who as a little girl had kept up with the cricket matches at Dunston while her brothers and Denys were down from Eton. Now twenty-one, at first glance the tall, blue-eyed Rose might have seemed an unusual choice for Denys. She was quiet and introverted, with no interest in balls and parties, and she did not talk much in company. She herself questioned why Denys was drawn to her, concluding that he liked the fact that she was "unsociable and shy." But there was something unusual about Rose, and she was courageous, both characteristics Denys went for in his women. During the war she had driven an ambulance in France, and there was a modest and private determination about everything she did. The intermittent romance between them lasted many years. She was one of his great loves.

In September of 1920, after almost a year in Europe, Denys sailed for Mombasa. As planned, he had secured a position with a London-based Abyssinian trading syndicate—itself a reflection of his reputation as an African expert, and a prelude to his later role as a spokesman for Africa in

Britain. He intended to make his first visit soon after reaching Kenya. Denys felt trapped on ships—he often referred to them as prisons—but he was happy to be on his way back. England was enjoying a brief Indian summer that year, and as the SS *Dunvegan Castle* moved out of port the tanned sails of the Hampshire barges were flat in the motionless air and varnished spirits gleamed in the tranquil sunshine. Farther south, war had left its mark. Discarded ordnance littered the brick-red coast of Portugal, wrecks disfigured the ports of the Mediterranean, and dismantled military engines rusted among the earthworks at Kantara, the entrails of a steel monster that had died in the heat. At Aden, where they docked at night, lanterns in the houses climbing the hill glimmered in an amphitheater of tiny lights. In the boats that hurried out to the ship, each with its own flickering lamp, Somalis held up cigarettes and ostrich feathers. On October 2, the palmy outlines of Mombasa appeared ahead, crenellated against a mackerel sky. Soon the ship was engulfed by *totos*. The air was heavy and humid. "Nothing exciting has taken place in Mombasa for the last week," the local newspaper reported promisingly. But Denys found that the Protectorate had developed a great deal in a year. To begin with, it was no longer a protectorate; it was a colony. The white population had decided to call it Kenya, after the highest mountain. (Equatoria was their second choice.) Victorious colonial powers had snatched bits of Africa from the Germans, and the former German East Africa, now British, had been renamed Tanganyika Territory.* Ex-soldiers had begun to arrive in Nairobi in large numbers, beneficiaries of the wildly popular land-grant lottery. Kenya, touted as a paradise, was the perfect refuge from the tired European world that had sent them to the trenches in the first place—or so they thought. Roads had opened, and the winner of Kenya's first motor race had covered the 113 miles between Nairobi and Nakuru at the wheel of a Model T Ford in a touch under four hours, albeit with a jockey astride the bonnet pouring water into the radiator as the car sped along. Denys dis-

---

* After unseemly squabbling, both Britain and Belgium received mandates from the League of Nations in respect of German East African territory. In 1919, Urundi and Rwanda were ceded to Belgium and the rest to Britain, much to the displeasure of the German and Austrian farmers now returning to properties they had worked before the war. Of all the countries whose people had fought on the side of the Allies, Kenya was the only one to lose land after the war. Jubaland, its northeastern province, was promised to Italy in 1915 in return for that country's participation in the conflict. In the mid-1920s, the deal was ratified.

covered that settlers had been busily forming fire brigades, football teams, and even a jazz band ("a sort of futuristic idea of harmony," sniffed the *Leader*). Three years later rugby was introduced, though in the first season a rhino invaded the pitch, had to be shot, and was towed off by a team of oxen. Progress came with its usual chaperone, nostalgia. Regrets were expressed for the good old days, "where erstwhile we were all a happy family. . . ." Meanwhile, the *Leader* struggled to keep its readers abreast of events in the puzzling world beyond East Africa. "What is Bolshevism?" wondered a columnist.

Denys had often spoken of Abyssinia at the bar of the Norfolk with George "Jack Flash" Riddell, one of the first white hunters. The Sandhurst-trained Riddell was a flamboyant individual who wore a wide-brimmed hat and bright-colored cravat, and in race week once rode his horse into the Norfolk dining room and hurdled over tables. Before the war, he had traded Lancashire cotton products for Abyssinian sheep and goats, wheedled his way around the local *ras* (head), and bought horses in the Danakil Desert. Europeans still knew little of Abyssinia, yet its civilization was as old as that of Egypt, and Christianity had flourished in its highlands since the fourth century. Riddell's stories spoke directly to Denys. At the end of the year, Denys set off himself. Although Abyssinia shared a border with northern Kenya, he traveled by ship up to Aden for the first leg of the journey. In nearby Djibouti he had arranged to meet Philip Zaphiro, a Constantinople-born Greek who rode around the country in the capacity of frontier inspector for British Southern Abyssinia. Denys now offered Zaphiro a stipend to act as local agent and interpreter for the syndicate. Terms were duly agreed.

Now Denys and Billea boarded a train for a three-day journey inland to Addis Ababa. Abyssinia was a disparate land, even by African standards. Besides the Christian Amharic highlanders, the population embraced pagan Shangalla in the west, nomadic Danakil in the east, and Somalis of the Ogaden Desert in the south. A cultivable belt was farmed by Muslim Gallas. Although Ras Tafari had not yet been crowned emperor and turned himself into Haile Selassie, in August 1917 he had been named heir apparent and regent, and was in the process of establishing a system of law courts, abolishing formal slavery, and generally modernizing—an auspicious time, therefore, for foreign investors to establish links.

Abyssinia was admitted to the League of Nations in 1923 and accepted as a legitimate trading partner by the European powers. Slavery persisted.

The ride across the plain to Dire Dawa was pleasant, if noisy, but by Afdem the remorseless glare of the sun had beaten European spirits into submission. At night, when the train stopped, first-class passengers slept in fly-blown hotels serviced by Arabs whose mouths were green from long hours spent chewing the narcotic khat leaves. At Hawash, the train began its laborious climb through its own soot-laden steam to Modjo, Akaki, and Addis Ababa itself. The capital was a new town situated eight thousand feet above sea level on a grassy, treeless plain raked by gulleys and surrounded by eucalyptus woods. The royal enclosure, or *ghebbit*, lay on a slight elevation, and a gallows tree stood in front of the cathedral. Most Abyssinians lived in circular grass-roofed *tukuls*, or mud huts, and the unpaved streets smelled of rancid butter, red peppers, and burning cow dung. The omnipresent white dress was relieved by the colored cloaks of aristocrats (who were always shadowed by a noisy mob of retainers) and the brilliant violets of mourning. Denys's syndicate was interested in the mineral wealth that might be lying inside the Entoto Hills, and these he explored on horseback, watching vultures circle in slow spirals above the cliffs and baboons lope below them among cabbage palms and coppices of yellow hibiscus. Then, after liaising with officials from the government and the legation, he and Billea set off northwest through Amhara, where heavy-bearded overlords rode about in white togalike *shammas* over long shirts and jodhpurs, their stiff curly hair frizzed out in a wide halo. Every fifty miles, the pink hills threw up a sandstone fort and a cluster of conical huts, and at the wells rows of youths chanted as they pulled up giraffe-hide buckets bulging with chalky water. Denys had a bad bout of dysentery as he followed the Blue Nile north, and he and Billea made haste for Khartoum and the facilities of the Grand Hotel, where laundry lists quoted prices for jodhpurs and nannies' uniforms.

FROM ABYSSINIA, DENYS returned to England to report to the syndicate board. Sailing from Asmara, he and Billea reached Marseille on June 15, 1921, and there entrained for Paris and London. Denys was still gaunt from the dysentery, but it was a hot month, and London looked fine. As usual, Toby had been on tenterhooks awaiting his appearance, and the night after his arrival Denys dined with him and Margaretta at their grand house in Manchester Square. Billea, who otherwise padded behind Denys at a respectful distance of five feet, stood silently in the corner of the dining room impassively resisting the sidelong glances of the parlor maids. Geoffrey Buxton was in London, and he, Denys, and Toby went to the City to see if they could raise cash for fresh East African business ventures. Kermit, too, was in town with his wife, Belle, and Denys took them to dine at Manchester Square before they all went off to Lady Cunard's dance. Toby's grueling social life had not slowed up with the years. The Queen and Princess Mary dropped in for tea, and the Dudley Wards for dinner, and while Denys was in London the Prince of Wales and the Duke of York attended a Manchester Square soirée. Toby had worked himself into a frenzy about the entertainment arrangements and only at the last minute hired the Douglas Sisters to sing. But he need not have worried. The royals lapped up Denys's stories of the East African sporting life and stayed till half past four in the morning. The next day, Denys drove Toby to Eton in a 1919 Cadillac that he had bought for £450. Motoring was a national obsession in the twenties. Toby was fanatically interested in the Cadillac, and spent an inordinate amount of time thinking about his own car; he was about to purchase the first of a string of Rolls-Royces. But at his old school Toby was appalled at "all the ghastly lozenges on the walls of cloisters" that had been stuck up to commemorate fallen Etonians. "Place ruined," he concluded glumly.

Unleashed, Denys toured the nightclubs of the capital and marveled at the transformation of the British woman. She had worked in the police force, in the munitions factories, and on the land while the men were fighting, and in the twenties she changed into a boy, cutting her hair into a bob, flattening her bosom and hips, and lounging unchaperoned in cocktail bars. She took to higher hems, glass beads, and plucked eyebrows, went hatless in summer, and threw parties that featured jazz on the gramophone and nonstop dancing. Dancing, like motoring, had become an obsession. Exotic varieties, such as the shimmy and the Charleston, flourished in the hothouse of London clubs, and even Claridge's had succumbed to live jazz. Denys drank deeply (but not for him the co-respondent shoes). He saw a lot of Rose and went up to Norfolk to stay with her at Dunston. The following year, she visited her brother Geoffrey in Kenya and met Algy Cartwright, the settler who had introduced Denys and Tania. This signaled the end of her romance with Denys; she married Algy in 1923, and moved to Kenya permanently. She and Denys remained close.

Meanwhile, in November Berkeley Cole, who had returned to England for medical treatment, joined Denys, Topsy, and a brace of Finch Hatton cousins for a Haverholme shoot. The hawthorns were crimsoned with haws, and the weak sun circled with a ruff of lavender cloud as beaters drove the pheasants out of Evedon Wood. Berkeley's heart had been troubling him for years and, back in London, Rose and Denys waited at the Ritz while he visited his cardiologist on Harley Street. The news was bad. Berkeley returned to the Ritz announcing that they must immediately start drinking the best champagne. In fact he had a few more years, but not many. His heart did kill him in the end. As for the champagne, its crucial role was a standing joke with Denys and some of his friends from Africa. He wrote a verse of doggerel about it, cribbed from Belloc.

And yet I really must complain
About the Muthaiga Club champagne.
This most expensive kind of wine
In England is a matter
Of pride or habit when we dine
Presumably the latter.
But on an equatorial stay
You must consume it—or you die.
And stern indomitable men
Have told me time and time again
The nuisance of the tropics is
The sheer necessity of fizz.

DENYS SPENT CHRISTMAS at Haverholme, and for the New Year drove to a party at John and Vi Astor's double-moated Hever Castle in Kent, a ride Toby described as "pretty exciting" on account of the Cadillac's lack of lights. Astor's American father's acquisition of Hever in 1903 was a characteristically emphatic expression of the power of the new order; a decade later, he snapped Cliveden up from the Duke of Westminster. Back at Haverholme, Denys found his father in bed with sciatica. Henry had only recently recovered from pleurisy, and his rheumatism was chronic. Nan was also poorly, and before she recovered properly she broke her leg riding. They had been discussing the possibility of selling Haverholme, the prospect of which lowered everyone's spirits. In addition, it was freezing, and in the middle of February Denys went down with such a bad cold that he took to his bed—and this despite the recent purchase of a calf-length greatcoat lined with musquash. It was his second winter on the trot in England, and he remembered why he didn't like it. The mornings at Haverholme were dark and liquid and wild, the afternoons too short, and the park so vaporous that from his bedroom window he could barely see the trees. He wrote to Tania telling her that he'd be home soon.

THE KAREN COFFEE COMPANY had been performing poorly, and shareholders were reluctant to continue pouring kroner into an African hole. Everyone had lost confidence in the profligate Blix, who had got the farm into appalling credit difficulties. Hostile telegrams had flashed between Europe and Africa, wrangling over the terms of a final loan. Geoffrey Buxton, a solid source of support to Tania, was involved in an abortive rescue package. Tania was faced with the threat of losing her farm. She would have liked to turn to Denys. But he was far away, and could not help her. The pattern of their relationship had been established, and she accepted it. She had to.

Tania had been in Rungstedlund in 1920, staying with her mother and receiving outpatient treatment from her venereologist at the national hospital. She returned to Kenya with her brother Thomas. He had decided, with her encouragement, to see if he, too, could carve out a life in Kenya. He had often thought about her vision of Africa, he said, on night watch in the trenches. He planned to buy a farm of his own, but for now he would stay with Tania; in any event, he had invested in the KCC. On December 30, 1920, they steamed into Mombasa on the *Garth Castle*. Blix and the servant Farah rowed out to meet them. Prices, Blix announced gravely once on solid ground, had gone through the floor. Drought had ruined the coffee, the laborers had not been paid, and there was no maize to eat. The value of flax had dropped to a quarter, and their flax fields at Eldoret had been abandoned. "Tanne sat as if paralysed," Thomas recalled. Blix took Thomas straight to the bank and relieved him of a large chunk of money to get Tania's silver out of pawn. Then, when they reached Mbogani, she found that her house had been occupied by persons unknown (though not unknown to Blix) and her china and crystal used as target practice. But again she knuckled down. All through 1921, she and Thomas worked to save the farm. He lived in a house of his own, close to the bungalow. At first he believed in the viability of the enterprise, and rather than buy his own land, as he had planned, he invested his remaining capital in the KCC. During that first year, he designed and built a factory near the coffee fields so they could process their own beans.

Eight years Tania's junior, Thomas was not neurotic as she was, and he had a lively sense of humor, a commodity she lacked. But they were exceptionally close. "I will never be able to thank you enough for what you have been to me," she wrote in 1918. He saw Tania as she was, not an idealized version. "It seems likely that from her childhood onwards, throughout her whole life, she had one shining goal—to be world famous," he wrote in old age. Many years later, she told an acolyte that the important things in life were to ride, to shoot with a bow and arrow, and to tell the truth. (She selected this dictum, in Latin, as the prefatory quotation for *Out of Africa*.) When the acolyte recounted this, Thomas reflected for a moment. Then he said, "She couldn't do any of those things." He was of a more genuinely liberal persuasion than Tania ("a Bolshevik," according to her), and less at ease with the feudal hierarchies she loved. Once, after returning from a safari, he told two English settlers how he had allowed three of his Kikuyu servants to share his tent during a violent thunderstorm. The Englishmen were deeply shocked, as if he had committed an act of treachery against their race. "And they were right really," Thomas noted. "If 40,000 white men have to maintain their dignity, their whole position over eight million Africans, then the gulf between them *has* to be kept insuperable. But we Scandinavians feel differently."

The April rains were good, and the fields foamed with flowers. A delighted Tania toured the farm in her wet-weather outfit of long khaki trousers, knee-length shirt, and clogs, accompanied by her dog, Banja, another Scottish deerhound. (She kept only this breed, she said, because they created a feudal atmosphere.) She had cut her hair short, and said she felt like Tolstoy, without the beard. But the struggle to stave off bankruptcy never went away. Time and again, Tania appealed to shareholders for further injections of capital. In the weekly struggle to find the wages, she sent Thomas to Nairobi on his three-wheeled motorbike to get a loan. When he returned empty-handed, she would set out in her old Overland car and wangle till she got the money.

The KCC chairman, their uncle, Aage Westenholz, had invested in the farm at the outset. Early in 1921, his patience exhausted, the sixty-two-year-old sailed to Kenya to arrange for loans and advances that would make it possible for Tania to buy the farm herself and relieve him and the board of their responsibilities. But it was impossible to secure the necessary funds. Collision with her family was traumatic for Tania. Her anger, often violently expressed, at what she perceived as their lack of support was unfair but curiously moving. Her faith in the farm—which meant her African life—was childlike in its simplicity, and she risked everything for it, including her dignity. In June 1921, she signed a last-ditch agreement with the board. It stipulated that she could continue running the farm in the position of managing director on condition that Blix had nothing to do with it. What could she do? Ngong, she said, was already engraved on her heart. She had to accept the board's terms or she would lose the farm. As for Uncle Aage's suggestion that she should move into a more modest house to economize, she agreed at first, then wriggled out of it once the old man was safely back in Denmark. He had traveled second-class, *pour encourager les autres*. The others were unmoved. Tania had to live in the grand manner. She made her servants wear white gloves at mealtimes, and each plate appeared at the table in an embroidered slipcase that was slid off as the plate was set down. Morning tea was served in Royal Copenhagen china on a silver tray, and each evening the twelve-seat dining table was laid with ranks of crystal glasses, even if there was nothing to pour into them.

In the last months of the year, the rains again failed. Thomas began to doubt the viability of the farm. Every year the coffee bushes bloomed and Tania talked about a harvest of 150 tons, and every year the crop yielded 40 to 50 tons and a profit that barely covered the wages. Too often, a black sky slid away after shedding only a few drops, the earth hardened, and the colors and smells of the bush faded. A bleak wind blew at those times. During Thomas's second year, he often made up his mind to go home. Although he loved Africa, it had no future for him. But it was hard for him to leave Tania. His departure would seem to her like a failure of her own. And she was alone—by this time Blix had moved out. In 1920, when Tania was in Denmark, he had passed through London, where Geoffrey Buxton invited him to a dinner at the Carlton. At the table he met the brown-eyed Jacqueline Birkbeck, who was married to Buxton's cousin Ben and known to everyone as Cockie. She was a friend of Iris Tree's, and of the same hue, though Cockie was less a bohemian than a dedicated partygoer. Cockie and Ben went to Kenya later that year, planning to settle, and Blix took them on safari. Soon he and Cockie were enjoying a clandestine affair under canvas, with love notes stowed in a gun barrel. Cockie was to ditch Mr. Birkbeck to become the next Baroness Blixen.*

Although the family pressured Tania to get rid of Blix formally, she was opposed to a divorce. "There is so much here that binds us together," she wrote home plaintively, "and it is impossible for me to stop believing in the good in him. . . ." As late as June 1922, when it was clear that they were to be divorced, Tania told Blix's elder sister that divorce would be for her "the greatest sorrow in the world." She admitted that she had not been a good wife, "but I do not think that there is anybody in the world who is as fond of him as I am." Besides the fondness, she had found out about her husband's affair with Cockie, and was anxious about the implications of two Baroness Blixens knocking around Nairobi—especially as she, Tania, would no longer be the incumbent. When it happened, it was exactly as she had feared, and hostesses dropped her from the guest list. But, divorced or not, she kept a firm grip on the title for decades, to the amusement, in later years, of egalitarian Danes. Early in 1922, she reluctantly agreed to file for divorce, but only because Blix wanted it—he was indeed going to marry Cockie. According to Thomas, Blix "harassed her about it endlessly." Thomas was more than bitter. "By his vicious lies," he wrote to Uncle Aage, "he [Blix] has made my position here in this country all but

---

* She lived until 1988, and never learned to boil an egg. At her funeral, guests were kept waiting for the arrival of the coffin, as Cockie had stipulated that she wished to be late for the event. The last line of her obituary in the *Daily Telegraph* read "Her species has become extinct."

impossible . . . he does everything he can to ruin Tania's reputation . . . at the same time presses Tania for money and assistance."

When Tania was agitated, she became emotionally manipulative. Early in 1922, her eldest sister, Ea de Neergaard, died after giving birth to a stillborn child. She was thirty-nine, and already had a daughter, little Karen, known as Mitten. The child was being cared for by Ingeborg, her grandmother, who decided she could not visit Kenya that year, as she had planned, because Mitten needed her. "But she [Mitten] does have so many years ahead to look forward to with you," Tania protested. Mitten was five and had just lost her mother; Tania was thirty-seven. On another occasion, she suggested to her mother that if her father were alive he would see that she, Tania, loved her parents more than their other children did. She identified with her dead father, whom she imagined had been suffocated by his wife's bourgeois milieu. "Father understood me as I was," she decided. It was her one great mistake, she wrote to her mother, to have accepted family help, and "I have suffered all the pains of hell for it." But there would have been no farm had her relatives not stumped up the capital at the outset. In the same letter, she told her mother, "You are the most beautiful and wonderful person in the world." Like most of us, Tania was a mass of contradictions.

DENYS HAD BEEN OUT of Africa for the whole of 1921, Tania for the whole of 1920. They were reunited at the end of the long rains, when fireflies came to the highland woods and skyscrapers of clouds toppled through the blue. He was still based at the cottage on the grounds of Muthaiga, but in August he stayed on her farm. He had acquired a Hudson, and they motored over to stay with the McMillans at Ol Donyo Sabuk (Buffalo Mountain), sixty miles away on the other side of Nairobi. It was as dry as the desert, but when they returned to Ngong they found that more than two inches of rain had fallen. It was still raining on September 8, when Tania and Denys drove to Lake Elmenteita to have tea with Delamere, who was eager to reveal his latest discoveries with sheep at Laikipia. Wartime illness had turned his hair white, and the locks emerging from his helmet gave him a patriarchal look. Tania took her houseboy's little daughter Mannehawa with her, as she often did, saying that she considered her an adopted child. Denys, too, had grown fond of the girl, and bought her shoes and scarves. He was becoming increasingly enmeshed in Tania's life. Late on New Year's Eve, when Tania was already asleep, he drove out to the bungalow with Lord Francis Scott, a prominent settler. They woke her up and went off for a midnight supper, returning to the farm the next day for lunch before another late night at Muthaiga.

The days and nights with Denys made Tania's life bearable. She had been ill again, and her hair was falling out. Her financial situation remained critical, and by November she had completely run out of money. She sold her couture gowns to a woman in Nairobi. Denys encouraged her to start painting again as a way of relaxing. ("He has a great talent himself but cannot be bothered to do anything about it," she wrote.) He offered practical advice, but he had little to give in the way of emotional support. Temperamentally, they were different. She was neurotic; he was phlegmatic. But he was susceptible to the black dog. He held himself, she said, to be an extremely rational person, yet he was "subject to special kinds of moods and forebodings." He would withdraw into himself for days and barely speak, and when she asked what was the matter he expressed surprise, as if he hadn't noticed how antisocial he had been. When he emerged from his gloom he was repentant, referring to his withdrawal as "bad temper." Tania learned to recognize a black period, and he learned to handle her emotional volatility, for the time being at least.

Some time after their reunion, Tania thought that she was pregnant with Denys's child.* She was deeply moved. She felt her hopes and needs and her immense store of love coagulate in her belly. Their child would bind them together and give their relationship the form and purpose it lacked. Her heart and her mind filled up with contentment. Then one night she began to bleed. She sent her watchman to Thomas's house with a lantern, asking him to come over straightaway. She believed she was having a miscarriage.

---

* Some commentators have since introduced doubts about whether Tania actually was pregnant in 1922, or just had a late period and mistook the signs. The important thing is that she believed she had been carrying a child.

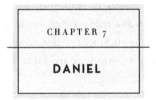

He never did but what he wanted to do.

—KAREN BLIXEN, *Out of Africa*, 1937

IN 1923, KENYA MADE THE FRONT PAGES AT HOME FOR THE FIRST TIME. Trade figures indicated that the colony had made a promising recovery from the upheavals of war and postwar inflation. The motoring craze had even seeped in, the latest Dodge causing a sensation in Nairobi when the first models chugged onto the Fisher and Simmons forecourt. Improvements included a larger radiator, greater clearance, and, bafflingly, "door handles both inside and out." But with the Dodges came greed and racial laws that would not have been out of place in early Nazi Germany. On the whole, settlers tolerated Africans not because they were there first but because the replacement of tribal wars with Pax Britannica was part of the imperial mission. Indians, on the other hand, were universally despised. They outnumbered the white population three to one. Most Kenyan Indians were *duka wallahs* who ran the tin-roofed trading stores strung from the coast to Lake Victoria. Settlers did not like the idea that others were profiting from colonial expansion. Indians were "sucking the lifeblood of BEA," according to the *Leader,* and as early as January 1919, Delamere had made a speech urging the administration to prevent further Indian immigration ("I think the Government ought to give up employing Asiatics"). He and his kind were incensed when Indians lobbied to be included on a common electoral roll. But the most crucial issue, the one with which, according to Tania, every white person in Kenya was obsessed, concerned land ownership. The Indian community had been calling for access to highland territory officially reserved for whites, and the settlers were determined to keep them out. "India for the Indians," went the rallying cry, "and the British colonies for the British." In 1922, the citizens of Southern Rhodesia, a British colony, achieved their longed-for self-government status, and Europeans in Kenya had their eye on the same goal, without Indians getting in the way. Worried that Whitehall might yield to Indian demands, Delamere led a deputation to London, where delegates politely threatened armed resistance (if there was a showdown, they already had a plan to kidnap the governor), and newspapers printed maps of Africa so that readers could see where Kenya was. A few observers were beginning to wonder whether the white man had the right to settle on other people's land at all, let alone elbow the Indians out. Although the war had added a million square miles to the empire, Britons were incubating doubts about the straightforward annexation of colonies. It was no longer universally accepted that the extension of European civilization in Africa was a desirable thing, or that the British race was superior to every other. Some newspaper commentators even branded the settlers fanatical racial bigots and Delamere a robber baron. Groups of freethinkers endorsed U.S. president Woodrow Wilson's ideas, enunciated at Versailles, about the desirability of self-determination for all nations, and a 1923 white paper asserted that "the interests of the African natives must be paramount." There was as yet no seismic shift of spirit—just a presaging tremor. And anyway, the colonial secretary who issued the white paper, the Duke of Devonshire, failed to note that the horse had already bolted: the most important Crown-land ordinances had already been enacted. One defined the borders of the highlands and forbade ownership to all but white Europeans. In 1923, those demanding ownership rights were Indian. In time, they would be Kikuyu. Their "reserves" abutted the fertile highlands. Even as the duke was delivering his conclusions to Prime Minister Andrew Bonar Law, in Nairobi Harry Thuku and a municipal worker called Johnstone—later Jomo—Kenyatta were developing ideas of Kikuyu nationalism and the rejection of colonial rule.* The winds of change were al-

---

* The massive disparity between African and European land ownership was a major cause of the (largely Kikuyu) Mau Mau uprising of the 1950s. Kenyatta, a mission boy, was born Kamau wa Ngengi.

ready beginning to blow, thirty-seven years before Harold Macmillan acknowledged them.

The British government eventually rejected Indian claims to the highlands and to political equality, but the opposition that had been expressed revealed that the settlers would soon be out of step with the Zeitgeist. Delamere and his supporters, battling still for a chain of linked white colonies across Africa, were marooned in the past. By the end of the twenties, the settler community in Kenya had become an anachronism, its members left to reflect on the transience of the paradise to which they had fled. Back at home, the most farsighted took the argument of self-determination to its logical conclusion and looked to a period of imperial tutelage that would lead to black self-governance.

AT THE END of January, Tania's coffee factory burned down. Thomas finally left for Denmark, "worn-down and frustrated," and his embattled sister immediately began writing anguished letters begging him to support schemes for further loans. "I would be so heartbroken if we gave it up now, so close to harbour," she pleaded. The problems—Tania used the Swahili word *shauri*—were entering an acute phase. She woke dreading each fresh encounter with creditors and fell ill with a variety of symptoms, including mysterious lightning-like pains.* In July of 1923, she was admitted to the hospital, though doctors were unable to reach a diagnosis, and the crisis passed. Through all her troubles, sick but indestructible, her optimism held. When a quarter of an inch of rain fell, she wrote to Denmark describing buds all over the farm that were "ready to burst when the next shower comes." But her lunches at Muthaiga with Denys were her real pools of joy. She told her mother that he was the kind of person who would improve with the years (whatever that meant), and compared him to d'Artagnan. That summer, he moved in with her.

---

* These lightning-like pains are classic syphilitic symptoms, and Tania experienced recurrent bouts in the twenties. She was suffering from *tabes dorsalis*, or syphilis of the spinal cord, and although her treatment had been partially effective, small numbers of spirochetes were still present in her body. (Some of her odd and undiagnosed symptoms represented a form of allergy to spirochetes.) Even if all spirochetes were eliminated, which is possible, by the mid-twenties Tania's nervous system was irreversibly damaged. There is characteristically a fifteen-year hiatus between early syphilis and the tertiary neurosyphilis that she was to endure.

The farm included two thousand acres of grassland on which *totos* herded their fathers' cows, and Kikuyu squatters occupied an additional thousand acres, living on small plots called *shambas*. In return for use of the land, they worked on the farm. Many had been born there, like their fathers before them; as Tania wrote, they very likely regarded *her* as a squatter on *their* land. They were obliged nonetheless to pay a hut tax to the government, and when Tania collected it the squatters complained that they did not want the roads, police, and street lighting their taxes were meant to finance. To the west, the estate sloped down to the Mbagathi, the river that formed the boundary between Tania's land and the Maasai reserve. The Ngong Forest lay to the east, the trees bearded with fungus, and at the beginning of the long rains jacaranda flowered purple in the undergrowth. On the farm, it was almost always hot during the day (she said you felt you had got "near to the sun"), but the nights were cold enough for *totos* to keep fires burning in the house. The furniture Tania had shipped from Rungsted included her father's painted grandfather clock, which her Somali butler wound on a Friday, the Muslim holy day. There was another clock in the dining room, an old German boxy one with doors that opened on the hour, allowing a cuckoo to emerge. The *totos* who grazed goats on the lawn crept in silently and stood in front of it, waiting for the bird to sing.

In the domestic rituals of the farm Denys found the familiar elegance of his youth, or the nearest a Kenyan household ever got to it. Gloved servants, linen napkins, polished silver, and a house blooming with candidum lilies—he had only to ship in some decent wine and he had found a home away from home. All the staff knew him and his ridgeback, Sirius. Among themselves they called him Bedar, "the balding one," or sometimes Makanyaga, which means "to tread upon," as they considered that he could tread upon inferior men with his tongue. They addressed him as Mr. Pinja-Hattern. He had shelves built in the study and installed his Proust and Swinburne and seven-volume Anatole France (in French), and he learned to master Poorbox, Tania's skittish Irish jumper. If news came that leopards had been at the maize or ostriches were eating the vegetables in the *shambas*, he picked up one of his rifles and went to the crime scene. He tried to help Tania in her titanic battle to keep the farm afloat, drafting letters to lawyers or others with whom she was in dispute. She wrote to her family about raising capital with Denys so that they could buy the shareholders out and own the farm together. When she decided that a servant needed to be punished, it was Denys who administered the beating. It seems an awkward role for a hero. At any rate, by August Tania had decided that the English were splendid. But Denys was often away.

He had formed a land-development company, Kiptiget, Ltd., with Tich Miles and four others and began touring the country to assess land for the firm, always tacking on days or weeks to hunt. Sometimes he returned unexpectedly, and Tania would ride back to her house to hear an aria floating through the French windows from the windup Columbia Grafonola that Denys had given her. At other times, he would send a messenger and she would find a naked youth standing on one leg outside her house. "Bedar is on his way back," he would say. "He will be here in two or three days." Denys brought marabou feathers and cheetah pelts, which she sent to Paris to be made into coats and hats, or sometimes he appeared with snake skins for belts, bags, and shoes. In Abyssinia, he bought her a ring fashioned from gold so soft that it could be molded to fit any finger. He came back, she said, "starved of talk," and they would sit smoking for hours at the millstone table outside the dining room. This was the emotional heart of the farm. From there they picked out a far ridge where they wanted to be buried, and sometimes they said, "Let us drive as far as our graves." When they got to the ridge, Denys would lie in the grass on his back and peel an orange, picking off segments as he watched eagles coasting overhead. Once he said he'd like to stay there forever. But they went home when the sun set and late light leaked from the west to outline the knuckled Ngong silhouette in silver. After dinner they read Shelley aloud, spreading cushions in front of the fire so Denys could sprawl out while she, cross-legged, invented stories infused with philosophical wit. Tania's accent, and her antiquated syntax and vocabulary, contributed to the exoticism of the tales. As in the versions she wrote down much later, characters supped rather than ate, bid rather than asked, and things happened on the morrow. Like many storytellers, she wove together fantasy and reality. She invested the facts of her own life with myth in the same way; much of *Out of Africa* departs from actuality. Story time developed into a ritual on the farm, and through Denys Tania experienced the liberation of her creative power. After the stories they smoked hashish or opium, he played the guitar, and they listened to records, though they rarely agreed on which. She wanted the old composers, and he, "as if courteously making up to the age for his lack of harmony with it, was as modern as possible in his taste in all arts. He liked to hear the most advanced music." He said, "I would like Beethoven all right, if he were not vulgar."

The preeminence of grand passion was notable later in Tania's published stories. Her characters tend to be personifications of good or evil, just as her moral landscape is painted in black and white. One longs for a touch of gray—the inconsistency that is the hallmark of humanity. But Tania was a storyteller first and a writer second (she once said she was a member of the storytellers' tribe), and she willingly subordinated characterization to plot. In her life, as in her art, she assigned roles, and again and again in her letters Denys is cast as redeemer. Once, when he had been with her for an entire month without a break, she wrote to Thomas and said she was happier than anyone else on earth. "That such a person as Denys does exist, something I have indeed guessed at before, but hardly dared to believe, and that I have been lucky enough to meet him in this life and been so close to him—even though there have been long periods of missing him in between—compensates for everything else in the world, and other things cease to have any significance." Many years later, the young writer Thorkild Bjørnvig, who knew her well, even intimately, said he did not think she ever recognized one living person as her equal except Denys Finch Hatton. She ended the letter to Thomas with a request that if she were to die he must *on no account* tell Denys what she had written. She repeated the demand in subsequent letters. It was a reflection of the degree to which Tania concealed her neediness from Denys, casting herself as the independent modern woman. She understood that if he knew that her life revolved around him he would leave. Even in death, she wanted to preserve his affection. It was a heroic effort. Her family saw the histrionic side of her, the side that did not bear witness to her ideals. And, in time, so did Denys. "He was happy on the farm; he came there only when he wanted to come"—a beautiful sentence in style and content, characteristic of the chaste elegance of *Out of Africa*. But what a world lies behind it. It was her triumph that for some years she let him come when he wanted to come, without telling him how very much she needed him to come when *she* wanted. As for Denys, he was taking advantage of the different moral code that prevailed in Kenya. At home, in England, he would not have lived openly with a woman to whom he was not married.

SIX DAYS A WEEK, Tania held a clinic on the farm between nine and ten, and if she could not treat a patient she drove him to the hospital run for Africans. Later in the morning, people would arrive to ask her to arbitrate in a dispute, or to appeal on their behalf in a government office. She had a more sophisticated understanding of tribal thinking than many immigrants—of how the concept of justice was fundamentally different in Africa, for instance—and she respected the habits and traditions of her staff and squatters. Her own life was subsumed within the workings of the farm, and of all the days of the week she liked Saturday afternoons best, as there was no mail until Monday, and therefore no bad news. All 132 oxen had Sunday off (they were inspanned before dawn on the other six days), so on Saturday evening Tania sat on the fence of their paddock smoking a cigarette and watching a tired little *toto* leading them in. All her people, she said, were "never reliable, but in a grand manner sincere," a description that might be applied to *Out of Africa*.

The fine-featured Somali Farah Aden, of the Habr Yunis tribe, was Tania's closest companion. Farah spoke English and French, the latter learned as a cabin boy on a French man-of-war, though on the whole he preferred to remain silent. A devout Muslim, he wore a turban, a white tunic, and a gold ring, and served Tania as butler, chauffeur, and financial controller. When he married in 1918, she had a house built for him and his bride (his second, and more were to follow). The wives brought their sisters to live on the farm. These unmarried women were friendly to Denys, but they were not permitted to talk to Billea: when he appeared, they vanished. Denys was crushed to be considered so harmless. Tania went to sit in Farah's house at the end of the day and talk with the women. Farah was her translator until she learned to speak Swahili—the lingua franca of the farm, injected with Kikuyu words and phrases.* He was proprietorial, and

* Swahili was the lingua franca of all East Africa, though few settlers progressed beyond the kitchen version. The *Leader* ran a column, "Swahili as She Is Spoke," mocking the Franglais of the day. The language evolved by white would-be Swahili speakers was classified as "Kisettla." Denys was quite good at it.

spoke of "our house" and "our horses." Tania went on to write about the relationship, describing their partnership as a unity, like a hook and eye; the romantic notion of the noble servant appealed to her.

When Paramount Chief Kinanjui arrived with his entourage, all work ceased. The Kikuyu Kinanjui ruled over one hundred thousand of his tribe. A tall man with a bony face and a slanting forehead, he wore a skull-cap made of sheep's stomach and lived on the reserve nine miles from the farm, attended by forty-three wives ranging from gummy hags to gazelle-like beauties with limbs wound around with copper wire. It was, in fact, the British who had given Kinanjui the title "Paramount Chief" when they secured his allegiance—a reliable tactic, and one they often used. When white grandees drove out to the farm, Tania dressed up her servants as if they were cabaret turns and made them parade through the drawing room offering cigarettes from slim gold cases. When one tripped and the cigarettes rocketed around the room, settling on the Persian rugs like miniature torpedoes, the guests sniggered and drove back to Nairobi to tell everyone that Tania was ludicrously affected. But she had genuine friends, among them Sir Northrup McMillan and his thin wife, Lucie.

The enormous Northrup had a special chair, which was placed on the veranda when he arrived; according to one servant, he was "so fat he had to spit sideways." In 1925, when he was fifty-two, he died of heart disease in Nice and was brought home to Ol Donyo Sabuk for a summit burial. A hearse was mounted on skis and a tractor drew it up the mountain. But the clutch plate burned out halfway up, so he was buried where the tractor stopped.

The most popular guest on the farm was the red-haired Berkeley Cole, who roared in from Mount Kenya in a car loaded with turkey eggs, wine, and oranges. He was lonely at Naro Moru, his remote ranch farm, and he, too, had financial problems. He helped Tania out, sending her a cat for Christmas one year to dispatch the proliferating rats. Berkeley walked as silently as a cat himself. When they sat talking in front of the fire, he seemed so slight that Tania thought he might at any moment fly up the chimney. He slept late, then walked into the forest at eleven to drink a bottle of champagne. Berkeley could speak the Maasai language well, and during his visits the old chiefs came over to discuss their troubles. When his jokes made them laugh, Tania said, "It was as if a hard stone had laughed." His heart remained weak, and Jama, his Somali servant, had learned to administer injections to assist his circulation. Berkeley told Tania that it would be unwise for him to have children, on account of his ill health. But he was an outcast at heart, like Denys. By keeping a mistress, he bought a solution to the problems of loneliness that are intrinsic to rootlessness.

Denys and Tania dressed for dinner even if they were alone—he in a brown velvet smoking jacket, she in a gown. When he was away, she spent the evening tapping in the dark study on her tiny Corona typewriter, its ink roll high and proud. The stories she wrote in Africa were little more than early scribblings. Writers have to stand up and live before they sit down to write, and it was what Tania experienced at Ngong, not what she wrote there, that lay the foundations for the literary prose poems that dazzled America twenty years later. If she was too tired to type, she sat reading in one of the red leather armchairs with Minerva, the house owl, perched on her shoulder. (The bird eventually swallowed the end of a window-blind cord, choked to death, and was found swinging in the breeze.) She did not benefit from breaks, as Denys did. Neither the skins he gave her nor the books and records he bought for her in Europe compensated for her drudgery. "It would be reasonable to expect a couple of months' holiday now," she complained to Thomas. Not long afterward, she informed him, "No one knows how I slaved." But the farm was also her purpose in life, and she wanted to be able to stay even more than she wanted to get away. "There have been many times when I have felt absolutely certain that I would not want to go on living if I had to leave this place," she wrote home. The investors had lost any vestigial threads of confidence—"This time I mean it," Uncle Aage wrote after the board decided that she was not to receive more money. But nothing seemed to improve, and one has the sense, from her letters, of a Greek tragedy creeping toward its denouement. Chinks of darkness began to appear in the bright light of her vision. "I think we have been too optimistic in believing that a neglected farm like this could be worked up to full capacity in a short time," she wrote sadly. She even talked of a new life elsewhere. The problem was that she had blind faith in coffee and never contemplated a literal root-and-branch change. After she died, Thomas remarked that she neither knew nor learned much about coffee. She relied instead on intuition, an inadequate business tool if deployed in isolation. It was always Denys who got her out of the trough. But if she lost the farm she would have to leave Africa. That meant losing Denys. It was her deepest dread.

IN THE MIDDLE of December 1923, at the end of the short rains, Denys drove up to inspect his property on the Nzoia River, north of Eldoret. He had gone into partnership with Arthur Cecil Hoey, an Englishman born in Wimbledon in 1883. In 1904, Hoey had walked a thousand miles across Africa with his brother and then trekked up to the Uasin Gishu Plateau. He was a burly man who held passionate views about the way forward in Kenya, and in his role as delegate on the Game Policy Committee had encouraged the establishment of the first game reserves. The subject had begun to fixate Denys, as he had witnessed a sinister rise in the random slaughter of big game from tourists' motorcars. He was an innate conservative, like his father, and in the case of animal slaughter saw real damage in change. In the future, he would take a public stand to defend the African landscape. But he did not prolong this December visit with late-night Hoey talk, as he had decided to break the journey home at Kekopey. It would mean missing Christmas with Tania, but the duck-shooting season opened on the twenty-fourth on Lake Naivasha and Galbraith and Nell Cole were hosting a house party. So Denys followed the Rift south to the funnel, where the two escarpments drew close, accompanied as ever by the inscrutable Billea, and arrived at Kekopey without warning on Christmas Eve. The increasingly arthritic Galbraith hobbled out to greet the car hunched over his sticks. His spirit was intact. He had recently followed a wounded lion through thick scrub on his sticks until he was able to shoot. He delighted in the company of his young sons, and that of his brother Berkeley, with whom he had always been close. The farm remained, as it had been during the war, a convivial refuge. Denys was relaxed and happy. At four in the morning on Christmas Day, he took the Hudson out with Dermott Dempster, Galbraith's manager, and they shot duck all day from Naivasha to Gilgil. On the way back, the car broke down. The Naivasha garage was closed, so they parked in the middle of the road and mended the springs with rawhide. It was dark by the time they reached Galbraith's farm. Delamere and his son Tom were there, and so was the

Stetson-wearing "Boy" Long, one of Delamere's managers. Twenty-one-year-old Beryl Purves was also a guest.

Beryl was tall and lissome, with arctic-blue eyes, long legs that scissored beneath her like a colt's when she sat down, and sandy hair bleached by years on horseback. Currently estranged from her husband, she featured regularly at Muthaiga and at the racecourse, where her father had been a leading trainer. There was something of the animal about her. Unlike Tania, who layered on white face powder and kohl eyeliner, Beryl had no interest in makeup. She was a Kenyan Circe, though, as Martha Gellhorn put it when she met her, "not your run-of-the-mill Circe." To Denys, she embodied the freedom of body and spirit that he identified with Africa. It was said that they ended up sleeping in the same room at Kekopey. Whatever happened, it was a casual, hedonistic encounter. But it was not the last of their romance.*

DENYS RETURNED TO NGONG in the New Year. It was the time when the purple wood pigeon came to feed on the Cape chestnuts in the forest, and he and Tania went out every morning at five to shoot them. The first spears of sunlight were turning the Ngong Hills copper when the birds came in, fast and thunderous as a cavalry attack. Sometimes Tania's friends drove out from Nairobi to join the shoot, rounding the corner to the house with their headlamps on. Then, after a week, Denys was off again for a six-week safari in southern Maasailand in a lorry he had acquired. That part of Maasai country, around the Mara River, was known to the early white hunters as the Mara Triangle. (It was later called the Maasai Mara.) Covering well over a thousand square miles and intersected by just two dirt roads south of Narok, the Mara was rarely traveled by Europeans. Apart from the two roads, Denys's map showed a large blank. The game there, already abundant, was annually augmented between June and September, when hundreds of thousands of animals veered north during the Serengeti

---

* Cockie Birkbeck, a confidante of Beryl's, told two separate writers that she helped arrange an abortion for Beryl in England in April 1924. Another woman, Genessie Hamilton, told a third writer that she paid for this abortion, which was performed by an osteopath. The baby had been conceived at about Christmastime. Several men were paternity candidates, but both Genessie and Cockie stated that Beryl thought the baby was Denys's. There is no proof, which is why I have included this material only in a footnote. But neither informant had a motive for making up the story.

migration, one of the greatest sights nature has produced. It was a varied landscape (*mara* means "mosaic"), the rolling hills alternating with savanna, woodland, and thickets. At first, Denys camped with Scottish prospectors panning in what had been touted as a gold rush, but he was unimpressed with what they were getting. He was hoping to find ivory, not gold.

The coffee harvest at the farm was a miserable seventy tons that year. "I really do believe that I have deserved to be given the VC for my work here just as much as you did during the war," Tania informed Thomas. Her life was a performance, and she was the heroine of every scene. But when Denys came back she was convinced that he was "the most wonderful being on earth." He was planning a three-month shoot in Tanganyika, and had obtained special permission to kill twenty-five elephants, telling Kermit that although the last two years had been a struggle, he felt that he had turned a corner. Then, in the middle of March, he got a wire saying his mother was ill. He left for the coast with one day's warning. "Goodbye," he wrote in a last note to Tania, "and thank you for so many pleasant days when I was so bad-tempered." Her commitment to him never wavered. Later in the year, she told Thomas, "I believe that for all time and eternity I am bound to Denys, to love the ground he walks upon, to be happy beyond words when he is here, and to suffer worse than death many times when he leaves. . . ."

DENYS ARRIVED IN LONDON on April 7, 1924. Toby drove him straight to Haverholme in the Rolls, complaining the whole way about his overdraft. Denys had not seen his mother for two years. He found her thin and frail and suffering from lung trouble and a weak heart, but no longer critically ill. The brothers went pike fishing, sitting at their childhood places on the bank under the clenched buds of early spring. The heraldic griffons stood proud on the bridge over the Slea, the wood cart rattled past amid wheeling clouds of primrose butterflies, and at six, in the familiar dining room, Albert the butler carried in the crested dark-silver plates. But the immeasurable timelessness of childhood had slipped away. Denys sorted through the boxes he had stored at the Priory. He found photographs he had taken on the Nandi border with Pixley years earlier and sent one to Kermit with a wistful letter. "I'd give most of the Rue de la Paix to be back there at that date with the friends I had then before the war, just starting off for a day's sport with those Nandi boys," he wrote. "Your news, friend?" He cheered himself up with a visit to the Buxtons and swanned about in John Astor's Cadillac before returning to London for business appointments in the City, dusting off his collapsible opera hat for a burst of Puccini before the Savoy Havana Band.

The spring weather was gorgeous, but ominous clouds hovered over the political landscape. That January, the king had appointed Ramsay MacDonald as the country's first Labour prime minister. In the cabinet, an institution previously the domain of the aristocracy and ruling classes, eleven out of twenty men came from a working-class background. They were faced with grave problems, working class or not; more than 1.2 million were unemployed, and strikes were proliferating among those who were in work. In continental Europe, a different kind of specter had risen. The previous year, Hitler had attempted to mount a coup in Munich, and now he was demanding that his government seek to have the Treaty of Versailles revoked. The German economy had spiraled out of control, and nationalism was burgeoning. At the Conservative Club, Denys read *The Times* over breakfast with sorrow and horror. The world he once knew had shrunk.

His mother seemed to be rallying, so he made plans to return to Africa at the end of May. Then the weather turned bad, and so did he—he went down with severe abdominal pains, and his doctor recommended an immediate appendectomy. Denys booked himself into a convalescent home and on May 7 had the operation at St. George's Hospital, on Hyde Park Corner. Toby visited every day. A fortnight later, they heard that their mother had had a relapse and was dangerously ill. Struggling to keep up, Toby noted in his diary, "Rammed a thorn in my eye, v. painful indeed." Denys went back to Haverholme while he was convalescing, joining Margaretta and Topsy, who were already there. In June, Nan suffered a double thrombosis. There was no question of returning to Kenya now. The may trees were in blossom, and on the pond in Evedon Wood the young herons were flapping on their nests. "It is sad to know how much my mother would have enjoyed it," Denys wrote to Kermit. By June 17, Nan no longer recognized anyone. Three days later, she died. They were all there. Denys wrote the inscription for her plaque in St. Andrew's: "No effigy would do justice to the beauties of her person nor any epitaph express the beauties of her mind, therefore neither is attempted here. But those to whom she left the world a void live in the humble hope that through the mercy of God it may be given to them when their time of departure comes to be with her where she is. Anne, Countess of Winchilsea and Nottingham, June 20th 1924."

TOPSY HAD BORROWED a flat in Kensington from a cousin, and Denys stayed there on his return to the capital. She always spoiled him with a bottle of Château d'Yquem, his favorite not just among Sauternes but of all wines. After they had retired one night, she looked through the glass panel in the spare bedroom door, expecting Denys to be asleep. But he was lying in bed with *Swann's Way* propped on his chest. One hand supported the book, and between the fingers of the other a cylinder of ash jutted from the end of a Player's Number Ten. She tapped on the glass. "Tiny, are you asleep?" she asked. "Topsy, you don't go to sleep when you're reading Proust," Denys replied without looking up. Ten-year-old Michael looked forward to his uncle's visits. "It was always a major event when he arrived from Africa," he recalled. Denys would sweep in with silver trinkets and large yellow and green bottles of scent for Topsy. "He wore a felt hat like a mushroom," Michael continued, "and his shoes, made by Peal's to a design of his own, had gently rounded square toes, making his feet look like boats. He had to have special trees made to fit the shoes." When the whole family was at Haverholme, Denys climbed the elms to collect rooks' eggs for Michael. He had a watching brief over his fatherless nephew. "Read the Bible," he advised him more than once. "It's a good book." The end of Denys's 1924 visit was inevitably muted, for him and for the rest of the family. But in the midst of his grief he forced himself to do the rounds, catching up with Hoskins, visiting Eton, and watching tennis at Wimbledon before trying out rifles and ordering wine for the farm. He and Toby had been investing in port in vintage years, and, as he wrote to Kermit, "I have often found it a pleasant thought out in Africa to remember those silent rows of black virgins steadfastly awaiting me in England, ready or getting ready, preparing in fact to pour out their life's blood for me and my friends any time after about 1938. I hope that you will crack one or two with me." By the time the port was drinkable, Kermit was a dying alcoholic.

On October 15, Denys took the boat train to Paris accompanied by Margaretta, who was on her way to visit her father at Cap-Ferrat. The leaves on the plane trees along the Seine were showing brown. "I am so sorry he has gone again, and am afraid that he will not be back for some time," Toby wrote.

WHILE DENYS WAS in England, Tania tried to write off her losses on the page, typing out fragments of the stories she liked telling, to take her mind off her situation. "All sorrows can be borne if you put them into a story," she once said. Indeed. She had also written a monograph on modern marriage. In this excruciating document, published posthumously when anything by Karen Blixen would sell, she argues that marriage has to be reinvented, suggesting that one must love "without the support of habit or outward conditions"—as Denys loved, in other words—and that a "love relationship" must be free of rules. She sent the monograph to Thomas, who retaliated with an article he had written on birth control. Intellectually, Tania recognized that her relationship with Denys was predicated on mutual freedom, which really meant his freedom, though she had convinced herself that it was what she wanted, too. Over the next two years, her lucubrations developed the idea of modern love, "which takes the form of a passionate sympathy . . . while one is oneself and striving for one's own distant aim one finds joy in the knowledge of being on parallel courses for all eternity." It was a protracted exercise in self-justification. She was trying to accept that love can exist, and flourish, without possession; she was willing herself to believe it. A laudable goal, but horribly hard to achieve. Tania genuinely valued sensuality and instinct above a rigid moral code, but sex itself was not important to her. Syphilis, even when no longer infectious, hardly stimulated the libido, and when she was an old woman she admitted to a confidant—albeit gnomically—that during these years "the love relationship could no longer be experienced as normal." To deal with the problem, she sought to sublimate sexual union to the higher plane (as she saw it) of spiritual union. She told Thomas, "I do not think I am capable of treating a sexual relationship in itself with any great seriousness. . . . I do not in the least like being caressed." Her friend the Russian diplomat General Polowtzoff once told her that he had never known anybody so sensual and yet "so little sexual." She took it as a compliment. The role of sex is often sublimated in her tales. In one story, she portrayed a woman of noble birth who has a disease that is obviously syphilis. The condition has endowed the character with "a mirthful forbearance with and benevolence towards the frailty of humanity"; syphilis, in other words, is presented as something ennobling. Karen Blixen even imbues venereal disease with religious overtones when she reveals that the woman became infected in St. Peter's Basilica in Rome when she kissed the foot of the saint's statue immediately after a mysterious cloaked young man smelling of "sweat and stable" had done the same (the bronze was still warm and "slightly moist"). But she also describes how the disease has shut down the erotic part of her character's life: "mystically she had become a maiden—an old maid."

WHEN DENYS RETURNED TO Kenya, he decided to look for work as a white hunter. It had taken him a long time to identify an occupation that made sense to him, but now, at the age of thirty-seven, he discovered his vocation. In ten years, he had become one of the best hunters in East Africa. He had learned how to kill a reedbuck neatly by feeling for the heart behind the foreleg, and watched his skinner turn the stomach inside out and stitch the liver and kidneys up in it to form a bag in which to carry the delicacies to camp. With a pair of field glasses, he could judge the size of a set of kudu horns to within half an inch. He knew the big tuskers would emerge from the trees immediately after a downpour, because they objected to water dripping on their backs, and he knew how the cut hide of a dead rhino hung down behind the head like a cape, white as freshly sliced coconut. It was useful, as a hunter, to be exceptionally strong, as he was. (His party trick was to tear a pack of playing cards in half.) On one safari, he was driving a Ford back to Nairobi late at night after heavy rain. At Nyeri he tried to drive across a river, as the bridge had disappeared, but the car tipped over, its roof coming to rest on the riverbed. He jumped clear, but his gun bearer could not get out. Denys righted the car and freed him. The only annoyance was that he had lost his bowler, and when they proceeded to the nearest house to summon help he borrowed a hat from the female occupant. He was also mechanically adept and could seal a leaking radiator with an egg, or, if there was no egg, a lump of dung: there was always plenty of that. The rituals of camp had become second nature, from rodding and re-oiling his rifles while Hamisi prepared dinner to setting up the gramophone and listening to Rachmaninoff in C minor belting away in opposition to the night noises of the forest. After a long expedition in Tanganyika, he would return through the low-lying country around Mombasa, a region poor in game and rich in tarantulas, disease-carrying insects, and urinating bats that haunted the trees in the thousands. It suited the mood at the end of a safari, like a dying fall of trumpets.

At this late stage in his progression from youth to maturity, Denys had learned to use his innate talents. It was a vital point on his journey of self-discovery. "I sure reckon I know about as much about the job as most of these folk who take parties out," he told Kermit, evidently adopting his friend's American phrasing. "So if you know of any pleasant people who want to shoot put them in touch with me. You know the sort of people I should get on with *and* the ones I should *not*. Don't send any of the latter!" Several dozen white men in Kenya were already hiring themselves out as hunters, and their stories were the currency of the Norfolk. Everyone knew how a tusker at Masongaleni had skewered the legendary Bill Judd, smashed him to a pulp, and knelt on the bloody remains (it was news in London, such was Judd's status). How a lion tore out Fritz Schindelar's stomach near Mount Longonot, or how Charles Cottar's wife carried on filming while a leopard attacked him. Or how Eddie Grafton had had his face ripped off by the horn of a charging buffalo and brave gun bearers had been sliced by a leopard's dewclaw. Fabulous figures such as Alan Black, Philip Percival, and R. J. Cunninghame emerged from the bush every few months to slake their thirst at the Norfolk bar and add to the repository of hunting lore, second only to the fisherman's in its fecundity. Many beasts, apparently, showed a Rasputin-like reluctance to die. One professional hunter reported that a client's .275 solid bullet had gone clean through a buffalo's arteries above the heart, his own four bullets from a .470 broke a shoulder and tore through heart, lungs, and guts, "and yet he came on until he was dead." Like gambling, hunting involved risk, the challenge of outwitting one's opponent, and the adrenaline-charged thrill of winning. Like golf and flying, it demanded total concentration, and Denys was bored by half measures.

While he was in England the summer his mother died, Denys had upgraded his arsenal in preparation for his new role. A serious East African hunter needed heavy-, medium-, and light-gauge rifles as well as a shotgun, as his quarry ranged from an eight-pound dik-dik to a six-ton elephant. To shoot the really big stuff, some favored a .505 Gibbs, which took three cartridges in the magazine and one in the breech and kicked like an ostrich, though overall, at that time, a .470 double was the most favored rifle in East Africa. One could get in two shots, as opposed to the single of a bolt-action gun, and it was therefore ideal for stopping dangerous game at close quarters. All doubles had side-by-side barrels in those days, not the vulgar over-and-under kind. Heavy barrels were easier to swing than light rifles, and they didn't fly into the air with the powerful kickback. Blix shot with a .600 Jeffrey, which was loathed by his gun bearer because it weighed fifteen pounds. Everyone had his favorite handmade gun—Bill Judd his trademark .577 Westley Richards, Bunny Allen a double .470 Rigby, John Douglas a .500 double-barreled rifle that especially suited him, as he had only one arm. The published journals of explorers and travelers crackled with lists of their firepower, and when big shots gathered they never exhausted the subject of bullets (with copper jackets, or without?), drops, castoffs, stock measurements, and trigger pull pressures, and they never agreed on anything.

Denys had settled on a secondhand Rigby .350, a medium-caliber bolt-action rifle that used 225-grain soft bullets and could deal with everything up to and including lions. He already had a 6.5 mm Austrian Mannlicher for antelope, and for his big "stopper"—to fell charging buffalo, elephants, and hippos with solid bullets—he asked his gunsmith to rebarrel his existing Lancaster .450 No. 2 to an ordinary .450, as it was hard to find ammunition for the No. 2. For his shotgun, required on safari to shoot guinea fowl or other birds for the pot, Denys was able to carry on with his standard, Birmingham-made Army & Navy twenty-bore, the weapon he used in Lincolnshire to shoot pheasants and rabbits.

Big-game hunting had been fashionable in the Protectorate since about 1906, and newspaper photographs of wealthy men crouched between an arc of ivory had thrilled boys of Denys's generation, who were already devouring tales of African adventuring from the pages of Henty. Sportsmen from America, Europe, and South Africa converged on the Norfolk to be kitted out with hunting gear by Indian tailors who customized bush jackets with cartridge loops sewn to fit the sportsman's barrel. Before the advent of motor vehicles, at least thirty porters were hired for each hunter, in addition to headmen, skinners, gun bearers, and the rest. Once assembled, the whole party vanished into the bush for three or four months. ("In those days," Bunny Allen recalled, "people not only had money to burn—they had time to burn too.") Until 1919, the wealthiest clients traveled with the firm of Newland & Tarlton, which had an office in Piccadilly and, on the ground, a limitless supply of mostly Swahili porters kitted out in dark blue jerseys with N & T embroidered on the front in red. (The porters were issued with boots but weren't required to wear them, so they slung them around their necks and kept them for display.) Their safaris were luxurious affairs, featuring Jaeger blankets, proper beds, and vintage wines served by uniformed waiters over a dinner supplied from a Fortnum & Mason safari hamper. Trackers salted kills where they fell and heads were sent to Nairobi by runner and thence to London, where they were mounted by the taxidermy firm Rowland Ward, or to New York, where Jonas Brothers of Yonkers turned them into rugs with fanged mouths at one end. For Teddy Roosevelt's 1909 safari from Mombasa to the Upper Nile, five hundred Africans were hired, porters carried four tons of fine salt, and Roosevelt personally shot 296 animals with his .405 Winchester or .450 Holland & Holland double. When Denys began to hunt for a living, he signed up with Safariland, the firm of outfitters that had replaced Newland & Tarlton. But by the twenties, the settlers' attitude to game conservation had polarized. On the one hand, wild animals were a menace to the agricultural community and farmers wanted them culled, or at least controlled. On the other hand, big-game hunters who constituted an important source of revenue were opposed to any controls. The government's job was to balance the conflicting demands of the two positions. By the early 1900s, licenses had been introduced throughout the empire to regulate the slaughter of big game, and reserves had been established well before the war, both reflections of a gradual dawning of awareness in the British consciousness. But still, every sportsman wanted his name in Rowland Ward's book of game records.* The white hunter was paid to conduct licensed tourists through the bush within the confines of legislation. He was to lead his clients to trophies and ensure that the killing was "clean," at the same time providing maximum thrill for minimum damage. He was a knight-errant, one of the most romantic figures in colonial history, combining a love of animals with a mastery of the natural world. Denys was perfectly cast.

At the beginning of 1925, Denys took out his first professional client, an American named Maclean. Piles of canvas and wooden crates snaked along the Nairobi street as Denys checked and rechecked an inventory in which tentage alone embraced mess tents, sleeping tents, lavatory tents, shower tents, and kitchen tents. When Metro-Goldwyn-Mayer and John Ford hired Safariland to outfit the four-month *Mogambo* shoot in 1952 (the stars were Grace Kelly, Clark Gable, and Ava Gardner), they even had a jail tent in case anyone got rowdy. Furniture included tables, chairs, a fridge, and sometimes, as when J. A. Hunter took out an Indian maharaja, a piano. Many hours were spent adding, multiplying, and dividing to ensure that the commissariat would not be found wanting: a pound of tea lasted one man a fortnight, and a one-pound tin of marmalade a week. Each porter consumed three pounds of *posho* (maize flour) a week, and no porter would carry more than fifty pounds. Biblical hordes of porters, at least, were rarely necessary after the first war, when motorized safaris began to displace the pedestrian kind. But the early white hunters regretted the advent of roads, arguing that a real hunter should cut his own thoroughfare with a machete.

AT THE NGONG FARM Tania's mother, Ingeborg, was approaching the end of a long visit. The servants adored her; they called her Old Memsahib, and when she let her hair down *totos* gathered around to stare—it was so long she could sit on it. As for Tania, on her eleventh wedding anniversary she got a cable informing her that her divorce was final. Denys was

---

* In his brilliant book *Hearts of Darkness*, about an earlier period of African history, Frank McLynn notes "a very clear inverse relationship [in Victorian explorers] between intellectual calibre and enthusiasm for the hunting of big game." The only contemporary parallel I can think of is the size of sports cars, and I believe in that case McLynn's argument stands up.

away with Maclean, but at the end of January they broke for an excursion into the Ngong Hills with Tania. The slopes were green after unseasonal rains, and the valleys were crowded with buffalo cows and their calves. The nights were cold enough to turn hands blue, and the bearers sat around the fire until late, listening to the gramophone as brindled wild dogs *hoohoo*ed from the forest. On March 5, Tania followed her mother back to Denmark for another course of Salvarsan injections. After the satisfied Maclean returned to America, his bag overflowing with trophies, Denys remained at the farm on his own. He lived there for most of 1925, departing only for his safaris. Later, his friends told Tania that they couldn't drag him away. He enjoyed his own company. He was reading Roy Campbell's new poetry anthology, *The Flaming Terrapin*, and making his way through the latest consignment of music he had ordered from Europe.

Denys was an odd mix—a charismatic loner with an immense capacity for friendship and a powerfully independent spirit. He liked a "rip" at the club, especially after a long session in the bush, but he could take or leave a party ("You know that Denys will never normally go out," Tania complained to her mother). When they were invited to a function in Nairobi, she often went on her own. If they did socialize together, they behaved formally to each other. "When you saw them in a group you never for a moment would think that they were having a love affair," Bunny Allen noted in the late 1920s. Above all, Denys hated small talk and had an intolerably low threshold for boredom. But the streak of frivolity had not vanished with the years. On the rare nights out at Muthaiga, he still lobbed bread rolls across the dining room or somersaulted over the cretonne-covered armchairs. On one occasion, when he was out on safari, Geoffrey "Tuppy" Headlam, an Eton master, sent him a cable asking, "Do you know Norman Tod's address?" "Yes," Denys cabled back.

He was a loyal friend once he recognized a kindred spirit like Hugh Martin, the head of the Land Office. A near-contemporary at Oxford, Martin was a career civil servant who had transferred to Kenya from the Malayan service. Inscrutable and Buddha-like in appearance, he was a committed cynic with a well-stocked mind, and came to Ngong with his wife, Flo, and their eight-year-old daughter, Betty. Once installed, he seldom stirred from his armchair, contemplating the world with Oriental detachment and swigging copious quantities of whiskey. But it was a bad year for friendship. Berkeley's health had continued to deteriorate. Toward the end of March, he went down to Soysambu, Delamere's farm, to collect fifteen rams that had been shipped over from Australia. He fell ill there and was obliged to retire to bed. "My rotten heart has got very dicky," Berkeley wrote in exasperation to his brother John. The doctor advised him to go back to Naro Moru and stay in bed for a month. This he refused to do, settling instead to drink Falernian wine and smoke the finest cigars. The situation at Naro Moru had improved and Berkeley at last had in view "a vista of success." The farm was running profitably, he had acquired more land, and his old friend Tich Miles had agreed to abandon the lonely job he had taken as a consul at Mega, in southern Abyssinia, and move south to work as Berkeley's estate manager. In addition, Berkeley was part owner of the fabled White Rhino hotel in Nyeri, and was involved in a promising local dairy scheme as well as a butchery business in Nairobi and a timber concession and mill. On April 21, he was back at Naro Moru, working as usual. He had breakfast and had just set out on his morning tour when his heart finally failed. He was forty-three. Denys was in the Maasai reserve with Maclean when he received a cable from Hugh Martin. He rushed to Naro Moru for the funeral. Above the farm, the Diamond Glacier hung matte on the sloping black shoulder of Mount Kenya, and the scent of witch hazel lay light on the air, like a top note. Berkeley was buried at a spot he had chosen on a bank of the river, in the fretwork of a thorn tree's shadow. The water there, he liked to say, glacier-cold and filtered through peat and black basalt, was so soft that you could work up a lather just from the oils on your skin. Martin cabled Berkeley's eldest brother, John, at home at Florence Court in Ireland. "Funeral everything you all could wish stop denys finch hatton came with me and all his friends came all together stop cannot realise yet what a loss we have all sustained stop deepest sympathy coming from all quarters." Galbraith was in Britain when he heard the news. "The more I reflect on the loss of him, the more I find how inevitably the world has changed for me," he wrote to their brother John. "We have been to each other the background of every thought or action all our lives and it is as if I had been cut in half." Perhaps the African Galbraith had killed had also had a brother. Profound love and random cruelty coexist more often than many care to recognize.

—

TANIA RETURNED TO the farm on February 1, 1926, listless and depressed. She had wondered, at peaceful Rungstedlund, whether to go back to Africa at all. Denys was on safari when she arrived. She had not seen him for eleven months. On March 5, he came to stay for more than two weeks. She was suddenly so happy, she said, that she had "nothing more to ask of life." She told Thomas that Denys was the only person who meant anything to her, and that her whole existence revolved around their relationship. But Denys had just received news from home that his father was very ill. He was about to dash back to England again.

Tania was plunged into despair. In moments of clarity, she could see that living only for her lover's visits came perilously close to living through him and submerging her own ideals. This was what she most feared. When he was with her, she said that perfect bliss and perfect despair fought for her attention, the despair fueled by the knowledge that she might never see him again. She compared his presence to lying in a perfumed bath, and his absence to a session on the rack. One of her staff remembered that she used to sit at her desk, put her head on her arms, and weep, asking the puzzled servant why Bwana Bedar had stayed away so long. Few women could tolerate such a precarious emotional life, and Tania was beginning to understand that she was not one of those fortunate few. "I will not and cannot go on living in this way, with this single element in my life," she told Thomas in an anguished letter. "It is an intolerable situation and I find it impossible to allow my immediate future to take the form of six months of utter desolation, emptiness and darkness, with the hope of seeing him again in the autumn, and being lifted up to the same unqualified happiness, only to be cast back into desolation and darkness—and so on and so on for infinity." By August, however, she was perfectly happy again. "One has freedom and peace out here," she told a bemused Thomas. "The really great passion in my life has been my love for my black brother . . . and my devotion to Denys fills my whole life with indescribable sweetness, in spite of constantly missing him." But a month later she was thrashing around again in the vortex of her conflict. She tried to convince herself that she did not actually want commitment, arguing that she could have married Geoffrey Buxton if she wanted a safe anchorage. (History does not record whether *he* wanted *her*.) "The reason for my giving up my life to loving the independence-seeking Denys and the black race so boundlessly," she decided, "must be because this is necessary for me; I cannot be possessed and I have no desire to possess. It can be cold and empty, God knows, but it is not cramped or stifling." Tania was vulnerable to violent swings of mood, ricocheting from suicidal despair to elation within twenty-four hours. The serene wisdom of *Out of Africa* was an ideal she never actually achieved for long, just as life on the farm was rarely the pastoral idyll that has enchanted millions. But what is the point of being a writer, if not to change grubby reality into something meaningful?

IN ADDITION TO THE news of Henry's illness, Denys learned that a buyer had been found for Haverholme; he was to lose his childhood home. He was disturbed, and conveyed his tense mood to Tania in a letter written in Mombasa just before boarding his ship. It concerned his Hudson, which he left with her on the farm. "Don't drive fast when the car is cold," he ordered her. "The red should be up to the lower edge of the white circle in the thermometer. Don't force your gears if you miss them: start again." The gears were evidently especially vulnerable. "They are so important," he continued, "if you want the car to run nicely." There was more: "Always let your clutch in smoothly otherwise you strain all its transmission." He hated the journey, was nursing an atrocious cold, and arrived in a chilly, showery London on the first day of the first general strike in British history. The coal miners had come out a few days earlier, their leader warning that the strike would be to the death, and the Trades Union Congress had voted to back them. CLASS WAR SPLITS BRITAIN, shrieked the headlines, and workers at the *Daily Mail* refused to print a leader denouncing TUC plans. A formal state of emergency was declared, troops were deployed, and the prime minister asked John Reith, the head of the BBC, to broadcast a message urging listeners to "Keep Steady!" The Establishment stiffened in its efforts to ensure that the strike cause the least possible disruption. Toby's colleagues in the City started driving trains, barristers were sworn in as special constables, and the Marylebone Cricket Club announced that there would be no interruption in the cricket. Strikers had little support outside the working classes. As the historian A.J.P.

Taylor noted, "The elderly Liberal leaders forgot their liberalism when threatened by (imaginary) social revolution." It was not imaginary, but it quickly lost any reality. On May 12, 1926, the TUC called off the general strike. The miners fought on until November, when, half-starved, they returned to the pits, worse off than they had been before. The strike was indeed to the death. It was the miners who died.

There were still virtually no buses running when Denys got to the capital, but the streets were thronged with black box-body cars. Car ownership had rocketed even before the strike, especially with the introduction of cheaper models, and Londoners had recently enjoyed their first taste of the traffic jam. Since Denys's last visit, white lines had been painted onto roads to separate motor streams, traffic lights had been installed in Piccadilly, and a one-way scheme had been introduced around Trafalgar Square and Hyde Park Corner. Now, during the strike, the petrol engine moved stealthily toward its inexorable victory over coal-burning trains. Toby, still a fanatic motorist, drove Denys and Margaretta to Haverholme in the latest Rolls. It rained hard for most of the three-and-a-half-hour journey. Their father had that week suffered an attack of what the doctor called apoplexy. It had partially paralyzed his right hand, but they found him better than they had feared. His hand was coming back to life and his spirits were reasonable, though he was demoralized, as they all were, by the prospect of packing up the contents of the vast house that had been their family home for so many decades. As Henry did not appear to want any help, after two days Toby, Margaretta, and Denys returned to London. But another specter was waiting. On May 21, Denys received a telegram at the Conservative Club from Tania telling him that she was pregnant again.

They had devised a code for such an event: the unborn child would be referred to as Daniel, a Winchilsea name. So the "love relationship" had obviously been normal enough. Denys was horrified. He was not interested in having a child; he was not prepared to have one. His inability to accept long-term commitment was pathological. He sent a cable straight back: "Strongly urge you cancel Daniel's visit." It was as if iron had entered the soul. Revulsion and sympathy competed for ascendancy and, later in the day, pacing around the high-ceilinged public rooms, he had misgivings about his heartless telegram. He cabled again: "Reference your cable and my reply please do as you like about Daniel as I should welcome him if I could offer partnership but this is impossible stop you will I know consider your mother's views. Denys." She responded with dignity. "Thanks cables never meant to ask assistance/permission—consent only. Tania." She was, in fact, never certain that she had been pregnant. Before she knew for sure, she began to bleed, and concluded that if she had been expecting a baby she was now having a miscarriage. Later that year, she told Thomas that she no longer wanted a child. But in her childless old age she admitted to her secretary that she had deeply wanted this baby.

A fretful Denys went back up to the Priory, where things had gotten worse. Henry looked awful, and on May 28 Denys reported to Toby that he did not think their father was well. Toby drove up the next day. It had turned even colder, and the red Shorthorns were clustered in the corner of the fields with their heads down. Denys, worried about Tania, felt guilty and confused. It was difficult to be out of communication. He sent her a note, enclosing photographs. "I am rather depressed and could wish myself back at Ngong," he wrote. "I want your news. What of Daniel? I would have liked it but saw it as being very difficult for you." He promised to write properly soon. No wonder he was depressed. He had made a frightful mess of things and dwelled miserably over what Yeats called "the foul rag and bone shop of the heart"—his heart, padlocked to all, and perhaps even to himself. In July he sent Tania another note, along with a picture, a piece of music, and an Egyptian book. The music, he told her, was for a dance in a Lesbian ballet (presumably Diaghilev's *Les Biches*, which he had seen at His Majesty's Theatre). No doubt this lifted her spirits. She did not reply, and he started to worry that he had the wrong box number. He sent her a consignment of bulbs for the garden, along with catalogs marking the ones he had ordered.

Henry again rallied, and in August Denys went shooting in Scotland for three weeks, which cheered him up. When he returned to Haverholme to help his father pack up, he found that the old man was not amenable to assistance. They sat over dinner at the long table, the wind from the North Sea rattling the loose panes and the weak electric light yellowing the old matte silverware. Packing crates lurked in dark corners, and only the discolored oblongs on the flaking walls indicated where ancestral portraits had hung for generations. Henry, white-haired and whiskery, sat with his shoulders stooped. He had been reluctant to sell the Priory, "on sentimental grounds," and clung to the shreds of his independence, refusing to let his children take over. Denys, as a result, felt useless. "In spite of his being very unwell," he told Tania, "he insists upon doing everything himself as long as he can stagger around: so that all I can do is stand around like the French clown at a circus." He stretched his long legs under the table as steam from the poached halibut rose a fraction before evaporating in the cold air. The silence was punctuated only by the clink and scrape of cutlery as Henry worked his knife slowly with his weak right hand.

Denys found the atmosphere depressing, and told Tania that he would be returning to Africa in October. "I shall be glad to see Ngong and your charming self again," he wrote. "Those sunsets at Ngong have an atmosphere of rest and content about them which I never realise anywhere else. I believe I could die happily enough at sunset at Ngong, looking up the hills, with all their lovely colours fading out above the darkening belt of the near forest. Soon they will be velvet black against the silver fading sky—black as the buffalos which now come pushing softly out of the bush high up under the breasts of the hills to feed with sweet breath unafraid upon the open grass of the night. I am much looking forward to seeing you again Tania: you might have given me something of your news— nothing—no word even of Daniel." He went on to tell her that he was bringing out a new Hudson, and that he was planning to stay at the coast for a few days, as he had determined to buy a piece of land he had seen and build a small bungalow "so that we can visit the sea from time to time. It is a nice place and will be right away from anyone else. Do not tell of this." He asked her to write to him in Mombasa, "to say whether you are alive and well, or ill and dying. How is Farah: where is Billea, and has he learned to drive your Hudson yet? Is Kamau still with you, or has he stolen all the tools and *torokaed* [run off]? I must talk to my father—Goodnight Goodnight." How could she resist? She wrote him a letter. He was not, after all, to be a father. He replied from the Conservative Club, thanking her for a "charming letter" and agreeing to her request to buy some cosmetics ("I have got your Rubinstein muck"). It looked as if they had made up.

IN LONDON, MEN WERE wearing Oxford bags and the carefree image of the twenties persisted in the face of the strike and its consequences for working people. Charleston flappers kicked their legs sideways in the ball-rooms, Noël Coward and Ben Travers were packing the theaters, and everyone was laughing at the boot-eating scene in Charlie Chaplin's *The Gold Rush*. Denys did the cultural rounds, stocked up on safari equipment, and toured the country in his recently acquired second Hudson. Unlike the first model, this one had windows and a roof, "to keep this icy climate out." He visited Pussy and her brood in Stowmarket, Suffolk, and Iris, whose career continued at its usual rackety pace. Her marriage to the painter had disintegrated, and although not yet divorced, during a spell as an actress when she toured America with Diana Cooper she had fallen in love with a fantastically tall impoverished Austrian nobleman. She re-mained based in the United States, returning occasionally to visit her small son, Ivan, who stayed in England, and Denys caught up with them both. In 1927, a friend arranged for a volume of Iris's poems to be pub-lished in New York to procure desperately needed cash. Called *The Trav-eller,* the collection included a poem titled "Wild Geese," which she had written for Denys. Iris was already counting the cost of her youthful abandon, and many of the poems she wrote at this time express regret ("Oh that I had waited fast behind the fret / That loosed me into shim-mering illusions"). The weight of her repining grew heavier with the years. "Men are cumbersome," she wrote to her sister Viola later, after life had really put the boot in. "One has always to treat them like an ill-ness or madness."

Henry staged yet another recovery. He had taken a house in Park Lane as a London base, and in the long term was to live with Toby and Mar-garetta somewhere in the home counties. Denys was free to go over to France, where, as he was on both the kitchen and the wine subcommittees of Muthaiga, he wanted to order wine for the club and hire a chef. The raffish and anonymous nightlife of Paris in the twenties appealed to him. He looked in at Lipp's on the Boulevard Saint-Germain, warmed his hands at the charcoal braziers of the Rotonde, and mingled with the *poules* in the streets, where leaves were already floating from the plane trees to cling around the brightly painted entranceways. Ever since the previous year's Exposition des Arts Décoratifs, a cultish exhibition that fathered the Art Deco movement, clean combinations of curves and angles and sleek geometric shapes had appeared on the walls of his regular nightclubs and restaurants. Women had become more streamlined, too, and Coco Chanel had made tanned skin fashionable. *Les femmes du monde* were wearing exotic orange, violet, and silver gowns created under the influence of the Russian ballet designer Léon Bakst. The Catholic Church had recently attacked the "scandalous" attire adopted by postwar metropolitan women, as well as their growing involvement in sport, which the Pope found "utterly incompatible" with female dignity. Outrage spilled beyond Rome, and English bishops publicly expressed their alarm at the rise in hemlines, perceiving a parallel descent in morals. Doctors (male) weighed in with the diagnosis that shorter skirts could cause puffiness and chafing of the legs. In Paris, Josephine Baker took little notice, and Denys enjoyed her bare-breasted mating dance in *La Revue Nègre* at the Théâtre des Champs-Elysées. Meanwhile, in the galleries, the patrician portraits of Sargent seemed centuries old next to the canvases of Max Ernst and Joan Miró. But Erik Satie's pear-shaped piano music was too modern even for Denys.

As his father seemed to be stable, Denys began to make arrangements to get back to Africa. He had been thinking of visiting Kermit in America, but felt that he could not be away from his new safari work for so long. He went to Tunis for a week instead, to see more of the northern part of Africa, staying with friends who had a house there. Back in Italy, a country now firmly under the control of the bowler-hatted Mussolini and his pet lion, Denys ended his tour at Rome, a city he loved. On October 25, he set off from Genoa in the German ship *Tanganyika* for what he described as "17 days prison." He wrote to Tania when he arrived at Mombasa, saying that he didn't think he would ever go to Europe again by sea. He was glad to be back, and told her, "Homeward bound I feel that I am, for now Ngong has got more of the feeling of Home to me than England." He said he hoped to stay with her over Christmas, and that he was greatly looking forward to seeing her. But he neither hurried to Ngong nor took out a client. He went to stay with his friend Sheikh Ali bin Salim, the *liwali* (governor) of the coast. The sultan's representative in Mombasa, bin Salim lived in a palatial residence on the mainland coast, where the red flag of the sultan was hoisted each morning and servants offered cigarettes, figs, and Turkish delight from inlaid brass platters. Installed in one of the whitewashed guesthouses on the grounds, Denys sat in pools of black shade under the mango trees or descended the long flight of stone steps to be rowed to town by the sheikh's team of Swahili oarsmen. The air on the coast was so damp that the ropes of the boat sweated a salt dew. Denys had shipped the new Hudson out with him, and after a few days proceeded north to see if he could get the land he had been looking for on the ocean. Toward the end of November, having selected his plot, he finally appeared at the farm.

Tania and Denys took up their old pleasures, sitting on the bench picking out their graves or riding into the hills to track a single impala ram running with a harem of eighty females. The plains were heavy with the scent of lilies, and hundreds of plover fed on new grass. In the evenings, Tania told more stories by the fire. She had a paneled French fire screen with pasted-on Oriental figures cut out of an illustrated paper, and the glow of the flames lit an unfolding narrative, the panels crowded with animals like an Elizabethan tapestry. Denys was an attentive listener. At the surprise reappearance of a character, he would chip in, "That man died at the beginning of the story, but never mind." They played Schubert's "Frühlingsglaube" ("Faith in Spring"), and when it came to the line *"Es blüht das fernste, tiefste Tal"* ("The farthest, deepest valley is blooming"), they agreed that it was a certain valley they could see from the farm just after the rains.

But *shauries* (problems) continued to plague the farm. Epidemics had immobilized the workers, Tania had been quarreling with Dickens, her manager, and Farah had been sulky. Most serious of all, she had no money and she was fed up with being "poor," saying that she hated her poverty more than her syphilis or her nose or her loneliness. It was becoming increasingly hard to conceal her neediness from Denys, and when she did reveal it he was only partially capable of an appropriate response, blindly refusing to put her at the center of his life or to engage with her on any profound emotional level. "Denys was a loveable person, but he was also very selfish," Ben Birkbeck's second wife, Ginger, recalled. The boundary between selfish and elusive is porous. It was Denys's elusiveness that attracted Tania (and so many others). Having overtly rejected commitment, he did not see his behavior as selfish. But actions engender commitment as well as words, and he had been living with her for three years, albeit intermittently. He could have raised capital and bought out the Karen Coffee Company shareholders so that he and Tania could own the farm together. They had discussed it, but Denys was never serious about the project. He tried to help in the titanic battle to keep the farm afloat, but as his life was acquiring shape and structure hers was falling apart. He knew that she was desperate. At the very least, he had to co-opt someone to stay on the farm with Tania when he was away. The obvious choice was Ingrid Lindstrom.

Ingrid, a hardworking Swede, had immigrated to British East Africa with her husband, Gilles, in 1918. Another indefatigable pioneer, she saw experiment after experiment fail—she once had a whole flock of turkeys devoured by *siafu* (giant ants)—but she kept going, producing four children while she was about it. Petite and fair, with gap teeth, she was a loyal friend to Tania. "She was difficult, but she was lovely,"* Ingrid recalled years later. Now Denys devised an elaborate scheme whereby he would wire to let Ingrid know when he was leaving, she would take the train from Njoro to Nairobi the day before his departure, and he would pick her up and drive her to Ngong. Tania would not then be alone. According to Ingrid, Denys was taking precautions because Tania had threatened to kill herself. ("Tanne liked to use suicide," she remembered.) Death never seemed far off to Tania, and in many of her tales it hovers on the margin of life. She was not afraid of dying. Once, when she was sailing back from Rotterdam, a gale blew up. Ingrid's sister Ette de Mare was also on board. "I hope we're not going down," she said fearfully to Tania. "I wouldn't mind," Tania replied. After Denys had actually vanished, however, it seemed to Ingrid that Tania got over the loss almost immediately, tackling life with relish. "She was double," Ingrid said. "It was hard to get inside someone like that." Whatever was happening in Tania's internal world, by the end of 1926 the cracks in her relationship with Denys had opened, and, in the gaps between, crisis was rising.

---

* Ingrid said that she did not recognize her own portrait in *Out of Africa*. She appears as a bizarre mix of ancient Swedish peasant and laughing Valkyrie. Tania had turned her into an archetype, as she did with many of her characters, including Denys.

CHAPTER 8

STUNTING

Denys could, like the pied piper, have made us go
wherever he pleased at the crook of his little finger.

—KIT TAYLOR, JUNE 1975

A FRICANS IN KENYA WERE NOW MOSTLY CONFINED TO SPECIAL RE-
serves and required to supply labor and taxes; the white community, on
the other hand, was enjoying the first good years since the war, what some
historians call the Sunbeam Period. Plantation crops, mainly coffee and
sisal, were flourishing east of the Rift and Britons had established themselves in the western sector, which until then had been dominated by
South Africans. Gilgil and Nakuru had developed into livestock centers,
the administration had extended the railway, and the architect Sir Herbert
Baker, Lutyens's formidable rival, had built schools as well as a neoclassi-
cal Government House for Sir Edward "Ned" Grigg, a governor with
more than a touch of the matinee idol. It was in this prosperous interlude
between the First World War and the Depression that Kenya became fashionable, and in paraded the set who gave life to the Happy Valley soubri-
quet that dogged Kenya for a generation.

After the languid Etonian Josslyn Hay married the divorcée Lady
Idina Gordon in 1923 and set up home on the slopes of the Aberdares,
news spread of a sybaritic clique based in the Wanjohi Valley, a hundred
miles north of Nairobi. The loose association of idle toffs, remittance
men, beauties, and oddballs thrived on champagne, cocaine, morphine,
and sex, and when their friends from England returned home gasping

with tales of debauchery and servants who cleaned the family silver with Vim, Happy Valley became a synonym for orgies, wife-swapping, and drinking—above all, drinking—and a gossip-column staple in London and New York, especially as the image of wanton abandon merged into a nameless fear of the primal desires lurking below the surface of sunny Africa. "Are you married," people in England asked, "or do you live in Kenya?" Lady Idina in particular was emblematic of the untamed female. She stalked the polo grounds like a divine but rackety temptress in a shimmering confection of plum-and-emerald silk slung with ropes of pearls (there were always lots of pearls). The daughter of the eighth Earl de la Warr, she went through six husbands and lashings of boyfriends, including Oswald Mosley. (Joss Hay also went on to join the Fascists.) At one of her cuckolded spouses, an industrialist, Lady Idina once raged huskily, "You maker of shirts, how can you understand us, who have been wanton through the ages?" Hay, meanwhile, a suave figure with foxy good looks, pale gold hair, and a glimmering smile, rested on his shooting stick at the racecourse in a white silk suit, polka-dot bow tie, and panama. In London, *Tatler* magazine had featured his romance with the older Idina as its cover story. Hay devoted his life to the pursuit of pleasure. On the ship that transported him and his bride to Mombasa, a woman locked him in a lavatory after she heard her husband returning to their cabin while she was sucking Hay's penis. In the Men's Bar at Muthaiga, he divided women into three categories—Droopers, Boopers, and Super-boopers—although in their state of semipermanent inebriation most of his chums fell limply into the first category themselves. Like many of the truly debauched, Hay himself did not smoke or take drugs, and he drank little. He liked to gamble and once air-freighted a pair of fighting cocks and a hen to Wanjohi, a project that ended when his cook inadvertently roasted the birds for dinner.

When Evelyn Waugh visited Kenya in 1930, he mixed with the Wanjohi crowd, lolling on their cushions at night picnics and nibbling small hot sausages at the cocktail hour in baronial highland mansions. At the end of it all, he hazarded that these were settlers who "wish to transplant and perpetuate a habit of life traditional to them, which England has ceased to accommodate—the traditional life of the English squirearchy." They were, he concluded, quixotic "in their attempt to recreate Barsetshire on the equator." But the few hedonistic aristocrats who inhabited Happy Valley led a very different life from that of the hardworking farmers who struggled for decades to bully the land into productivity. "They were a group as representative of Kenya," as a contemporary Anglo-Kenyan puts it, "as beefeaters are of London." They fueled a myth of glamour and hedonism, but all they were doing was seeking escape through sex and stimulants. The story of Tania and Denys, on the other hand, is about transcendence through love; through living out deeply held personal values; and, eventually, through art. And the truth was that the coterie at the heart of Happy Valley, when they were not drunk or bombed out on cocaine, were often suicidally depressed. Unhappy Valley would have been a better name.

DENYS HAD BEEN BACK in Kenya for less than four months, but he wanted to see his father again before he moved out of Haverholme. A bad bout of dysentery delayed his departure, but Tania nursed him back to health in time to sail on March 5, 1927. When he finally got up to Lincolnshire in April, he was relieved to find the old man fit. The sale of the Priory was nearing completion. A new house had been found near Basingstoke, in Hampshire, and Henry and Toby were to take possession in July. Denys walked through the Haverholme grounds for the last time toward the end of the month. He had just turned forty, and stood on the cusp of middle age looking backward at his youth. A bloom lay over the park, and gusts of cool air from the North Sea rippled the pheasants' feathers as they scattered from the lawns. Fenland steeples peeped up among the trees along the horizon, and at the end of the day, streams of the retiring sun poured through a broken hedge onto the stile he raced to with Toby when their governess released them from the schoolroom. It was too lugubrious, and Denys hurried back down to the Conservative Club. The staff there adored him. One valet remembered him sixty years later. "I had many a talk with him when I was laying out his clothes or running his bath," he recalled. "He told me of the safaris he went on and all about the animals. I thought he was a great man, and his tales of Africa kept me enthralled. I have always remembered him because he had time to talk to me." Denys's heart and mind had stayed behind among the shadows of the Rift; it was

England that seemed foreign. Calling at the Café Royal or at Ciro's, he noted that young women's hair, which had been getting shorter and shorter for years, had now vanished completely under brocade skullcaps. He wrote to Tania to tell her that he was longing for Africa, finishing the letter, "I bless you whenever I think of you, which is very often."

After only two months he left on the SS *Crispi*, for once finding the journey "quite pleasant." Disembarking at Massawa, an Eritrean Red Sea port, he got hold of a car and motored inland to Asmara: it was "a wonderful road, rising 6500 feet in about 20 miles." Continuing south on the *Crispi*, he got off again in Mogadishu to spend two days in Italian Somaliland as a guest of his friend Conte Capallo. Much had changed since his first visit. The arrival of the Fascist governor Cesare Maria de Vecchi, later Conte di Val Cismon, in 1923 marked a new phase of colonial "development." De Vecchi launched large-scale agricultural projects, built extensively, and generally ramped up the economy—greatly, of course, to the benefit of Italy (whereas the British weren't doing much with their slice of Somaliland to the north). But his regime was vile. Capallo had worked in Somaliland for years, and was attached to the people. He took Denys south to Kismayo, the port, previously in Kenya, that was ceded to Italy along with the rest of Jubaland in 1925. Denys was shocked at what the Italians were dishing out to the Somalis. "They have a madman of a governor there," he told Kermit, "which is a pity; he is playing the devil with the Somalis: forced labour very badly organised—families split up and sent to work 150 miles from their houses. The inevitable insurrections are suppressed with every brutality: women and children butchered in cold blood after the men have been rounded up and flattened out with machine guns. All decent-thinking Italians are disgusted by this regime." Capallo knew personally four Somali dissidents who had been tortured for an invented theft. Two died; Denys met the other two. Meanwhile, the governor was building a palace. "If I have ever seen a region in need of the intervention of the League of Nations, it was there," Denys told Tania later.

DENYS HAD ABANDONED almost all professional pursuits except hunting with clients, an occupation that turned out to encompass more than he or anyone else could have imagined. It led him to the serious study of photography, to a campaigning involvement in conservation, and to flying as a bush scout. All three were fed by his love of Africa and, finally, provided appropriate purpose for his energies and talents. From now on his schedule of assignments for Safariland gave his life sense and pattern, and when he got back to Kenya in the first week of June he started on his longest safari to date, a five-month photographic expedition with a single client, the American manufacturing tycoon Frederick B. Patterson. Denys had been offered the job the previous year and wrote to Kermit for advice: "Do you know aught of one 'Patterson' whose chief call to fame I believe is that he has made a hideous amount of money out of some patent penny-in-the-slot machine for correctly registering the sale of buns and ginger pop?" The inventive Patterson, a fastidious individual close to Denys's age, with springy dark hair and sloping shoulders, was a fanatic snapper. Photography was a craze among Americans with money in the twenties, and the possibility of returning from exotic lands with gorgeous black-and-white prints depicting elephants in their own environment or the aluminum backs of hippos in a wallow gripped the imagination of inquisitive travelers like Patterson. He had been negotiating with Safariland for almost a year, and his friend the Duke of York had recommended Denys as his white hunter. Patterson had business in Europe and sailed from New York in March to spend six weeks in London before proceeding to Africa. While he was there he met Hatton, as he called him. He found his future guide "a walking encyclopedia" who could "rattle off all the names of African animals and tell of the quarter-mile where one could find them on the map." The pair met again at the Voi station at midnight, when Patterson stepped off the Mombasa train. "Hatton," he recalled, loomed from the sidings to shake hands and "seemed eight feet" tall. Denys had a Dodge and two Chevrolet trucks waiting, and they set off along a hoof path that corkscrewed through the encircling darkness of the Taita Hills. Sitting next to Denys in the Dodge as the trucks dropped behind, Patterson wondered if he would ever see his luggage again.

For their first base camp, Denys had selected Maktau, west of Voi. It had been one of his favorite areas since his soldiering days, and he and Patterson hunted for a month before proceeding southwest across the

Serengeti plains to Lake Jipe.* The party consisted of a hundred Swahili porters who walked barefoot ahead of the cars, two skinners, and two driers (there was to be some trophy-shooting in addition to the photographs), Hamisi and his mess boys, Billea, now an experienced headman, and Kanuthia, a young Kikuyu with watchful eyes who worked for many years as Denys's driver. Each hunter also had two gun bearers (Patterson said that his pair did not leave his side for five months) and a personal team of Marsi boys. At first, the nocturnal snort of a rhino left Patterson rigid with fear till dawn. His doctor had ordered him to drink only filtered water, and the breakage of his filter precipitated a crisis. He gulped down quinine grains and followed specific medical instruction to take no fewer than one and no more than two glasses of whiskey per evening. He fretted day and night about the dirt that might be scratching his Graflex lens. But he was enchanted with Africa. He and Denys walked all day, following the musky smell of waterbuck to places where yellow-barked fever trees grew like inside-out umbrellas and Fischer's lovebirds flashed among the branches in mustard streaks. Before dinner, filmed in sweat and dust, they sat at a water hole and pulled ticks off their ankles, the delicate scent of spoor mingling with the dank, earthy smell of hoof-plowed soil. Stentorian troupes of baboons prattled out of sight while an advance guard of old males scouted for leopards; zebras sniffed the air and bared their teeth; and just before the light died velvet-eared giraffes drank warily, tempting prey when their legs were splayed. Then Hamisi baked bread in a tin box and served up ostrich eggs as appetizers.

Once, because Patterson wanted to photograph lions at night, they staked out a zebra carcass after supper. "We waited for an hour or two, peering through the starlit night at the grey blur which marked the kill," Patterson recalled. "Then, without warning, came a blood-chilling concert from the dusky bush beyond." Soon they saw the lions.

"How many are there?" Patterson whispered.

* The region known as the Serengeti plains in Kenya, east of Kilimanjaro, is not the same as the more famous Serengeti National Park created in 1951 in today's Tanzania, which is west of the mountain. The Serengeti ecosystem in fact covers an area in excess of thirty thousand square kilometers—more than double the size of the national park—and it includes chunks of Kenya, such as the Maasai Mara game reserve. In Denys's era, the term "Serengeti plains" was applied to large stretches of land on both sides of the border, east and west of Kilimanjaro.

"Three, I think," Denys whispered back. Then he clutched Patterson's arm. "No, by George! There are five—*six*!"

When they sat at dinner the next night in the light of glass-globed candle lanterns and a smoky red moon climbed above the brown hills, Patterson asked Denys how he got into the job. Denys smiled amiably and swallowed some more wine. "Oh," he said, "it just happened, if you know what I mean."

Photographing big game was a test of nerve, and the hunter's job was to compensate when the quarry refused to cooperate. Near Njoro, Denys killed a charging rhino six yards from Patterson's lens. Then, after making sure his client was safely scrubbing up in camp, he had to go out and shoot meat for more than a hundred hungry mouths as flies bit hard on his neck, tracking a kongoni antelope through sansevieria grass with spikes sharp enough to penetrate the sole of a shoe. When he made a kill, his boys carried the limp animal back on a pole, chanting while the tongue dripped blood onto heavy-grained grasses. After six weeks, Denys was ready for a break. He had proposed Patterson as a temporary member of Muthaiga and deposited him there when the safari routed through Nairobi. He himself escaped to Tania.

INGEBORG HAD BEEN on the farm for a second three-month visit, and after she left Tania was ill. She had two minor abdominal operations and had to stay in bed for three weeks. But by the time Denys stopped off she was better, and when he drove up she was out inspecting the plantation with Charles Taylor, a coffee farmer who was advising her. A founder of the Coffee Board, Taylor was the doyen of Kenyan planters. Later, at Denys's suggestion, Tania invited him and his wife, Kit, to stay for dinner. "I never knew two people who were on the same wavelength as those two were," Kit noted at the end of the evening. "I was aware of a very deep harmony between them, but on the surface a kind of delicate detachment." Tania sat quietly at one end of the table, the scarlet tones of her shawl flashing in the crystal glasses. Denys, deeply bronzed, presided at the other end in his brown velvet smoking jacket. Kit noticed Denys's "clear steady eyes, with that distant horizons look one often saw in Kenya," and the way he used his hands without actually gesticulating. He told safari stories in the still darkness. "He began to weave a spell around Charles and me," Kit recalled, "till we felt we were with him in the strange, beautiful places he had just come from . . . the dining room was dark and the polished table seemed like a pool with only the glimmer of the candles reflected in it. Tania sat very still and silent as if a sudden move might break the spell. In the shadows her face looked small and white, and her dark eyes huge, like a little woodland witch or something out of legend."

THE REFITTED PATTERSON safari journeyed to the banks of the Uaso Nyiro in the Northern Frontier District, an attenuated landscape accurately described by one jaded traveler as "miles of damn-all." Close to the Lorian Swamp, where Denys had promised elephants, the cars were charged twice by rhinos, adding what Patterson called "zest" to the journey. The Lorian itself consisted of fetid reed beds, olive *mswaki* thickets, thousands of flies, and millions of mosquitoes, and at night Patterson recorded "a pandemonium of trumpetings and crashings all around our camp." But they got their elephant. The next day, as they crossed a stream in pursuit of another one, an adolescent crocodile silently clamped its jaws around Denys's right leg. Remembering the drill in a surge of adrenaline and an explosion of water, Denys jabbed at an eye with his index finger. The jaws slackened and Denys floundered to the bank, bleeding into the mud before collapsing. He was lucky: crocodiles usually made off with a limb at the very least. But the episode was a bother. Denys could not hunt with a nasty leg wound. After dispatching a runner to the railway a hundred miles away with a letter summoning a replacement hunter, he sat it out in camp, prevailing upon the faintly irritated Patterson to dress his leg.

By the time the party broke again, in Nairobi, the wound had healed. Denys went about his business. On Government Road the heat solidified like colorless jelly, and the cattle gathered at the far end seemed to walk on stilts. On the wide steps outside the post office, an Indian letter writer crouched over dirty scraps of paper while a Kikuyu stood beside him declaiming his sentences. Denys went in to collect his mail and his cables. When he came out, he walked to the bottom of the steps and stood on the edge of the dusty road. The Kikuyu had finished his letter. Denys opened a cable and learned that his father was dead. Toby was the fourteenth earl.

Both he and Topsy were with Henry when he died in his bed at his new Park Lane house. "He looked v. peaceful," Toby wrote in his diary, "and about 45." In fact, he was seventy-four. Henry had lasted two months without Haverholme.

AS PATTERSON WAS DUE to sail from Mombasa in the second week of October, they spent the last leg of the safari moving toward the coast. "Hatton was talking of a return trip to England, but his eyes kept sweeping the horizon," Patterson noted. "He loved every inch of this country. . . ." They saw sable running, scimitar horns thrown back almost to their tails. Many hunters considered the sable the most beautiful antelope in Africa, and it made a good ending. Finally they reached Mombasa, and Denys shook Patterson's hand.

"Till we meet again," he said. "You will come back."

Patterson turned toward the ship that was to convey him back to what he called "civilisation," though he spoke the word more ruefully now that he had lived without it for five months. He returned to America extolling the beauty of unspoiled Africa, noting that the tentacles of that "civilisation" were creeping ominously toward the "healthful wonderland" that had so enchanted him. "Every tale I have ever read about African wildlife falls short of the real thing," he wrote. He had nothing but praise for Denys: "I could not have found a better person for the job. He was a true sportsman, a fine companion and a fair dealer with the natives; a man fearless in the face of danger and most considerate at all times. . . . Never once did I see Hatton lose his head in a tight corner. . . . He is popular with everybody. . . . The great thing is, I think, that he loves Africa: people, country and animals."

Denys arrived back at the farm to find that Tania had crashed his Hudson into a ditch, thumping her head on the steering wheel and smashing the car. But he had brought records back from his last trip to England, including the Kreutzer Sonata, which he loved (so much for Beethoven being vulgar), and they resumed their postprandial routine of music and stories. During the day, he interrupted her as she sat at the typewriter in her dark mahogany study pounding out missives home. Tania said that she was happier than she had ever believed it possible to be. Although they had not had enough rain and the berries had shriveled on the coffee bushes, she was buoyant, assuring Anders, her youngest brother, that she was not going to let the company go bankrupt, no matter what the board thought. As for Denys, he appreciated fine cuisine, and the house had become famous for its table. The cook, Kamante Gatura, was a favorite of Tania's. She had noticed him as a boy in 1921, herding goats. His father, a Kikuyu elder, had a *shamba* (small plot) on the farm. After he died, Kamante contracted a leg infection, which Tania tried to treat, dressing the suppurations herself, but the disease had advanced too far, so she sent the patient to the Scottish mission hospital. When Kamante was cured, he came to work as her dog *toto*—the servant in charge of feeding the dogs. He also came back a Christian. Awakened by the howling hounds in the middle of the night, Kamante and Tania had often sat together picking giant ants—*siafu*—off their fur. When the cook was found murdered, Kamante was apprenticed to the kitchen and subsequently became chief cook himself. He was angular and his legs remained skeletal; there was, she said, something of the gargoyle about him. She taught him dishes from a recipe book and sent him to Muthaiga and to friends' kitchens to learn how to prepare new meals. When guests were expected, she scribbled menu plans in the back of her battered *Mrs Beeton* cookbook: *soufflé aux tomates, jambon froid Richelieu, artichaux à la Milanese.* But Kamante memorized recipes by naming them after events that had taken place on the day they were shown to him—the sauce of the gray horse that died, or the stew of the lightning that struck the tree. The only thing he never mastered was the order in which dishes were to appear, and if Tania did not draw pictograms beforehand the chocolate mousse would appear in advance of the consommé. He himself ate corn on the cob.

DENYS WENT OFF NORTH on his own account, traveling light with a few boys. He valued his solo safaris; the eye stared more sharply inward when there was no client to worry over. At dusk, he listened for the hoot of the spotted eagle owl and watched the finely barred underparts of the bird's yard-wide wings lofting toward the outcrops of Somalia. When he looked out beneath the tent flap at dawn and watched life returning to the plain in the strengthening light, like sap rising, or when he stepped beyond his camp to watch night deepen over the river, stillness rose in him, a primitive quietude that conquered despair, and at those moments he knew it was the only victory worth having. The incommunicable content Denys found in the landscapes of Africa nourished his emotional self-sufficiency. Tania projected her inner world onto the exterior environment with such remorseless intensity that there was no liberation from the bondage of self. Then Denys became ill again. By the beginning of December he was laid up at the farm, "horribly thin" and worried that he would not be well enough for a safari he was booked to lead on January 4. A doctor was called. It was his old heart trouble. But he was well enough to drive to the French mission with Tania on Christmas Eve for midnight Mass. They heard the mission bell tolling through the warm air even before they had cleared the wattle plantation. When they drew up outside the small church, the yard was thronged with beaming converts.

They spent the week quietly together. On the last day of the year a friend came to borrow a rifle, but after he had left with it Denys remembered that he had not explained an idiosyncrasy of the weapon, which meant that the hair trigger could be inadvertently demobilized. As the friend had already left on safari, Denys and Tania determined to set out before sunrise and catch up with him. They took Denys's Kikuyu driver, Kanuthia, and drove along the new Narok road, hoping to meet the safari caravan, which had taken the old road, at Narok itself. But neither Denys nor Tania knew if the new road had been completed. The stars were still out as cold air flowed over their faces, sharp with the scent of olive bushes, burned grass, and what Tania called "a sudden quelling smell of decay," and silhouettes of slim gazelles and lumpy eland loomed in the yellowing mist. About fifteen miles from the farm, Kanuthia pointed to a dark bulk on their right. It was a lion feeding on a giraffe corpse. The Maasai thereabouts had recently complained to Tania about a cattle-eating lion, but she had not been able to find it. Denys jumped out of the car and fired two shots at 250 yards. There was no time for skinning, so they covered the lion with branches and hurried on. But the road ran out after six miles, so they turned back, facing the eastern sky as the sun tilted over the plains and the hills. (The friend, it turned out, never used the faulty rifle.) When they reached the giraffe again on their way back, another lion was on it, a magnificent one with a black mane intermittently lifted by the wind. Behind him, the sky was crimson as a wound. Denys shot and the lion flew into the air, coming down with his legs gathered under him. Kanuthia got four bottles of fat from the skinning. Then they sat on the grass, shadows of vultures at their feet, and drank a bottle of claret with bread, cheese, raisins, and almonds that Tania had brought to celebrate the New Year. Was it an auspicious beginning? She thought so, and wrote to her mother to say that if 1928 continued to be so exciting there was much to look forward to. In *Out of Africa*, she transformed the lion hunt into a love scene. She made the first lion a female, shot at the closer distance of "twelve or fifteen yards," and killed the second lion herself. Her bullet, she wrote, "was a declaration of love."

Four months after the Narok road incident, Tania's manager, W. H. Dickens, refused to shoot a marauding lion on the grounds that as a married man with a small daughter he was unwilling to risk his life. After Tania and Denys had done the job themselves, she took up the theme in a long letter to her aunt Bess. Dickens, she claimed, was right: one had to choose between "the lions or family life," and she ended with what seemed like a gracious acknowledgment that Dickens's wife "gets just as much out of, sees 'the highest and greatest' in her baby daughter Anne's first tooth and evening bath" as Tania herself did from the lion hunt. This was nicely put, but one can have the first tooth and the lion. Or can one, really, without each being compromised? The Dickenses regularly functioned as ciphers for the undesirability of the married state. "Who can judge," Tania asked the bemused old aunt in Zeeland, "whether Dickens is actually happier than Finch Hatton, or Mrs Dickens happier than I?" Who indeed? Tania herself, apparently. "I myself think that I am much happier and get far more out of life than Mrs Dickens, who is always pretty sulky." Denys had compelled her to embrace the unorthodox, but it did not come naturally to her as it did to him, and the effort created tension which emerged most forcibly in her relationship with her family. She told her younger sister that she did not regard illness, poverty, loneliness, or "being let down" as misfortunes at all. These were bourgeois trifles. Instead, her greatest burdens had been imposed on her by people with so-called good intentions. Furthermore, her failure to find conventional domestic contentment encouraged her to indulge in the myth that the artist, in order to achieve greatness, is obliged to renounce convention.

The writer, in other words, must be isolated from real life in order to develop her talent—this is the price she must pay. But what can "real life" possibly be? The washing-up, perhaps, and who wants to do that? The pram in the hall had not yet been established as an enemy of promise, but a long line of artistic figures before Tania had conveniently decided that their destiny excluded them from the tedious minutiae of daily life, and that responsibility for the latter fell to smaller people. "Oh yes," wrote Amandine-Aurore Lucile Dudevant after she had abandoned her husband, son, and daughter in Nohant to take a nineteen-year-old lover, change her name to George Sand, and embrace the literary world of Paris, "*vive la vie d'artiste*. Our motto is freedom."

ON JANUARY 4, DENYS left on his safari, but he saw a lot of Tania that month. He turned up unexpectedly and stayed with her for a week while the safari broke; Will Dickerson, his second gun, was with him. Only six days later, the magneto on one of the lorries gave out thirty miles into Tanganyika. Denys drove nonstop to collect a replacement in Nairobi and appeared at the farm for dinner and a few hours' sleep on the dash back. He got up at one, and Tania went with him as far as the dam in her coat and nightgown, walking home when he went on. In the middle of March he was back, "accompanied, unfortunately," Tania reported home, "by his slave Dickerson, who is a bit of a bore." More scintillating guests were made welcome. A week earlier, Tania had run into Joss Hay, high priest of the Happy Valley set, in the bank. His father had just died, making Joss the twenty-second Earl of Erroll and high constable of Scotland. En route to London after the news came through, Hay was lashed with a rhino-hide whip on the platform of the Nairobi station by a cuckolded husband.

Fifteen years younger than Denys, Hay had been similarly fêted at Eton for his charm and good looks before being expelled for fornicating with a maid. He was addicted to speed, and in Kenya was often sighted racing along the rutted roads in Lady Idina's Hispano-Suiza. When he had his own Buick coupe, a passenger in the backseat once bounced right out of the car. Hay didn't notice for several miles. Tania invited him to the farm for an afternoon "bottle," and he asked if he might bring Alice de Janzé, a rich American heiress who lived in Happy Valley but was preparing to leave the country—she was being deported. Alice was frail and gorgeous, with oceanic eyes, a natural pout, and Cleopatra hair. She was in her late twenties and had lingering consumption; a spurned suitor once said she smelled of death. At Muthaiga, where love affairs germinated like valley grass, she had fallen in love with Raymund de Trafford. He was a remittance man from a grand County Limerick family, a former officer in the Coldstream Guards, an asthmatic, a gambler, and a committed drinker. Evelyn Waugh, who stayed with him in Kenya, called him a "fine desperado"; when the de Trafford cook was absent, Waugh had to forage for food and found his host in bed with his finger in a tin of grouse paste. The previous year, de Trafford and Alice had liaised in Paris, where he told her that his Catholic parents would not countenance their marriage. When he left for Calais, she boarded the train with him at the Gare du Nord and entered his compartment. She knelt in front of him, kissed him, then shot him and herself. Both recovered, and they went on to marry, then to divorce. Alice became known as "the fastest gun in the Gare du Nord." De Trafford continued as before. His elder brother eventually offered him £10,000 to be castrated. De Trafford, always short of cash, reflected for a moment, and said he would have one ball cut off and take £5,000.

When Tania welcomed her to the farm, Alice had just been acquitted of attempted murder, though the Kenyan government had asked her to leave the country anyway, on the grounds that she was an undesirable alien. She had been having an intermittent affair with Hay since 1919. But before the pair arrived, Lucie, Lady McMillan, appeared unexpectedly with two vast American women on leave from their cruise ship. (Cruise operators were just beginning to offer Nairobi stopovers, entraining wealthy passengers up from the coast.) They had gone for a drive in the hope of seeing a lion. But something even more exotic was lying in wait. Sipping tea from Tania's Royal Copenhagen china while Farah stood impassive in a corner, the dowagers spoke of the scandalous behavior of the Kenyan fast set of which they had read so much lubricious detail. The worst offender, they thought, was their fellow American Alice de Janzé. At that moment, Hay's Buick screamed up the drive in a typhoon of dust, and a minute later Jezebel herself glided across Tania's parquet.

Tania generously offered Alice the farm as a base before she was deported. Contrary to her bravura statements about the inferiority of women, Tania was close to a number of her own sex, notably the gap-toothed Ingrid, whom she told Ingeborg she loved. She liked joining the chaos of the Lindstroms' farm at Njoro, where barefoot children ran about feeding the chickens, and she enjoyed girlish talks about clothes. Her sartorial style was all her own. At a Muthaiga dance at which the other women wore variations of the clinging hip-waisted, calf-length dresses that were *le dernier cri,* Tania appeared in a hooped gown with panniers sewn with sprays of flowers, introducing a note of fantasy with a white astrakhan fez. But there was always an element of fantasy about Tania, as there is in the lacquered phrases of her prose. She blackened her eyes with kohl before anyone else used eye makeup, and it had an odd effect, as if she put it on just for fun; when she overdid it, she looked like a louche cabaret artiste. Throughout her life she was attracted to glamour, and in her old age, when she visited America as a literary luminary, it was Marilyn Monroe whom she asked to meet. When the audience was granted (with Arthur Miller in tow), Tania was spellbound. But her women friends accepted the posturing. "I knew her very well for many years," recalled Genessie Long (later Hamilton), who lived in splendor at Nderit, near Lake Nakuru, with her husband, seventy horses, and herds of dappled Shorthorns that grazed miles of parklike meadowland. "Like all my friends, I was devoted to her." Denys's old girlfriend Rose Cartwright said Tania was "a wonderful person without pretence. She was courteous, loyal and always most considerate of her servants and other people." Above all, Tania identified with unconventional women, and this was what drew her to the pantherine Beryl Markham (previously Purves, née Clutterbuck, subsequently Schumacher). But there were things Tania did not know about her friend.

IN 1936, BERYL WAS to win global fame as an aviatrix when she crossed the Atlantic solo and nonstop from east to west—the hard way, against the winds. She was the first pilot to do so, and the first woman to cross the Atlantic in any direction. She crash-landed her plane, the two-hundred-horsepower *Messenger,* in a bog in Cape Breton, but that didn't matter. All the press reports—and there were thousands—noted the slacks she wore.

Some people said she had whiskey rather than coffee in her thermos. But she did it.

Beryl was born in Leicestershire in 1902. Her father, Charles Clutter-buck, was a failed army officer with a talent for horses. He moved to Kenya in 1904, working, at first, as Delamere's dairy manager. His wife, Clara, followed him out with their two small children, Richard and the three-year-old Beryl. Clutt, as he was known, bought fifteen hundred acres at Njoro, between the Mau Forest and the Rongai Valley, which in those days was teeming with game. He cut down the ebony, teak, and ma-hogany, cleared hundreds of miles of creeping plants, and traded salt with the Dorobo, taking in exchange skins of colobus monkeys, which he used as bedspreads. He called the place Ndimu Farm and built flour and timber mills. By 1907, Clutt had more than a thousand Kavirondo and Kikuyu on the payroll. But Clara left him for a colonel and moved back to England, taking their son. Beryl was left to run wild with the Kipsigi, wearing a cowrie shell on a leather thong around her wrist to ward off evil spirits. She ate with her hands, her first language was Swahili, and she could hurl a spear as well as her male *layoni* (pre-circumcision age group) Kipsigi playmates. Clutt had a thoroughbred stud at Njoro, and Beryl practically grew up on horseback; she told a friend that she felt better on a horse than she did on her feet. It was said that even as a young girl there was no horse she could not ride—one of her many African names was a long and com-plicated one meaning "she who cannot fall off a horse." She had two and a half years of formal education before she was thrown out of school, and in 1919 she married Alexander "Jock" Purves, a freckled Scottish army captain who played rugby. Beryl was sixteen—though it was said that Clutt could not remember exactly when she was born and aged her as he did the horses, all of which became a year older on the same date. Purves was twice her age. In 1920, Clutt had to sell everything to satisfy his cred-itors, and Beryl began to train horses herself.

Tania was one of the few people who supported Beryl through years of flaky behavior and did not judge her. Beryl was a man's woman (actually, she liked men and horses equally) with few close female friends, and she grasped the hand Tania held out to her. In April of 1923, she moved to the farm for several weeks, bringing her horse, and told Tania that she and Jock were estranged. She no longer cared for her husband, she said, but he refused to give her either a divorce or an allowance, "so she is pretty stranded, but full of life and energy, so I expect she will manage," Tania concluded. They went out riding together, socialized with a pair of young Norwegian men, and skidded into Nairobi in the rain for parties. (Denys was away at the time.) Tania welcomed the prospect that they might one day be neighbors: "Beryl and I could always have some fun together," she told her mother. Beryl went back to Purves briefly before leaving him for good and taking refuge with Delamere at Soysambu, where she seduced his son in the hayloft. This was also the Christmas she was intimate with Denys at Galbraith's house party after he had been out shooting duck. She fitted in an affair with "Boy" Long, the Stetson-wearing glamour boy who was at that time Delamere's manager. Purves found out about Tom and Boy (but not about Denys) and dealt with both problems by beating up Lord Delamere outside the Nakuru hotel. As far as he was concerned, Delamere was guilty by association, having fathered Tom and employed Boy. Beryl's promiscuity was legendary. There was no doubt that she liked sex, but she also attracted gossip; one of her biographers observed that if all the stories were true "Beryl would never have risen from a re-clining position between the ages of fourteen to eighty-four." But Beryl was no mere femme fatale. She was brilliant at doing things: she turned herself into a hugely successful horse trainer, a world-record-breaking pilot, and a bestselling author. Even her critics admired her skills. "She was always up at dawn to be with the horses as usual, no matter what the night had brought," said an otherwise censorious fellow trainer.

When Beryl went back to England for the first time, in January 1924, it was Tania who saw her off at the station. Beryl was wearing a saggy hand-knitted suit. "I was so sorry for the poor child," Tania wrote. "She is so boundlessly naïve and confused, and has more or less fallen out with all her friends. . . . A year ago she was the most fêted person out here, now she is travelling home second class and when she gets to England she will have only £20 in her pocket." But Beryl found a wealthy lover and came back to Kenya in July "dressed like Solomon in all his glory." She began training horses again, winning the St. Leger in 1926. Purves agreed to a divorce, and the following year Beryl became engaged to Bob Watson, who was to inherit the Sunlight soap empire, but she broke it off and five months later agreed to marry Mansfield Markham, the mustachioed heir to a colliery fortune. In London's *Daily Express*, the two betrothal announcements were telescoped together and looked as if they had appeared three days apart—speedy even by Beryl's standards. But she did marry Markham. Delamere gave her away; Hoey, Denys's partner on the Nzoia farm, was best man; and Tania provided a bouquet. The newlyweds stayed at the farm and gave Tania a large bed before returning to England, where Beryl was kitted out in full designer trousseau and presented to the king and queen. The Markhams returned to Kenya in March 1928, bringing bloodstock, and immediately drove out to Ngong in Mansfield's yellow Rolls. They asked Tania to mind their dogs while they went house hunting, and eventually settled on a farm called Melela, at Elburgon near Njoro, close to Beryl's childhood home. From April to June, Beryl triumphed at the racecourse, but at Melela the going was far from good: Markham wasn't interested in horses, and Beryl refused to play bridge. But soon she was pregnant.

EARLY IN 1928, DENYS learned that he had been selected to take the Prince of Wales on safari during his forthcoming tour. It was the most prestigious assignment: Tania had already noted that people were talking of nothing but the royal visit, and one settler wrote to the *Standard* describing it as "the most momentous occasion in our history." A complex network of subcommittees had sprung up, its representatives stooped under the mantle of their responsibilities. Denys had in fact been second choice for the job: J. A. Hunter was asked first, but he was booked to take out a party of American clients and could not break his contract. It was an honor just to be second. But Denys hated protocol and, according to Tania, he was in "absolute despair" over his duties.

Denys had just begun to take his photography seriously. "It is true that some sort of a Kodak was always taken with a large quantity of film and the best intentions; but if my companion had a camera as well I generally found that my own completed the trip unopened, like the arrowroot," he wrote of his pre-Patterson safaris. Now he found cameras more absorbing than guns. He went out specially to get pictures of buffalo, spending four days following a herd and positioning his concertina-snouted camera until he got the shots he wanted. In July he sent a selection of pictures to Toby, asking him to see if he could get them into *Country Life* to accompany a chunk of inspirational text that he would write later on the importance of protecting the ageless abundance of Africa. When Toby dutifully took in the prints, an editor bought them as a royal safari tie-in. But there was no time to wait for Denys's copy. The photographs duly appeared, captioned with text that was not so much staff of life as staff of *Country Life*. At the same time, Denys had photographs displayed at the Kenya game department's first exhibition in Nairobi and his buffalo shots were praised by the *Standard* critic.

Through the lens of his camera, Denys had seen another Kenya: a pristine and ancient landscape in grave danger from the depredations of immigrants and their toys. He was among the first to recognize that although white men had spent the early years of settlement protecting themselves from game, the time had come to protect the game from the white men. The game department had appointed Denys an honorary warden, one of forty selected to balance the conflicting interests of farmers, hunters, and conservationists, and he was helping the chief warden, Archie Ritchie, gather data for a census that would define migration patterns. Ritchie was a majestic figure often seen in Nairobi behind the wheel of another yellow Rolls—this one distinguished from the first by the rhino horn mounted on the bonnet. Denys was especially concerned to do something about illegal practices proliferating within a parallelogram of land on the Tanganyikan Serengeti plains sixty miles west of the southern tip of Lake Natron. There were few human residents and a wonderland of game unique even in the Africa of the 1920s, but for two years parties of amateur hunters had been motoring across the border to shoot indiscriminately from cars. Americans competed to see how many heads they could bag in a day; one group killed twenty-one lions without getting out of their vehicles. Denys had twice reported the slaughter to the chief game warden of Tanganyika. But nothing was done. Now he began to brood.

In August of 1928, Tania, recovering from flu, drove Denys's new Hudson to Gilgil, where she stayed in the small hotel run by her friend Lady Colville, a cheery Frenchwoman who was widowed when her husband, a baronet in the Grenadier Guards, was knocked off his bicycle in Bagshot. Tania was preoccupied by the contents of a letter she had just received from Blix informing her that he and Cockie were to marry. Blix had taken up hunting professionally after he was relieved of his responsibilities on her farm; to a man practically born with a gun in his hand, East Africa was paradise. He had worked on elephant control and traveled through Uganda and the Congo's Ituri Forest, writing copious notes about the Wambouti pygmies he encountered in places where it rains every day for two-thirds of the year. He was there in 1925 when he learned that his mother was ill. He walked 260 miles to the Stanley Falls, caught a steamer down the Congo, and arrived in Sweden before she died. He had one episode of what Tania referred to as his "old illness," but it was a temporary setback in an otherwise unjustly healthy existence. In 1928, he and Sir Charles Markham motored 2,800 miles from Kano in Nigeria to Algiers—theirs was the first regular car to complete the journey straight across the Sahara. They continued to Paris, where they partied in the Big Bar of the Ritz for three days while the dirty vehicle and its sets of antelope horns caused a stir on the Place Vendôme.

A client had recently asked Blix to develop a five-thousand-acre farm in Babati, Tanganyika, and he and Cockie were to settle there. He and Tania had stayed friends; he was indulgent toward her. When she published her book *Seven Gothic Tales* in 1934, he congratulated her warmly, remarking privately, "We could have done with four gothic tales instead of seven." But now he and his new wife were sure to turn up in Nairobi, and Tania saw how invidious her position would be with another Baroness Blixen swanning around Muthaiga. She confided her anxieties to Lady Colville. "You will be the Honourable Mrs Denys Finch Hatton," purred her friend. This she would never be, but it would have solved the problem. It would have solved a number of problems. Was Tania still hopeful? Denys was devoted to her. Ingrid noticed how tender he was when he was with her, and how attentive to her needs. But around the middle of 1928 she also observed that a quarrel was simmering.

IT WAS ANOTHER YEAR of savage drought. The grass turned to straw and then powder. Tornadoes of dust danced across the plains in a macabre ballet as the hot, dry wind sucked the marrow from the animals' bones. In September 1928, Denys left to hunt bongo in the Kijabe Forest with a client. After three weeks, the safari party broke before continuing into

Uganda, and on the twenty-third Tania returned from the game reserve to find Denys waiting. They had a Schubert evening, and he experienced the monumental lifting of the spirit that comes from communion with a genius like Schubert. But he could stay for only one night. He had to get back to his client before a lightning visit to greet the Prince of Wales, who had a round of official duties before his safari. Everything in the country now seemed to revolve around the royal tour. Roads were under repair, including the one out to Ngong; shops were advertising new frocks; and Grigg, who had once been the prince's political adviser, refurbished the ballroom at Government House at a cost of £7,000.

Grigg had also summoned Tich Miles, the "third musketeer" who had served in the Scouts with Denys and Berkeley. After the war, Tich had joined the King's African Rifles in Jubaland, surviving two episodes of the usually fatal blackwater fever before being sent to Mega, in southern Abyssinia, as British consul. Mega was a three-day march from Moyale, the Kenyan frontier post, and there was no road. Tich's job was to pressure Amharic provincial governors to control their subjects and to open the wells on their side of the border to Kenyan cattle herders, neither of which task they were willing to undertake. Tich sat alongside them at the government palace, sipping *tej* (a drink made from fermented honey and flavored with bitter leaves) and talking with gusto in broken English and Amharic while slaves behind him swatted away flies. A Lawrentian figure who went about with armed bodyguards as the governors did, Tich lived in a kind of palisaded Saxon stronghold with neat beds of dahlias and red-hot pokers in the garden. He loved English flowers and tended his display with devotion; it was an antidote to the wilderness that surrounded him. After more ill health, he at last found an escape when Berkeley suggested that he go to Naro Moru as estate manager. Then Berkeley died, so it was more *tej* and flies in Mega. Tich was often joined by his spinster sister, Olive, known as Dolly, a wiry adventuress with a loud voice and a taste for ghosts and gardening. Both concealed soft hearts beneath their leathery armor. When Grigg engineered a two-year posting for Tich as his aide-de-camp at Government House, the two Mileses returned to a heroes' welcome.*

---

* In 1930, Tich's posting as aide-de-camp to the governor expired, so he went back to Mega. He missed company and hated the job. It was a life sentence, and he was dead within four years. He was, as Grigg once said, a slayer of dragons.

At the end of September 1928, the SS *Malda* steamed into Kilindini Harbor amid a thronging flotilla of yachts. Edward and his brother Henry, Duke of Gloucester, were standing at the bow rail in military regalia. Later that night, at the ball at Government House in Mombasa, the two princes had to shake five hundred hands. Denys, who had raced across the country from a safari he was leading up the Nile, paid his formal respects before returning to his client.

Slight as a jockey, with fair hair, fair eyelashes, and a shy half smile, the Prince of Wales, known to his family as David, was thirty-four. He had a poor relationship with his father, who did little but bark at him over his shortcomings, of which there were many. He was not cut out for the role of heir. Letters from his foreign tours reveal a preoccupation with "our set" and boundless self-pity over his duties. Life was "merely an existence," he wrote from one outpost, referring elsewhere to "these foul tours." On another occasion he wailed, "I've got four terrible months ahead of me in India," and he complained ceaselessly about the official "stunts" he was forced to endure. ("I've not had any fun here," he told a woman friend from South America. "I can't tell you what these Argentine officials have been like—stunted me to death and B-A is a silly place really.") There was much talk about him being sunk, by which he meant depressed, without an adequate supply of dances and women. En route from Honolulu to Acapulco at the age of twenty-six, he sulked to the same friend, "I suppose there are some divine new tunes at home now which I shan't know curse them though!" But at least he found something to like in Kenya. After a week in Nairobi, he wrote to Gwendolyn Butler, née Francis, whom he called Poots. Her second husband was one of his equerries. "Darling Poots, well here we are in this wild place and it sure is wild this race week it's been a matter of the survival of the fittest . . . they sure are a wild crowd these settlers and great fun too some of them though. I do miss my friends and wish to god Fredie [Freda Dudley Ward, his mistress] and you were here to enjoy it all and laugh with. It's exactly what we said before I left about it being a waste to come out to East Africa without the person you love and are keen on. Of course, I've not been on safari yet and am d———d glad I haven't planned a long one as we are a stag party. But the atmosphere and whatever the charm of this country is has got to me all right and I know even now that I'll want to come back again. Much love, from your very very old friend and spotted doggie."

The prince's rackety career was on a cusp when he sailed into Mombasa. In the years after the war he had been popular with the public, both at home and in the dominions, and his tours, while bristling with incident, had sustained the illusion that he took his duties seriously. In the view of his courtiers, 1928 marked the beginning of his decline; seven years later, his public life had been subsumed in its private counterpart. A raft of irreconcilable differences already lay between him and his advisers, and it was becoming increasingly difficult to conceal his failings. At the end of the African tour Joanie, Lady Grigg, confided in her diary that he was "the most unpleasant and uncivil guest I've had in my house."

Joanie had invited Tania to stay at Government House for the first week of the royal visit. The white pillars and cobalt shadows breathed an alpine freshness after the dust of Nairobi, and at luncheon Their Majesties gazed on their sons from gilt frames at either end of the room while velvet-slippered Somali footmen in scarlet and gold drew down the blinds to blot the volcanic glare of noon. Tania was determined to lobby the prince on the subject of the taxes the administration levied on her farmworkers. She had met Poots in England, which helped her cause, and His Royal Highness listened to what she had to say. Naturally, she found him "absolutely charming" ("I am so much in love with him that it hurts," she told her mother), and she brought off a characteristic coup when she drove him out to the farm for tea. He walked among the *shambas* with Tania and questioned the puzzled residents about the number of goats and cattle they owned, what they earned, and what they paid in taxes, writing down the figures in a notebook and concentrating on the fiscal problem for at least an hour. His brother Prince Henry was occupied with equally pressing matters. A shy, heavy-jowled figure with a whinnying laugh, he was the most Hanoverian of the three royal princes and a model of decorum compared with his eldest brother. But then Beryl appeared, and, after all, Beryl was Circe—albeit a pregnant Circe. "Harry is enjoying himself and has got off with a nice woman," the Prince of Wales confided to Poots after a week in Kenya. Unlike his dwarfish brother, the duke was tall, and a fine match for the still lean, slim-hipped Beryl, who glided around the paddocks on race days wearing close-fitting slacks and men's shirts with the top buttons undone. The next weeks unfolded in a series of trysts at which Beryl was smuggled into bungalows and camps, keeping her husband quiet and making sure she didn't spoil romantic encounters with morning sickness. But her liaison with the Duke of Gloucester was no mere fling. Before he left, he agreed to meet her in London. He said that he would be waiting for her on the wharf.

When the safari he was leading up the Nile ended, Denys returned to Nairobi on the night train from Kisumu to be on hand in case the prince, who was staying with Delamere at Soysambu, wanted to go shooting. But HRH was too busy enduring the usual round of stunts—at a reception in Gilgil after a golf tournament, one settler tried to make him shake hands with her dog—and behaving like a rutting stag in between.* His assistant private secretary, Captain (later Sir) Alan "Tommy" Lascelles, a dark man with a pronounced center part that ran over his crown like a stripe, knew Denys from England. They had been contemporaries at Oxford; Lascelles was close to Alan and Viola and to others within Denys's circle. Chaperoning HRH through Africa had already reduced him to paroxysms of despair, his attempts to run a smooth schedule thwarted by the prince's leaping into bed or the nearest bush with any woman who came to hand. The crusty Lascelles was unimpressed by "the farmyard morals" of the settlers, and "the all-pervading eat and drink for tomorrow we die philosophy." At a dinner in Kitale 100 of the 150 present "were tight before the soup was off the table." He had been on the prince's staff for eight years, and was so browned off that he was on the brink of resignation; he looks furious in the official photographs, his brows furrowed and his part gleaming in the sun. Starting off in the job full of optimism, Lascelles had consistently tried to make the prince fit to be king. But it was a hopeless task. He finally resigned in 1929, but returned to royal employment in 1935, working once again for the prince when he became King Edward VIII. "Though I have little doubt that the change is ultimately for the best," he wrote in November 1936, when he was one of only twelve people in the world who knew that Edward was going to abdicate, "I am in-

---

* Husbands in those days seemed to consider it an honor if a king or his heir slept with their wives. It was not considered adultery. It did not count.

clined to think that as the years went on, the Hyde side would have predominated more and more over the Jekyll—the pity of it all is heart rending." He continued, "Nothing but his own will could have saved him, and the will was not there."

Almost as soon as Denys reached the farm, a runner appeared brandishing a cleft stick with a cable from Delamere summoning him to Soysambu. The prince wished to make safari plans. A plane was waiting at the airfield, and Tania drove Denys there as fast as she could. He was allowed no luggage, as the pilot said he was too heavy already. The props were turning when they raced onto the strip. As the plane took off, a clearing sky laid bare the high plateaus that stretch down the spine of eastern Africa, and triumphant shafts of sunlight fell on a herd of elephants moving over them like gray lava. It was Denys's first flight over the Rift, and as he looked down into the entrails of the Longonot Crater he realized the potential of planes in Africa. One could cut out backbreaking weeks of sweat and delay as cars sank up to their axles in mud and clients looked at their wristwatches, as well as penetrate thousands of miles of virgin hunting ground. One could even scout elephants from the air and keep hunters in touch with a moving herd. Clients would pay well for the service. Denys was awed by the spacious magnificence of floating in a tiny plane, cut free from the earth, in another dimension. He returned to Tania after the trip raving about the view. As with photography, he had found another way of looking at the world.

The prince vanished to Uganda, leaving Denys a clear month to finish his preparations. The royal brothers were to take separate safaris before continuing overland to South Africa for Christmas. From now on, Denys spent every waking hour checking and rechecking supplies among the tiers of sun-dried hides in the Safariland offices, negotiating with headmen, and studying maps unfolded on the millstone table. A week before the start, he and Tania were invited to a private dinner in the dining saloon of the royal train. It was the kind of social event he hated, but Tania was in heaven. Seated next to the host in the dark paneled carriage, she talked innocently about her Africans and their ritual dances, called *ngomas*. As she was leaving, the prince announced that he would dine with her on Friday in order to watch a *ngoma* on her farm. But *ngomas* were scheduled according to sacred law; they could not be whipped up on a whim. The next day Farah was dispatched on a frenzied diplomatic mission to Paramount Chief Kinanjui. He returned to the farm on Wednesday night. "Memsahib," he told Tania as she emerged from the house anxious for news, "they are coming."

On Friday night the moon was full. Three thousand of Kinanjui's people had gathered around a giant oval of fires close to the freshly whitewashed boys' huts. Flashes of dyed red flesh and narrow waists trussed with beads kaleidoscoped with feathered spears and fur-braided chests as naked young men gyrated around a tumescent central fire, oiled limbs buckling and pumping to the throb of skin drums and chants that rose and fell like a wave. Toward the outer edge of the crowd the elders (*mẓees*) stood limp, monkey-skin cloaks drawn close. Later, Tania served dinner in the house for the guests of honor. The prince and two of his aides—Lascelles and Captain the Hon. Piers "Joey" Legh, a Grenadier Guardsman who had introduced the prince to sex in an Amiens brothel—joined Denys, Tania, and two female guests. One was Vivienne de Watteville, a twenty-eight-year-old beauty who had just spent three months photographing elephants near the Tanganyikan border, camping on the southern buttresses of Ol Donyo Orok with a six-foot Nubian gun bearer and a cook who fried the croutons in lion fat. She slept with a .318 next to her camp bed, and spent the evenings in the company of Plato and Plutarch, with a gramophone on which she played Schubert's Trio in B-flat Major, music that reassured her "that all I felt had been felt before." The other female present was an "absolutely ravishing" Beryl, whom Tania placed next to Denys. The nine-course menu included what Kamante described as "a very strange fish got from Mombasa, it is the crab one with many legs and arms." Denys provided the wine and the cigars. Outside, the dancing continued, even when a fight broke out. The royal party were delighted with the spectacle (they didn't see the fight), and Tania was gratified. The elders were proud. Several weeks later, when she thanked them formally and presented each with a goat or a rug, one old man made a speech in which he said that their hearts had been pleased to see her wearing a special frock, "for we all think that here, every day on the farm, you are terribly badly dressed."

The safari was preceded by a crescendo of parties. At one event a settler was bundled out of Muthaiga for offering His Royal Highness cocaine. There was no resident club band then, and when the prince got fed up with the gramophone he and a female guest picked up all the records and threw them through the ballroom window. At least he had stamina. He went to bed well after dawn, emerging from the sour air of the Muthaiga bar into the bone-white light of a Nairobi morning, and was saddled up on the racecourse before eight. The other benighted competitors had to force their horses to slow down to let him win the KAR Trophy—and to let the duke come second. Lascelles longed for the safari to begin so that he could hand over responsibility to Denys and relax, or so he thought. "I *fiche* myself completely of all anxiety, for I know nobody in the world who inspires me with more complete and childlike confidence than he [Denys] does," he wrote home. "He was always a remarkable chap, but he has come on tremendously since the days when I used to know him in England. . . . He has organised the whole expedition for me down to the last sheet of Bronco."

ON DEPARTURE DAY the rains sheeted down, warm and heavy, and the road to the first camp, at Kajiado on the southern fringe of the Kapiti Plains, was impassable. Denys abandoned his plan to go by road and co-opted the assistance of the controller of the Uganda railway, who conjured a train that was part passenger and part freight. The vehicles—spare tires roped to the sides and crates protruding from every aperture—were simply driven onto the train. Denys sent one lorry out to try the road, like Noah's dove. (It was never seen again, though the driver eventually materialized, asking for money.) At two o'clock, according to the prince's diary, "practically everyone in Nairobi" came to see them off. Rain continued to flood country so recently paralyzed by drought, and when the royal train drew into the Kajiado station it was met with relief by the district officer, Clarence Buxton, a cousin of Geoffrey's, who had himself been bogged down all night on the Athi Plain. (This Buxton was famous for trying to get the Maasai to play polo on donkeys. He was later exposed as an adulterer and transferred to Palestine in disgrace.) The next day it was dry, and they were able to continue by road. The convoy consisted of four Albion lorries in the charge of a KAR sergeant; Delamere's loaned Buick, driven by the prince; Denys's Hudson, driven by him, with Lascelles in the passenger seat; two Willys-Knight safari box cars driven by Legh and Kanuthia; and, at the rear, a Rolls-Royce provided by the Nairobi reception committee, driven by one Inspector Burt.

The prince had borrowed Grigg's motion-picture camera, and when Denys spotted a bull elephant in the Ol Mberesha Hills, HRH and his aides set out after it on foot. They got the pictures, but when a second elephant charged, Denys brought it down with a head shot with inches to spare. In the cool morning air, a tiny whorl of thin blue smoke rose through the bullet hole. It was the first of several uncomfortable incidents. The prince was apparently impervious to danger and wholly insensitive to the responsibilities his presence placed on others. When Denys judged that a charging rhino was close enough and shot it, the prince rounded on him.

"How dare you shoot without an order," he snapped. "I wanted to get him right up to the camera."

"Your Royal Highness," Denys replied, "suppose you look at the matter from my point of view. If you, the heir to the throne, are killed, what is there left for me to do? I can only go behind a tree and blow my brains out."

The two men had little in common. HRH never read a book and had no interest in classical music. He loathed being alone. But he could distinguish an independent spirit from a toady, and secretly liked to be dominated. Mature and unafraid, Denys had his measure, correctly hazarding that a firm line would have a more positive effect than craven capitulation. By speaking out, he established a basis for friendship. For once, the prince began to display genuine interest in his subject land, listening attentively as Denys spoke of Kenya and its people. Instinctually not a wanton slaughterer, he was shocked at the stories of orgiastic killers zooming around the plains of Tanganyika in motorcars, and over the next weeks proved an enthusiastic student as beer cooled in the canvas water buckets and skinners salted the hides. For his part, Denys was encouraged to have found an influential ally, and, as it turned out, the future king's enthusiasm for photographing game did influence the fashion for shooting with cameras.

The next afternoon they entered Arusha, bush capital of the northern province of Tanganyika. Denys had asked Blix to be his second gun for the main part of the safari.* Still managing the remote farm, Blix had driven to Arusha with Cockie and pitched camp near the small hotel where the prince was staying. He was shaking a cocktail in his tent when a little man came in.

"I'm the Prince of Wales," said the man, "and should like to make your acquaintance."

"You could not have chosen a more suitable moment," Blix replied, pouring from the ice-cold shaker.

Still wearing the wilted *terai,* Blix, unlike many hunters, did not take himself too seriously. He laughed a lot, which made his fleshy cheeks wobble, and judged that 75 percent of a white hunter's role was to be a glorified butler and keep clients amused, both tasks at which he was adept. The next day everyone proceeded to Babati, the scratchy settlement near the Blixens' farm. Their only neighbors were the Popps. Mrs. Popp left her farm once a year to have a baby in Arusha: it was her annual holiday. Blix sustained himself with regular visits to the Fig Tree, a bar run by a drunken Scot and patronized by a pair of Estonians who had escaped from the French foreign legion by swimming to Marseille from a distant island. But there was to be no drinking till the prince got his lion; Blix's attitude toward lions, HRH said later, was that of the prophet Daniel. When at last an old male bounded from a covert, the prince shot with a borrowed .350 double-barreled Express. He missed with the first bullet, but hit the lion in the chest at 140 yards with the left barrel. He ran up. The lion lay still, then got to its feet and limped off. Then it swiveled around to charge. The prince finished it off with both barrels. This time even Denys had broken into a sweat.

The prince had to leave for another round of official duties, and while he was away the safari moved to Blix's farm itself. There Blix co-opted the help of his friend Chief Michaeli, a redoubtable M'bulu who presided over several thousand of his tall tribe. Dwelling in pits dug out of the surrounding hillsides, the agricultural M'bulu had been in the highlands for many generations; according to their legend they migrated there from Lake Na-

---

* Denys also hired Andy Anderson, Pat Ayre, and the war hero and game warden Monty Moore VC. To look after the Duke of Gloucester, he hired Alan Black and, to back him up, Sydney Waller. Bunny Allen helped out.

tron. Chief Michaeli, keen to impress a future white king, obligingly summoned five hundred of his *moran* to assist the hunt. When the royal party returned, they all tracked buffalo together, and if the prince sat on a rock to rest the five hundred spread below, crouching with their spears between their thighs. If Michaeli appeared, they rose like a wave. Back on the farm at the cocktail hour, the boys squatted by the lorries, removing thorns that had worked their way into the tires while the prince fiddled with his Crichton ice-making machine, a device unknown to Africa, and one that Cockie coveted. She and the prince were getting on famously, and when he invited her to join them for the rest of the safari she accepted with pleasure, though she was a rotten shot. This was to prove awkward for Denys.

The night they reached Kondoa Irangi, the prince played his accordion before retiring, slept badly, and threw a boot at a noisy hyena in the night. In the morning, they received a cable informing them that George V was unwell. The sixty-three-year-old king had developed pleurisy, and that morning a truck had rumbled through the gates of Buckingham Palace with a set of the new X-Ray machines. Over the next days Reuters' wires indicated that he was rallying. But on November 27, en route for Dodoma, the party got a private cable written in a code no one knew. "There was something ominous and exasperating in the uncertainty as to what the absurd code words were hiding," an aide recalled. They pushed on to Dodoma, each man alone with his thoughts, and found there a rash of panicky cables urging the prince to return at once. Several were from the aldermanic prime minister, Stanley Baldwin. "I remember sitting, one hot night . . . deciphering, with the help of dear Denys Finch Hatton, the last and most urgent of several cables from Baldwin, begging him [the prince] to come home at once," Lascelles wrote. Just as he and Denys finished decoding the missive, the prince appeared. Lascelles read him the cable.

"I don't believe a word of it," said the heir. "It's just some election dodge of old Baldwin's. It doesn't mean a thing."

"Sir," Lascelles replied, "the King of England is dying; and if that means nothing to you, it means a great deal to the rest of us."

"He looked at me, went out without a word, and spent the remainder of the evening in the successful seduction of a Mrs Barnes, wife of the local commissioner," the exhausted Lascelles wrote in his journal. "He told me so himself the next morning." But the prince was bluffing, at least to some degree. "Imagine," he told Cockie, "I could be king of England tomorrow." When she asked him what he would do in that case, he replied that he would set the clocks at Sandringham back to the right time, as his grandfather Edward VII had kept them half an hour fast to counter his wife's tardy tendencies, and George V had maintained the practice. (When he ascended, this was indeed one of his first tasks—almost as soon as he had left his father's deathbed.)

At four in the morning on November 28, HRH left Dodoma for Dar on the governor's train. He had capitulated. Denys went with him. They stopped to pick up telegrams, dictating replies to a station babu who typed them with one finger while his wife dispensed tea, a beverage that consisted mainly of sugar and raw ginger. As the massy African darkness moved outside the ill-fitting window, Denys watched the Prince of Wales smoking and fingering the cables. They arrived at Dar and drove straight to Government House, where they learned that the HMS *Enterprise*, which was to convey the prince forty-seven hundred miles to Brindisi, would not arrive for three days.

It was a tense interlude. "One sat and waited, one stood and waited, and HRH went to a children's party," an aide recalled. They sailed to Zanzibar in the governor's yacht. The prince called on the sultan, dined at the residency, and sailed back. On the morning of December 2, the *Enterprise* appeared on the delphinium blue of the Indian Ocean and HRH was on his way home. He had asked Denys to go with him, but he had a booking to take out Baron Napoléon Gourgaud, a sporting Frenchman, so they said goodbye on the deck of the *Enterprise* and Denys hurried ashore to find a ship to take him up to Mombasa. Meanwhile, King George deteriorated. He was administered oxygen, Queen Mary took over his duties, and on December 4 a council of state was appointed to act in his place. Millions gathered around their wireless sets. But on the twelfth surgeons operated to drain an abscess on his chest, and the king again rallied. On the voyage home, the prince wrote a long letter thanking Denys: "What a mess up this all is, and this ship is vibrating at 20 knots to beat any face massage machine." There was nothing to do but eat and sleep, he whined, and he expected every radio message to say that his father was dead. It was "a curious contrast to the happy life of our safari the first ten days. It was great fun and I was enjoying it all so much. . . . We miss you very much now . . . besides knowing more about hunting in Africa than nearly everybody, you kind of get the form of people so amazingly well. . . . We look forward to seeing you in England around May." To make up for his disappointment, the prince had decided that if his father recovered he would return to East Africa to complete what he had started, and that no hunter but Denys would be good enough. (He did, in a little over a year.) Lascelles was too seasick to leave his bed, but Legh also wrote to tell Denys how much they missed him: "It was very sad saying goodbye to you. . . . We all wish you were with us." He promised to deliver the note Denys had given him for Toby. "I do not think I have ever spent a more interesting fortnight," Legh said. "In all the ten years I have been with HRH I have never known him enjoy a trip more and I do congratulate you in putting up such a wonderful show in such a ridiculous short space of time. . . . I hope you will have an enjoyable safari with your frog." The prince later sent Chief Michaeli the King's Medal for Africans, and Cockie an ice-making machine. Denys received an engraved blue, black, and gray enameled Raymond Templier cigarette case. The king recovered.

> A man never forgotten or explained by his friends,
> who left nothing behind him but affection, a memory
> of gaiety and grace, a kind of melody or aroma ...

—ELSPETH HUXLEY, *Forks and Hope*, 1964

SIX INCHES OF RAIN HAD FALLEN AT NGONG, AND TANIA, IN SUNNY SPIRITS, was looking forward to another quiet Christmas with Denys. But when he arrived back from the royal safari and told her that Blix had been with him, her mood darkened. When she learned that Cockie, too, had joined the party, it turned to thunder. She could not understand Denys's insensitivity. As a Parthian shot before he left with his French client, she told him it was "a law against nature" that he was friendly with Blix; "so would it be with you I believe if Bror had been your sister's husband." Many years later, Tania told a friend that Blix had never wanted her to have anything to herself. Now he was taking her lover. But Denys could no longer reach her emotionally. Ingrid remembered that the quarrel "left a reserve of bitterness in both of them, to be tapped later." In her fiction, Tania frequently wrote of the pain of love. "He often wondered," she said of one character, "how it came to be that, with the dagger in the heart, one might be stabbed anew twenty times a day." One has indeed wondered; she puts it awfully well.

While Denys was away with Gourgaud, Tania learned from Thomas that their seventy-two-year-old mother was seriously ill. She left for Denmark immediately and remained at Rungstedlund for more than seven months. Denys at first stayed at the farm while she was away, and then, on May 22, left Kenya himself. Convinced that bush flying had a future, he had decided to return to England, requalify as a pilot, and ship a plane back. He sailed to Marseilles, hopped over to Tunis for ten days, and turned up in London on July 2, 1929. Toby, alerted by his cables, went to Victoria Station but missed him, and the pair were eventually reunited at the Conservative Club. On one of those fine summer days when the English countryside is as lovely as anywhere on earth, they motored to Ewerby to visit their parents' graves. From there, Denys went on to Eton to see his nephew Michael. Finding the boy absent, he wrote him a note and weighed it down with a small ivory elephant. "Learn as much mathematics as you can," he ordered the child. "It is useful. And read general history: it is amusing." Michael remembered seeing him later that summer in London, where Denys, his dark English suit draped with a navy Somali shawl, was stocking up on homburgs at Lock's on St. James's Street, and on his trademark square-toed boots and shoes at Peal's, where his lasts were stored.

In August, the whole family converged on Toby and Margaretta's new Hampshire home, Buckfield House in Sherfield-on-Loddon, near Basingstoke. Built of red brick in 1898, Buckfield had twenty-five bedrooms and a two-mile drive, but none of the dreamy romance of Haverholme. The Drexel millions had contributed a tennis court, a plantation garden, and a swimming pool, and the mini-estate was run by a team of servants—including a pair of footmen and the master's wartime batman, Fen, now transmogrified into a butler who had a habit of rummaging deeply in his pockets whenever he was asked a question, as if he might find the answer in their depths. Toby's eighteen-year-old son, Christopher, had just finished at Eton. He was less confident than his handsome sisters and had a cast in one eye. The idea that she had borne an ill-favored infant displeased Margaretta, who regularly informed Christopher in public that he would "not get far with looks like that." Toby, who had been on a diet and lost nineteen pounds, rarely crossed her; he walled himself off from the bits of her he didn't like. As for Topsy, she had turned to the church after Ossie died—she had nowhere else to turn—and Toby and Margaretta's fashionable world was foreign to her quiet circle. She leaned even further inward when Anne, her daughter, was knocked down by a car as they both got off a tram on a visit to Michael at school, sustaining head injuries that affected her short-term memory for the rest of her life. At her coming-out ball, Anne was the only debutante without a single partner on her dance card. So her brother, Michael, then twenty, danced with her. He had turned out a lot like Denys.

DENYS'S EARLIER EFFORTS to induce the Tanganyikan authorities to suppress the killing of game from cars had failed. It was not surprising: few had time to worry about the East African herds, and fewer still considered conservation a remotely important issue. Nothing was going to happen without legislation and sanctions. But this time Denys did not simply move on to the next project. For the first time in his life, he had found something he believed in, a cause that was worth commitment. It was a kind of awakening. While still in Kenya he went public with a philippic to London, writing a long article for *The Times* extolling the pleasures of shooting with a camera. It appeared with a selection of his pictures. Speaking of "an orgy of slaughter" in Tanganyika, Denys proposed closed districts and, to compensate for the loss of gun-license revenue, a charge for photographic licenses. The piece ended with a rhetorical flourish: "Is it too much to hope that the appropriate influential bodies and individuals in England who have the interest of natural science and study and photography of wild animals in their natural surroundings at heart, will bestir themselves in time to get the necessary action taken before it is too late?" It was uncharacteristic of Denys to enter public life; he considered self-advertisement vulgar at any price. But he had been deeply moved by the undefiled abundance of East Africa and was responding passionately to the carnage he had witnessed, acting in the tradition of the great nineteenth-century explorers who had spoken out against killing for its own sake, among them Livingstone, Burton, and Stanley. Denys had suddenly seen the ruin the white man and his money might bring to a whole continent, and the prospect was too much to bear. He emerged from his foray into print as the archetypal Homeric hero, excelling in debate and action. But taken as a whole he was not Odysseus, tossed around by fate against his will and all the time longing for home. He was more of an eternal wanderer on a perpetual quest for knowledge and experience.

Still, though, nothing happened to control the killing. Inspired by Marcuswell Maxwell's lion photographs in *The Times* (the bizarrely named photographer had recently made two trips to East Africa), Denys wrote a second article, and it was published while he was in London. He was supported by the Prince of Wales, who that same week publicly condemned the practice of massacring game from cars. Recognizing the insidious influence of testosterone, in his piece Denys attempted to dispel the popular notion that cameras were for girls and that real men went around weighed down with bandoliers of ammunition, staggering back to the cave at dusk with another mammoth over their hairy shoulders. He did it by conjuring the danger of wildlife photography. "A treacherous eddy of wind, or the whir of gears in a motion picture camera, can instantly galvanize a placidly feeding pachyderm into four tons of rapidly advancing angry elephant," he wrote. He followed the article with a letter condemning both the "hideous abuse" and the government that condoned it. This time Douglas Jardine, chief secretary to the Tanganyikan government, sprang up in a huff to defend himself. Over the course of the next week, he and Denys traded insults on the letters page of *The Times*. But Denys had a battery of facts with which to blast his opponent into submission. When he cited proposed amendments to a 1927 report to the League of Nations indicating that *no controls at all* were to be introduced in Tanganyika, he concluded persuasively that it would be "the beginning of the end." This made Jardine look a nit, and flushed the argument into the open. Others weighed in, many of them old colonial hands ("In Nyasaland in my time . . ."). Parliament even debated the topic, and Sidney Webb, secretary of state for the colonies, asked the governor of Tanganyika for a report. The *Times*'s man in Dar wired a dispatch with the news that a game warden had been sent to the Serengeti plains. "Mr Finch Hatton's crusade," the journalist concluded, "has already begun to produce its effect."

The story spread like a ripple, appearing in provincial publications from the Rochdale *Observer* to the Hull *Daily Mail*, in which the hero appeared as Denise. In November, the Tanganyikan government published a notice in the official gazette proclaiming part of the Serengeti plains a game reserve. Amendments to the game laws were announced at the same time, and in a parliamentary debate on "The Preservation of the Fauna of the Empire" Lord Onslow, supported by the archbishop of Canterbury, urged the enforcement of the law against hunting by car in East Africa. Julian Huxley returned from a fact-finding tour arguing for game reserves, but Secretary Webb took some persuading, as socialists perceived reserves as places where rich people could shoot at leisure. In the end, the conservationists won their case. "Within a few years," Huxley wrote later with some satisfaction, "National Parks were established in all three East African territories." The episode indicated how much Denys could accomplish if he chose. He did not care that his outspoken public comments had earned him enemies in the safari trade and among farmers gunning for a hunting free-for-all. Progress has always come chaperoned by bad blood. Most of Denys's proposals were adopted, sooner or later. They were part of a legislative process that reached its logical conclusion, in Kenya, when hunting was banned outright in 1977.* By then, of course, it was too late.

Issues surrounding the conservation of game impinged on the ongoing debate over the entire future of colonial rule. Did animals belong to the Africans, as Jardine implied when he proposed that "natives" should be exempt from hunting restrictions? Denys argued that restrictions should apply to African and foreigner alike. But public opinion was shifting ever further from a belief in the automatic wisdom of imposed white law. In January 1928, questions had been asked in the House of Commons about the alleged employment of women and children to build Kenyan roads. The Nairobi authorities indignantly denied the accusations, and on the farms settlers expressed irritation at what they perceived as ignorant interference by London do-gooders. But many at home believed that the gradual delegation of authority to native chiefs and councils was the only logical solution in Africa. The issue of the rights of indigenous peoples in the colonial project had moved forward with agonizing lack of haste since the war, but it did move. In May 1921, when attempts were made to reduce African wages, Harry Thuku formed the nontribal East Africa Association. When he started advocating civil disobedience, he was arrested and deported to Kismayo, then still in the Kenyan province of Jubaland. At the

* Hunting was banned in Tanzania for five years in the 1970s. This led to an explosion of poaching and a dramatic drop in government revenue, so it was reintroduced, on a strictly controlled basis.

ensuing protest march in Nairobi, twenty-five Africans were killed. Settlers didn't like it at all. Responding to calls for African education, an editorial in the *Standard* spoke for many when it proclaimed, "It is a terribly serious sign that certain elements among the natives within the Kikuyu tribe advocate reform." In February 1929, Jomo Kenyatta went to England at the head of a delegation to present the African case to the British government. Thirty-four years later, he would be elected the first president of an independent Kenya.

DENYS HAD SAILED to England this time chiefly to requalify as a pilot and to select a plane. He went to as many air shows as he could, inspecting biplanes, triplanes, monoplanes, and any other kind on display. At the beginning of September, he motored to the coast with his nephews and nieces to watch the Schneider Trophy run, an air race over the Solent. An English pilot won in a Supermarine RR 56 flying at 332 miles per hour. Aerial experimentation had made spectacular progress since the painfully unglamorous Wright brothers mounted a small engine onto a gossamer frame and hopped over the sand dunes of North Carolina like fledglings. Over in the equally unglamorous Wolverhampton, it had been enough for a plane to circle the airfield *on the ground* at Arty's air show. Now long-haul flights were generating unprecedented public interest—Lindbergh's 1927 Atlantic crossing the most dramatic so far—and chic aviatrixes in flying jackets were ousting film stars from the front pages. In May of 1930, a Hull fish merchant's daughter, Amy Johnson, flew De Havilland's twelfth Gypsy Moth to Australia in the record-breaking time of nineteen and a half days. The plane had no lights, brakes, or radio, and Johnson had never been abroad before. People compared her to Joan of Arc. In England it was fashionable for the superrich to own a plane, and many chose the Moth, a milestone aircraft that launched a fabulously successful period of British light-aircraft design and production. In outposts like Kenya, settlers had become obsessed with the potential of flight. As early as 1919 the *Leader* reported eagerly, "Few portions of the British empire have more to gain than BEA from the conquest of the air." On May 12, 1926, Tania had driven to Dagoretti Junction in Ngong, the car loaded with servants, to see the first planes in the colony arrive from Kisumu. In October that year, John Carberry, an Irish baronet with a bogus American accent, flew a De Havilland 51—an ancestor of the Moth—from Nyeri to Nairobi, a flight the *Standard* described as "epoch-making."* In 1927, the Aero Club of Kenya was founded, using the Dagoretti airstrip; the following year, when it changed its name to the Aero Club of East Africa, the government asked its members to select the site for a Nairobi Aerodrome (now Wilson), which was first used on February 19, 1929—though there were no runways until 1933, and game roamed the strip for a long time after that.

Denys booked lessons at an airstrip on the outskirts of Bristol, and put in practice hours at the Hendon airfield in North London. His companion at Hendon was his old girlfriend Rose Cartwright, who was temporarily back in England and working as a social correspondent for the *Daily Express*. They had remained close. Denys sometimes took safari clients to stay at the Cartwrights' farm at Naivasha. Rose—stable, self-effacing, and the least flamboyant of Denys's lovers—was able to handle even the most demanding guests. On one occasion, Denys arrived with an American family and, after settling them in, asked for his own dinner to be sent up to his room on a tray, explaining privately to Rose that the clients were "too abominable for words." Rose's marriage, however, was troubled. Her husband, Algy, was a regular of the Muthaiga club set, known for his prowess at scaling the Doric columns, but he was a peculiar man and few settlers liked him. He had a butcher's business, among other interests, and one week was allegedly short of meat and sold a hyena. The Cartwrights had a son in 1924, and in 1928 Rose became pregnant again. When her daughter was born, she asked Denys to stand as godfather. Now, reunited in London, they were able to share their unhappiness. Denys told Rose

---

* John Evans-Freke, as he was born, became the tenth baron and third baronet Carbery at the age of six in 1898. The barony, as opposed to the family name, was spelled with one *r*. In 1920, he renounced the title and changed his name by deed poll to John Evans Carberry, with two *r*'s. He was a tall, handsome, and satanic figure who hated England so much that he became an American citizen (though he was deported from the U.S. for bootlegging) and a Nazi sympathizer. His first wife divorced him for cruelty; his second, Maia, was an aviatrix who died when her plane crashed near Ngong in 1928. In 1930, he married June Mosley; she dealt with the problem by drinking. Carberry flew with a pipe in his mouth. It was he who, at the bar of the White Rhino, dared Beryl to fly the Atlantic.

that he could not tolerate Tania's emotional demands. "If I don't move out of the farm, we will lose all that we have been to one another, even our happy memories," he said. In 1935, Rose left Algy.

When he was not in Bristol, Denys checked in to the Conservative Club. That year, he went to the Russian ballet at Covent Garden every night of its season. In the afternoons, if he was not flying at Hendon, he idled in Hatchard's on Piccadilly to peruse books in the news for their "obscenity." The furor surrounding *Lady Chatterley's Lover* the previous year had risen in a more generalized crescendo of public indignation despite the fact that Lawrence's novel was available only in Italy; and the *Sporting Times*, Toby's bible, had described *Ulysses* as "enough to make a Hottentot sick." Denys thought it amusing, seldom finding himself in sympathy with pious expressions of public morality; and it was not yet closing time in the gardens of the West.

As Denys's visit was drawing to a close, Tania came over from Denmark for a week. He drove her up to Lincolnshire to show her Haverholme, and then down to Buckfield, where they stayed for five days. Topsy was there, and Glyn Philpot, the artist, who was about to paint Margaretta. Neither an Edwardian nor a modernist but a little of both, like the age itself, Philpot was among the most financially successful portrait painters of his generation, and Tania was gratified to be in such illustrious company. She walked the grounds with Philpot talking of North Africa, where he had traveled. But she was too preoccupied to enjoy herself. She was again embroiled in financial negotiations to keep the farm, and this time they involved Denys. He had offered to lend £10,000 to keep the Karen Coffee Company afloat. It would not be a personal loan: the money was to come out of Kiptiget funds (Denys remained a director of the land-development company). He instructed his solicitor to write to Tania at her London hotel to set out terms. The proposed rate of interest was 9 percent, "to be secured by a first debenture upon the undertakings and assets of the Karen Coffee Company," and the KCC board was to be assured "that money is ready and available so there will be no delay in getting it." Denys was in a difficult position. He wanted to help, yet he had just received a telegram from his advisers in Nairobi cautioning him against lending, as the prognosis for the 1929–30 harvest was poor. But he did not back out. The terms of the loan were settled by the end of October, when Tania was back at Rungstedlund; but the deal, crucially, was not signed.

Denys passed his test with flying colors, but there was no time left to purchase a plane before returning to business in Kenya. Toby had offered him £100 so that he could take a commercial flight back to Africa instead of sailing and therefore have an extra ten days at home. But suddenly Denys rang from London to say that he had decided to leave by ship from Marseille the next day after all. A distraught Toby hurried up to town to spend the last night with Denys, who, meanwhile, had dashed over to his lawyer's office to make a will—his preoccupation with flying had not blinded him to its vertiginous casualty rate. He left his guns and hunting equipment to Toby, and made Topsy his residuary legatee. In the event of her predeceasing him, her children were to receive £4,000 each and Toby the rest.* Tania was not mentioned.

WHILE DENYS WAS steaming back down the African coast, panic descended on Wall Street, and by the time he reached Mombasa the stock market had crashed. Disaster soon spread to Threadneedle Street. Kenya was already in a state of agricultural crisis: drought had been followed by a locust invasion during which many farmers saw their entire crop destroyed a week before the harvest. Dusk had fallen on the Sunbeam Period, and the high living of the royal tour turned out to be the last spree in Kenya for many years. The colony was wholly dependent on agricultural production, and by 1930 the price of all principal exports was well below production cost; coffee prices were so low that beans were used to stoke Brazilian railway locomotives (imagine the smell). Petrol, on the other hand, became so expensive that farmers used oxen to pull their cars. Historians regularly suggest that the first cracks in the colonial system appeared in the aftermath of the 1929–30 slump. The crash certainly thinned the settlers out; many finally packed their hopes away with the soda siphons and boxes of sparklets and sailed back to the old country. The flow of visitors also dwindled, reducing the influx of capital, and the administration cut back drastically on development programs.

---

* When Denys died, he left nothing like the sum of £8,000. His estate was valued at £1,487 (£52,327 in today's terms).

—

LOSS, LIKE A BANEFUL predator, was waiting for Denys among the purple shadows of the Rift. On October 6, Galbraith Cole had shot himself at Kekopey at the age of forty-eight. He had had an arthritic crisis and could not face another long period as an invalid. He asked Nell to let him kill himself, and she did; they had often spoken of it. He had spent his last weeks lying on the veranda, looking across the lake with his one good eye at the changing light on the water and the sun setting over the Rift, or listening for the gunfire crack of fighting hartebeest locking horns. When he wanted to inspect a particular flock of sheep, he had it driven past him. The rains had already begun to fall when he shot himself, and the feathered rushes of Elmenteita were swaying again in deep water, shadowing the endless cycle of life and death in the valley. Algy and Dr. Burkitt went to Kekopey to help Nell, and they buried Galbraith overlooking the lake by the light of a hurricane lamp. The wagon carrying his coffin took the top off the gatepost, which would have annoyed him. Nell spoke of "twelve unclouded years of the most perfect companionship that anyone ever had."

Denys went to his property at Takaungu, on the coast. He had bought the land in 1927, and had the house built the following year on the ruins of an Arab settlement. Situated thirty miles north of Mombasa between two deep tidal creeks, it was an isolated spot reached by a rutted track through a sisal plantation off the Mombasa-Malindi road. (It remains hard to access even now.) The house was a low Moorish-style dwelling built from blocks of porous coral stone that were plastered and whitewashed, and it was dwarfed by a row of swaying palms. At the front, an arched colonnade faced the sea and a low wall ran between the arches, broken by steps that curved down to a sandy beach. A pair of carved doors with worked brass-copper bolts opened from the tiled colonnade into the dark, cool interior, and Denys had designed that part so that when the moon was full it shone right through the house. At those times, Tania wrote after she visited, "the beauty of the radiant, still nights was so perfect that the heart bent under it." One could always hear the murmur of the breakers at Takaungu, and the low rustle of palms—a ceaseless dirge charged with the unresolved melancholy of all beach houses. Denys slept with the doors open, and the breeze swept sand onto the stone floor. He liked to lie under the mosquito net watching the sun rise over the ocean, or, before the monsoon, the row of high-pooped dhows that ran noiselessly close to the coast, a file of brown shadow-sails against the cyclamen dawn. Many flew the red flag of the sultan of Zanzibar and displayed a cargo of Persian carpets. "The scenery was of a divine, clean, barren marine greatness," Tania wrote. When the tide was out, they could walk a long way over the beach picking up shells before retreating to one of the caves below the house until the water returned and the caves filled up, "and in the porous coral-rock the sea sang and sighed in the strangest way." The long waves came running up Takaungu Creek then like a storming army. In the afternoon, Swahili fishermen came in loincloths and turbans selling spiked fish, and out in the ocean waves broke on the reef like a curl of lemon pith bisecting the blue. After a long safari, Denys would walk down the steps and bathe in the bleached silence of midday, or go to look at the ancient stone walls at the south end of the beach, catching sand crabs and brittle stars in the coral pools. In the other direction, the pale gray and yellow rocks of the coastline wriggled up to Mtwapa Creek, where, in a band of gathering green, he could watch the mating dance of the Usambara, a coastal tropical butterfly, in the orange flowers of the *Cordia africana*.

Occasionally, Denys had guests at his refuge. Once, when he heard that Bunny Allen, the young hunter who had assisted on the Duke of Gloucester's safari, was down in Mombasa competing in a boxing competition against a Royal Navy team, he sent a runner with an invitation. Bunny, who wore a gold earring in honor of his Romany forebears, was still in his early twenties, and Denys was already established in his mind as "a great hero." At that time, Bunny had a Rugby-Durant safari car with wooden wheel spokes and a geyser-like radiator that made excellent tea. He went on to become a leading white hunter himself. He had a courtly manner irresistible to women, a love of parties ("I was always ready to give the drinks the go"), and a tendency to get into scrapes. He once lost a finger in a motor accident, and the digit was returned to him a week later by an Indian trader. Tania was at Takaungu when he arrived. "And what a difference," he noted, "from the Karen Blixen one met at the Muthaiga Club, at a polo tournament, at a race meeting, or anywhere with a lot of people about. Under those conditions she was so reserved as to be almost cold. You could almost feel the icy blast of a Scandinavian snowstorm—not the wonderful glow of her heart. Denys reacted in complete sympathy to her feelings. Until Takaungu, I had not seen their warm, loving side. It was a complete revelation. . . . Whenever he left he kissed her. When he returned he kissed her. She did exactly the same. They would go for long walks on the beach, holding hands the while. They would pick up a shell, putting their heads together as they examined it. Constantly he would read to her as she sat at his feet." It was nonetheless Denys's house. He was considering turning it into his Kenyan base, and was devising schemes to improve it. This was incompatible with a life shared with Tania, and anyway, as even the awestruck Bunny noticed, she found the heat at Takaungu uncomfortable and merely "put up with it" for Denys's sake. He carried on with his plans, irrespective of her, or of anyone. He had stepped up his commitment to the area by buying shares in the Kilifi Sisal Plantation. Although it was a laborious crop, sisal grew tolerably well on the waterless coastal plains and was in perennial demand in the foreign markets, as its fiber made the toughest ropes in the world.* The spiky leaves were so hard that settlers used the points as gramophone needles. In the slump, sisal fell from £40 to £12 per ton, but prices came back and the crop became the country's second most valuable export, after coffee.

TANIA'S 1929 VISIT TO Denmark to visit her sick mother had been less than joyful, despite the fact that Ingeborg made a good recovery. Thomas, his own life now crowded with a wife and children, found Tania "weak, self-absorbed, futureless, emptier than I had ever seen her before. I couldn't imagine what was going to happen." She had kept in touch with the farm through detailed monthly reports sent by Dickens, her farm manager. The usual relentless roster of problems had presented themselves: mealybugs, frost, oxen poisoned by arsenic, then the locusts. "Locust eggs are hatching and the factory field and other areas are full of tiny hoppers," the report read ominously. Dickens, whose African name was Murungaru,

---

* Sisal was introduced to East Africa in 1893 by an entrepreneurial German who imported two thousand bulbils from Florida. Sixty-four survived the voyage, but it was enough. In due course, the crop became Tanganyika's major export, and sisal plantations continue to flourish in the Kilifi section of the Kenyan coast.

"straight as a club," had entrenched ideas about European discipline and scorned the less rigid Kenyan approach. His bête noire was Farah. Farah was not handing over money for vegetables he had sold; Farah was selling paraffin to the farm school at a high price ("I think it is very wrong of Farah to profiteer on the company like this when he trades on the company's land rent free"); "Farah I am sorry to say is showing no interest in your affairs." It was a far cry from the idealized depiction of Farah in *Out of Africa*. But Dickens's overall prognosis was good. In July he told Tania, "The whole of the coffee is looking well on both estates." At the beginning of September, he reported that "everything is looking very well and indications show prospects of a very heavy flowering in October and November." As late as October, he was confidently asserting that the coffee was "in tip-top condition." All through the long sea voyage back to Africa, Tania was preoccupied with the harvest. On a good day, she reckoned they might pick seventy-five tons. When she was in a less robust mood, she thought they would get sixty—this was the minimum figure, the one they were bound to pick.

Tania got back to Mombasa in the middle of January 1930, and Farah met her. In the African way, they did not at first discuss the vital matter of the harvest. But before she went to bed that first night, she had to ask him—how many tons? Stars prickled in millions outside the window, and the boom of an ostrich broke the surface of the night like a fin. "The Somalis," she wrote, "are generally pleased to announce a disaster. But here, Farah was not happy, he was extremely grave . . . and he half closed his eyes and laid back his head, swallowing his sorrow, when he said, 'Forty tons, Memsahib.' At that I knew I could not carry on. All colour and life faded out of the world around me. . . ." But she did carry on. She focused on the Kiptiget loan Denys had promised. It had not yet come through; it seemed that terms had not been agreed on, after all, and negotiations dragged on. Tania made special trips to Nairobi in search of news, as the loan was now the only way out. She and Denys were briefly reunited at the end of January. He told her that he was going to bring a plane out to fly her over Africa, and they chose a place for a landing strip on the flattest part of her farm (now Ndege Road in Karen). They went through the motions, but their relationship had taken on the dreariness of all irresolvable love affairs. He could not give her the commitment she wanted, however minimal. His sense of self was so entrenched that he could not betray it; he looked to a further geography than stories around the fire screen. After he left to prepare for the second royal safari, Tania learned that the crucial loan had fallen through. She took the blame, she wrote to Uncle Aage, "for having raised and maintained a false hope and for having such unreliable friends."

IN THE SECOND WEEK of February, the Prince of Wales returned to Mombasa and proceeded immediately to Government House for breakfast. He was received in the dining room by the Griggs, Denys—and Blix. Denys had again hired him, in open defiance of Tania. Actions are so often more powerful than words, and this was as forceful as a right to the jaw. Flourishing as usual, Blix had recently formed a safari company with Hemingway's idol Philip Percival. He was still exploring on his own account as well. He had recently trawled the area from Makindu to the Yatta Plateau for a month with Dick Cooper and eighty staff. Proceeding down to Malindi, following the Athi to the sea, they stopped after one particularly arduous morning to enjoy a gin and lime before lunch. Bearers set up chairs and bottles. As the hunters took their first sip, a rhino charged. He put one foot through the case of soft drinks, skewered Blix's hastily vacated chair on his horn, and continued his tanklike trajectory through the bush. Silence returned to the camp and the men picked up their drinks, brushed themselves down, and took a second sip.

Denys had planned an ambitious two-month safari for the Prince of Wales through Kenya, Tanganyika, Uganda, Congo, and the Sudan. "I am longing to get away to Africa and the sun more than ever," HRH had added to his letter approving the arrangements. "Especially as I haven't any horses and golf is a damn rotten substitute for hunting." He brought a small group of aides (though not Lascelles, who had finally resigned in disgust), but refused to take a doctor into the bush, so Governor Grigg, terrified lest the heir should fall sick on his turf, sent one along disguised as a chauffeur. This time the prince had brought his own motion-picture camera, a device he referred to enthusiastically as "my new hobby." But heads and ivory had not yet lost their appeal. The highlight of the first month was a seventy-mile trek in pursuit of an elephant reported to be heading toward the Pare Mountains. Denys, Blix, and the prince followed the spoor across remorselessly shadeless plains, camping light and eating cold bully beef and tinned beans. By the third day, dried out and foot-foundered, each man privately feared that he would not be able to get his boots on. But at four o'clock on the fourth day, with just a few inches of water remaining in the canteens, Denys sensed that the elephant was near. He crept forward and saw the animal in a clearing, tugging grass with its trunk and mowing with its toenails, the forefoot swinging like a scythe. Denys reckoned each tusk weighed out at 125 pounds. He signaled to the prince to creep forward and take a shot. But HRH stepped on a twig, the wing ears flared, a brief scream of alarm broke the stillness, and after a vi-olent crashing of branches there was nothing in the clearing but hot, still air. "We sat down where we stood and not much was said, but the words uttered were sincere and vigorous," Blix said. Then they had to walk thirty miles to the railway.

When they got back to camp, Denys found a letter and a telegram from Tania. The farm was now barely able to stagger from day to day and she was practically begging for money. Denys had already offered to put up a further £2,000 on behalf of Kiptiget to buy the first mortgage back from the bank. Tania now revealed that she needed another £500, to keep the place going for three more months until the time was favorable for sale. Denys tore a page from an exercise book and sat on a canvas chair outside his tent to compose a reply. Tania obviously thought—and she was mis-taken—that purchasing the mortgage would put him in an advantageous position as a potential purchaser. "If I wanted to buy the house and grounds, I should have to come in for it at the sale as any other would-be buyer, and should be in no better position by holding the first mortgage," he explained. He repeated his willingness to put up £2,000 of company money, "as I cannot see that Kiptiget will stand to lose anything when the sale comes even if they have to buy in to get their money. But I am unwill-ing to put up the further five hundred for manning the place another three months. Surely the [Karen Coffee] Company will do that in their own in-terests if they have reduced the bank debt at one fell swoop by some £12,000!" So Denys was not aware that his £10,000 loan had not in the end been ratified. It was a pity: had he known, there was a ghost of a chance that he could have done something, as he would certainly have made an offer of another kind. As it was, what more could he give her? He was still willing to bail her out of minor financial embarrassments. Shortly after this exchange of letters, he paid off a debt of eight thousand shillings that she had incurred five years earlier with a Nairobi lawyer. "I am sorry that I cannot do more to help," he wrote. "I have not the money myself, and must consider Kiptiget shareholders' interests primarily. I am very sorry to hear you are so seedy. In haste for the post, Denys." Squashed up vertically along one margin, he added, "I will do anything I can to prevent your house and grounds going to the enemy. Denys." Desperately seeking to show concern, he found a tiny space to squeeze in a final thought: "You are having a bad time poor thing. I wish I could help more—will not your brother find the £500 wanted?" He sent the letter by runner and rail (it was thirty-five miles to the station), along with a note to his Nairobi solicitor repeating his offer to buy the mortgage.

When the safari party entrained to the capital, the prince was joined by his current sweetheart, Thelma, Lady Furness, the twenty-six-year-old daughter of an American consul whose identical twin sister, Gloria, married Reginald Vanderbilt. Toodles, as the prince called her, had ostensibly come to Kenya on safari with her second husband, the hard-living Marmaduke, Lord Furness ("Duke"), but he wisely stayed out of the way. She was a sleek, lean creature with bobbed hair, plucked eyebrows, and dark lips, and she was deeply in love with the prince. He got off his train early and went to meet Thelma in Nairobi by road; members of the welcoming reception at the Nairobi station were puzzled when only sheepish aides emerged from his carriage. The whole party stayed at Government House for a week, as they had in 1928. But this time Cockie was there, so it was impossible for Tania to join in. She was even excluded from balls and receptions, and had to rely on newspaper reports that included fulsome references to Baroness Blixen's gowns. Joanie Grigg was embarrassed, and so was Denys. Tania wrote to Uncle Aage expressing her unhappiness, ending the letter, "But I thought that the only dignified attitude under the circumstances was to stay away from it all and pretend to be completely cheerful." When Denys went to the farm, however, her dignity departed, and she made what she called "a scene of the first water." The histrionic side of her repelled him. The next day, back at Government House, he sent her a note. "Your talk disturbed me very much last night," he wrote.

"Do not think that I do not see your point of view: I do absolutely. But I feel that just now you are looking on the very darkest side of things. I would like to see you before I go off and shall try to get out later. I am sending Kamau to collect a box of papers and a Jaeger dressing gown." There is something inexpressibly bleak about this letter. But he did visit her, and so did the prince, who drove out for tea. But mostly, Tania was left alone with her humiliation.

On the next leg of the safari, in Maasailand, Denys had arranged to be resupplied by plane. He engaged Tom Campbell Black, a pioneering East African aviator who was to become famous for his long-distance exploits. Flying alternately a Gypsy Moth and a Puss, Campbell Black sometimes arrived with Beryl in the passenger seat.* The safari was progressing well. The prince's tent was erected at the end of the line, with that of the royal mistress next to it. "This was our Eden," Toodles wrote of the silky nights by the fire when the others had diplomatically turned in. "Each night I felt more completely possessed by our love, carried ever more swiftly into uncharted seas of feeling. . . ." In the navigable waters of morning, Denys was relieved to see the prince in playful spirits. One morning he bet Denys that he could not stick a photograph of his father on a rhinoceros's bottom, producing from his pocket two postage stamps printed with the kingly image. Never one to balk at a challenge, at noon Denys went out and found a target dozing within one hundred yards of camp. Stationing the prince to observe from a safe distance, he inched forward until he was able to stick one stamp on each cheek, surely a historical precedent. Less happily, Denys was suffering from an embarrassing infestation. He had been caught in a storm on the way to a convoy of supply lorries stuck in mud and was obliged to accept local hospitality. But the blankets were crawling with bedbugs. "What [the creatures] left of Finch Hatton," the prince gleefully noted, "returned to camp early next morning."

A more alarming disease, however, was incubating elsewhere. Toodles had to rejoin her husband and, against the advice of his equerry,

---

* Campbell Black was a great love of Beryl's, though their affair had not yet taken wing. In old age she kept his photograph on the wall over her chair, and she told several people that he was the love of her life. But he went off with an actress without telling her. Beryl read about it in the press.

Grigg, and everyone else, the prince insisted on driving her to the railway alone. The heat was appalling. Halfway across the plain, the color drained from his face. "Darling," he said, "I've got to stop for a bit, I feel frightfully seedy." With that he slumped over the wheel. Toodles had only driven along the boulevards of Beverly Hills. Eyeing a rhino as her lover breathed in sharp gasps and sweat trickled down her back, she thought, rather late in the day, about her "responsibility to the empire." But before she could take the wheel the prince came around. He was able to drive slowly to the railway, where the "chauffeur" diagnosed malaria and a train carriage was converted into a hospital ward. After a week in Nairobi, the patient was dancing at Muthaiga. Toodles and her husband went home.* The party then proceeded by train and car to Masindi in Uganda, and from there, through blue gum forests and emerald valleys blazing with alpine flowers—"perhaps the most beautiful 45 miles in Africa or in the universe," according to the prince—to the escarpment that tumbles two thousand feet to Lake Albert. In the Congo pygmies danced, leeches enjoyed their first taste of royal blood, and a driver misunderstood instructions and lost the baggage. In the sudd, they steamed along torpid creeks lined with hippo landing stages, and the prince, who was experimenting with color film, photographed Nile lechwe, the semi-amphibious antelope that live only in southern Sudan, as well as Shilluk hunters who were hanging flaps of hippo meat over the hide rope slung between the spears fencing their camps. Greater Nile geese and giant shoebills landed on heaving rafts of decomposing vegetation, egrets rose in white cirrus clouds above the papyrus, and the vibrations of the ship's screw drove everyone slowly mad. The mosquitoes were infernal. On April 12, the party reached Malakal and flew to Khartoum in an RAF plane, following the White Nile north. At Port Said, they all boarded the SS *Rawalpindi*—Denys was returning to England with the royals. He was determined to buy his plane. It had been a tremendous safari, one of the high points of the prince's touring career. "Finch Hatton was responsible for lions, elephants and rhinoceroses, for Quaker oats, cartridges and candles," HRH concluded in his diary. "All things were on the head

---

* Later that year Toodles, about to go on holiday to America, asked her friend Wallis Simpson to look after the prince in her absence.

of Finch Hatton, and all things went without a hitch. He never made a mistake. He forgot nothing. He foresaw everything. At last, his charges took off their solar [*sic*] topees to him and said that he was the most efficient man in the world."

THE LONDON NEWSPAPERS were full of the Depression, but Denys took a sanguine view. "Everyone says they are more broke than ever this year," he wrote to Tania, "but there seems to be just as much money being spent on inane amusements as ever: more Rolls-Royces, new fashions, extravagant parties, and everyone who has money placing it abroad in concealed concerns to avoid income tax, supertax, etc.—the rats abandoning the sinking ship." It was true that the Depression never developed into an industrywide condition, as it did in the United States. It was localized, the coalfields of the Midlands and Wales and the ports and shipyards of the north suffering hard. Little changed in the capital. Unemployment, however, was steadily rising, and that year reached two million (it was two and a half million in Germany). But Denys found something more important to complain about than the plight of workingmen. "The trouble is that the land which cannot escape is taxed to death, and English agriculture is at its last gasp," he fulminated to Tania. "Australia is bankrupt: Germany full of unemployed: America ruled by gangs of gunmen—France seems to be the one country which is doing well. She kept her head when we were giving away everything; and took everything she could get." Denys may have had the common touch, but he was at sea in the new democratic order in which land and title did not determine all things. He was so enthusiastic about France that at the beginning of May he went over to Paris to hear *Parsifal*. He liked Wagner, but found the opera too long and sneaked out to have dinner in the second act. He also heard Wagner's comic opera *Die Meistersinger*, "which is very exhilarating," and afterward bought the record, writing to Tania, "Shall be quite ready to start back for EA all the same and hear it with you at Ngong."

By the second week of May 1930, Denys was back from France and staying with Philip Sassoon at Trent Park in New Barnet, thirteen miles north of Trafalgar Square. Since worshipping at Denys's feet at Eton, Sassoon had conquered London. An MP since 1912, he had risen to a senior position in the Tory administration, which had recently lost office, serving for five years as undersecretary of state for air. Few would have predicted, in those far-off Eton days, that it would be Sassoon, a foreign Jew, who got to the top rather than Denys Finch Hatton. A strange flitting little figure, Sassoon had become famous earlier in his career for snapping up secretaryships to important people (Lloyd George, for example). "Christ has risen," his friend Diana Cooper informed him by telegram one Easter Day, "and will shortly be needing a secretary." Sassoon was a lavish host, presiding over elaborate house parties in a double-breasted silk-fronted blue smoking jacket and zebra-hide slippers. Within the previous month alone, guests at the thousand-acre Trent Park had included the Prince of Wales, Prince Albert (later George VI), Lord Londonderry, Euan Charteris, Hugh Cecil, Diana Westmorland, and Freda Dudley Ward. Sporting facilities included a nine-hole golf course with professionals on hand, tennis courts, a boating lake, a swimming pool, and a furrowed landing strip surrounded by tall trees. Sassoon had been fascinated by all aspects of aviation since the war. He was one of the most forceful advocates for a strong air force, sat as chairman of the Royal Aero Club, and had a Moth of his own.* Gardens that smothered the landscape in their opulent embrace featured crowds of statuary, a pair of king penguins, and the bent figures of eighteen gardeners. The house itself was more English than the other Sassoon residences and had recently been refaced in eighteenth-century rose brick and stone bought from Devonshire House in Piccadilly when the latter was demolished; more grand houses were coming down than going up, and Sassoon was moving in on territory vacated by the landed classes of an older England. His good taste extended well into the ruinously decadent. He gilded the drainpipes, bound the telephone directory in white buckram, and in the guest rooms, where cocktails were delivered to the dressing table before dinner, cut flowers were dyed to match the curtains. There was a story that he had the Union Jack hauled down one day as the colors clashed with the sunset, though at least he did not dye his doves pastel shades like his friend Lord Berners. At Sassoon's death in 1939 it was said that his baroque was worse than his bite.

---

* The Labour administration returned in 1929, serving for what turned out to be a brief hiatus, and when the Conservatives came back to power in 1931 Sassoon was reappointed undersecretary of state for air, a post he held for another six years.

The Prince of Wales arrived for a golf lesson, bringing his African photographs to show Denys, but the latter was in a black mood. He had not gone to Trent Park to be social; he had gone to try out Sassoon's Moth, but the "pestilential" weather had precluded any flying. "This is a cursed country," he ranted. The others had been golfing in the rain, but Denys was allergic to cold English showers and thought his housemates mad. They had made him play one morning, and the single session was quite enough; he retired to the library. "This afternoon I have *kata'ed* [Swahili for 'refused'], and am spending a pleasant indoor afternoon by myself," he told Tania in an uncharacteristically long letter. She had not written to him, and he was anxious for her news. He felt a degree of responsibility toward her and wanted to help; he knew that she was having a difficult time. He urged her to go to his beach house at Takaungu. "I feel it would do you a lot of good to get away from Ngong for a little," he wrote. But to get there she would have had to take the train to Mombasa and then make a complicated journey north involving two ferries. (Nyali Bridge was not completed until 1931.) How could she do it, with the farm in turmoil? And anyway, Takaungu was too low and too hot for her. What Denys could offer was not enough.

He had been busy looking at planes that spring and was disappointed that the next batch of the new Puss Moth monoplane would not be ready in time for him to buy one before he started back. He test-flew a Bluebird, but didn't like it nearly as much as the Moth. He also took up a DW2, which needed only twenty yards' clearance for takeoff—a great advantage in the bush ("One could land it on your lawn!" he told Tania in excitement. "The Ngong side of the house!"), but it was slow, cruising at 60 miles per hour, whereas the Puss cruised at between 100 and 110. In the end, he bought a custard-yellow Gypsy Moth with the registration G-ABAK. A twenty-three-foot two-seater biplane with a thirty-foot wingspan, the Moth flew up to 102 miles per hour with a range of about 320 miles, and Denys immediately whizzed down to Buckfield, landing in a field beyond the lawn to the delight of his nieces and nephew, who squealed as their glamorous uncle unfolded his long limbs and emerged from the plane in his goggles. But later he crashed into a tree and repairs to the Moth delayed his departure.

When Denys finally got back to Kenya, he stayed in Mombasa. His

French client Gourgaud and his wife, Eva, had returned for a second safari and they were all to meet up on the coast. Denys cabled Tania inviting
her to join them for a week before they went into the bush. She had been
taken with the Gourgauds when she met them on their previous safari;
they were the right type, as Baron "Napo" was the great-grandson of
Napoléon's aide-de-camp Gaspard Gourgaud. But she could no longer
leave the farm: the situation there was more critical than ever. She had had
a miserable time in Denys's absence. In March 1930, she was locked in dispute with Dickens, who was threatening to resign. There had been three
attempts to murder Farah, who had long been at loggerheads with another
Somali faction. Tania was having nightmares and took an African baby to
bed to comfort her. Then locusts arrived in their brassy mass, darkening
the sky for twelve-hour stretches and shrieking the way a blizzard shrieks
in northern latitudes. They flew in a belt that extended from the ground to
the treetops, whirring against faces, sticking in shoes and collars, and settling in such dense abundance that when they landed on the branch of a
tree it snapped. Their jaws were not strong enough to chew the coffee
leaves, but they left the maize fields a dustheap.* Tania lost weight, and
did not perk up even when Beryl came out to ride with her.

Denys went through the motions when he reappeared, running errands and commissioning an Indian carpenter to make shelves so that he
could keep the rest of his books at the farm. Tania even drove to Nairobi
to fetch some of them, including his sixteen-volume Voltaire. But they
both knew it was over. She could not tell her family, but tried to prepare
them. "My black brother here in Africa," she wrote to her mother, "has
become the great passion of my life. . . . Even Denys, although he makes
me tremendously happy, carries no weight in comparison. It is lovely for
me that he exists . . . but he can do just about anything he likes for me and
still not greatly affect my feeling of happiness or unhappiness, and in general I find it hard to take anything concerning Denys really seriously. But
with my black brother it is something quite different; it is a matter of life
and death." It was hardly a sibling relationship. Her attitude to "her"
Africans was feudal: she was their mistress, not their sister. But a fresh

---

* The desert locust was bad; another species was on the way, the migratory locust, which arrived
in 1931, the worst year of all. When oil from insects crushed on the line prevented trains from gripping, the swarms even disrupted the railway.

anti-English phase was understandably looming. "I am finding it difficult to stand the English," she wrote. "The mere fact that they are always so skinny shows their uncongeniality."

MEANWHILE, G-ABAK JOINED the fragile flock of wings on the Nairobi airfield. The Africans on the farm christened it *Ndege*—"bird" or "plane"— but Denys and Tania called it Nzige, the Swahili word for locust. If he dive-bombed the house she rushed out, hands to her face, while boys and girls from the *shambas* ran around shrieking. Kikuyu elders trailed out to quiz Tania, as they could not understand why Denys didn't fall out of the plane. Once, after they had both been up, an old man named Ndwetti approached them as they walked back to the house.

"You were up very high today," he said. "We could not see you, only hear the aeroplane sing like a bee." Tania agreed that they had been up high.

"Did you see God?" Ndwetti asked.

"No, Ndwetti," Tania said. "We did not see God."

"Aha, then you were not up high enough," he said. "But now tell me: do you think that you will be able to get up high enough to see him?" Tania said she didn't know.

"And you, Bedar," said Ndwetti, turning to Denys. "What do you think? Will you get up high enough in your aeroplane to see God?"

"Really, I do not know," Denys said.

"Then," said Ndwetti, "I do not know at all why you two go on flying."

When they went up in the plane together, Tania sat in front of Denys. Rain and hail stung their faces. They flew down the east flank of Kilimanjaro above the streaky riverbeds that came off it like spokes, and over Lake Chala, the mysterious blue-green sea cupped in a volcanic crater. It was allegedly bottomless, and the lair of monsters various. Alongside the ridged hills east and west of Taveta, the water holes drew game as iron filings to a magnet, dispersed at one end and hurrying into an agglomeration at the other. When the hills flattened out, big-headed dots of wildebeest moved like running water across the yellowing gray plain—you could not see the gallop from the air. They scattered in puffs of dust when the shadow of the aircraft overtook them, and if Denys throttled down and lost height, particles of the dust burned his nostrils. The Serengeti plains, as warm with life as a tropical sea, were webbed with eland paths, and hot vapors pressed the undercarriage of the plane like heat from a fire lifting a flake of ash. As the Moth droned over the Rift, thin Grant's gazelles showed white against the burned-yellow grass of the valley floor. Lake Natron was garlanded with quivering flamingo pink, and as Denys turned back toward Ngong before day switched abruptly into night a softer shade of pink infused the cloud moving over the ground. "You knew then," Beryl wrote as she first looked down on ten thousand wild animals rolling like a carpet over Africa, "what you had always been told—that the world once lived and grew without adding machines and newsprint and brick-walled streets and the tyranny of clocks."

As Beryl noted when she went up with Denys, "the competence which he applied so casually to everything was as evident in the air as it was on one of his safaris or in the recitations of Walt Whitman he performed during his more sombre or perhaps during his lighter moments." His aerial experiences reinforced his developing conservation theories: from two hundred feet one could see a whole herd, as opposed to the single beast that loomed through the scope of a rifle. It heightened his awareness of the wealth at risk of depletion. Above all, flying brought Denys freedom and space, ideals of which formed the mainsprings of his character. The plane beat the road to most of Kenya by years. Aviation maps were drawn to a scale of one over two million, meaning that an inch on the map was thirty miles in the air, and many of those inches were labeled UNSURVEYED. What could be more thrilling than reaching the end of the map?* In the air, more than anywhere on the prosaic earth, Denys experienced a poetic intimacy with the wilderness. It was a physical expression of a spiritual yearning. When, reunited with his shadow, he put the chocks back under the wheels at the airfield or on some lonely patch of bush, he felt a satisfaction that could not be quantified by the number of elephants he had scouted. "Flying suits Denys so perfectly," Tania wrote home. "I have always felt that

---

* It happened to me once, on the West Antarctic Ice Sheet. I was hiking, and when I took the USGS map out of my pocket and looked at it I saw that I had reached a line the cartographer had drawn with a ruler and labeled "Limit of compilation."

he has so much of the element of air in his makeup . . . and was a kind of Ariel." She told her family proudly that he said he had brought this machine out here for her sake and that flying with him was the most transporting pleasure of her life on the farm. There was a disconcerting resilience about Tania. It was a mysterious kind of endurance that it is impossible not to respect. But she knew in her heart she had lost him, as one always does when one really has. The sense of freedom he had found in the air had made him feel even more imprisoned with her. She tried to ready her family. Pursuing the theme that Denys had the character of an Ariel, she concluded, "There is a good deal of heartlessness in this temperament."

IN NOVEMBER, DENYS FLEW to Lamu with Tania, circling the M'tepe dhows with their matting sails before landing behind the pocked fort. They walked in the sand dunes alongside the village of Shela, admired the plain ashlar beauty of the Arab mansions, and drank coffee served from brass jars by vendors tending tiny charcoal braziers. After three days, Denys dropped Tania at Ngong and departed on safari with Marshall Field, the son of the Chicago department-store magnate. Like the other white hunters, he was always thinking about where he might find fresh terrain for his clients. Between assignments, he had been scouting new areas in the company of the aptly named J. A. Hunter, an ace tracker and shot whom Denys revered. The pipe-smoking J.A., as he was known, was a sensitive Scot who had shot geese as a boy on the Galway Flats. Born the same year as Denys, he came to British East Africa in 1908, began his African career as a guard on the Lunatic Express, and by 1930 was living at Makindu with his wife, Hilda, and their six children. J.A. was solid, flinty and uncompromising, and more uxorious than those hunters who perceived women merely as bipedal quarry. Recently, besides searching for new hunting grounds, he and Denys had been trying to get motion-picture footage of a charging buffalo, a task that was becoming an obsession. On the soda flats of Lake Natron, their backs camouflaged with reeds, they had crawled to within thirty-five yards of the front line of the herd. But they were never able to overcome problems created by the dust kicked up by the disobliging beasts as soon as they heard the click of a shutter. Once it was so thick that a young bull ran straight into their truck, crumpling the bonnet.

At the end of 1930, after Marshall Field had returned to his father's shops, J.A. and Denys set out for southern Maasailand, a region they had both been warned off by reports of lack of water. Determined to see for themselves, they started out with a Chevrolet and a team of Africans and headed for the border. On the first day, the grass was so long that they hit an invisible rock and split the Chevy's sump. Denys patched it up and they carried on to the Mara River, across the cranial protuberances beyond Lake Province, creating their own bush trails. Eventually, they reached the plains of southern Maasailand. "Denys and I could scarcely believe our eyes when we saw the countless beasts ruminating there," J.A. wrote. ". . . The abundance of wild life naturally gave each individual creature a sense of security. . . . Lions, buffalo, rhino and antelope of every conceivable variety continued to graze unconcerned. Every slope as far as the eye could see, even through binoculars, swarmed with game." The security was often misplaced, as the living was easy for predators large and small. Denys and J.A. explored the plain among packs of gaunt hyenas, bloody jaws deep in entrails, and with the flocks of vultures too heavy to get off the ground. J.A. remembered the trip with nostalgia. "Denys opened up the Maasai with me," he wrote. "He was fearless and fair. . . . He was an undaunted hunter whose memory I cherish in my heart." Elsewhere, he said Denys was one of the bravest hunters he had ever met, which was high praise from one who knew them all. Right at the end of their Maasai tour, a herder asked them to go after a pair of lions that had been molesting his cattle. When they did, the beasts appeared suddenly, yards from Denys, and reared up on their hind legs preparing to dash him to the ground. "But Denys was quicker than the lions," J.A. wrote. "I saw him stop, shoulder his rifle . . . two shots rang out with scarcely a fraction of time between them. Both lions fell to the ground immediately, one of them first performing a miniature death dance as he fell." Most hunters using rifles can hit with the first shot, but few can fire accurately immediately after it with the second, because of the powerful recoil.

"Good effort," said J.A.

"I'd take any chance with you behind me, J.A.," Denys replied.

CHAPTER 10

TOO CLOSE
TO THE SUN

Denys would have greeted doomsday with
a wink—and I think he did.

—BERYL MARKHAM,

West with the Night, 1942

THE TRAGEDY OF THE FARM MOVED INTO THE FIFTH ACT. INTEREST HAD
not been paid on the mortgage for two years, and shareholders decided the
end had come. In the first months of 1931, the whole estate was sold to a
Nairobi property developer; the forced sale did not even cover the cost of
liquidation. The developer planned to build luxury houses and a golf and
country club, and as a tribute to Tania he was naming his new suburb
Karen. The baroness could remain on the farm, he said magnanimously,
until work began. She said that she would prefer to live in the middle of
the Sahara. But the final harvest belonged to the company, so she did stay
until it ripened, leasing her house for a shilling a day. She was giddy with
arrangements, pursued around the farm by squatters who ran after her
asking, "Why do you want to go away? You mustn't go, what will become
of us?" Determined to secure land for them elsewhere, Tania began negotiating with the government on their behalf—the talk of black brothers
had not all been cant. She compiled a list—each man noted with the number of his cattle, then of his goats, then of his women. (She had 157 squatters who owned between them 1,679 head of cattle, 1,506 goats,
and 238 women.) She typed and retyped documents on the high-rolled

Corona and ricocheted to and fro from Nairobi, trailing around offices, badgering officials, and dealing with unpaid debts: everything had to be settled before fresh land was allocated. Farah put on his brocade waistcoat and scarlet turban and walked behind her along the streets of Nairobi carrying a giraffe-hide whip inlaid with gold. She was deeply grateful. "No friend, brother or lover," she wrote, "could have done for me what my servant Farah did then."

Through Tania's prodigious efforts, most of the squatters were eventually resettled. In addition, she tried to find alternative employment for her staff. One man wanted to be a chauffeur, so she gave him driving lessons. In April, she began dismembering the house. She made inventories and advertised her furniture in Nairobi, inviting prospective purchasers to drive out to Ngong to inspect the goods and laying out china for viewing on the polished dining-room table where she had so often sat in the shadows with Denys. Many arrived only out of curiosity, eager for a glimpse of failure. Some came to buy. Lucie McMillan purchased furniture for the library she had built as a memorial to Northrup.* The cuckoo appeared to mark each hour as it always had, until it, too, was sold, and the house fell silent. In her beleaguered desperation Tania said she felt like Napoléon on the retreat from Moscow (no metaphor was too grandiose). She was too anxious to sleep or eat, and sometimes, in the middle of a meeting with a Nairobi official, she forgot what she wanted to say. As usual she was not well, and she had recently been diagnosed with chronic dysentery and severe anemia. "And during this time," she wrote in *Out of Africa*, "I thought something would happen to change it all back, since the world, after all, was not a regular or calculable place."

Denys moved out and went to stay with Hugh Martin, the whiskey-swigging head of the Land Office. Martin's marriage had collapsed, so he was living alone and had become more cynical and even less sober. It was awkward for Denys, abandoning Tania at this juncture. He sent her bottles of claret and books, offered to help with errands, and took her on spins over the Ngong Hills or down to the game reserve. Sometimes he went out to the farm to dine, sitting on one packing case and eating off another.

---

* I worked in the archive in the basement of that Nairobi library while I was researching this book. I often peered into murky corners (and there were many), wondering if a broken-down chair had once belonged at Ngong.

Without any friendly furniture the paneled rooms echoed with every cough and footfall. "He himself looked upon Africa as his home, and he understood me very well and grieved with me then, even if he laughed at my distress at parting with my people," she wrote of Denys. He encouraged her to make a plan for the next phase of her life and made her promise that she would write to Thomas asking for practical help. He talked of packing up his books, but he had nowhere else to put them: there was no room at Hugh's. He briefly considered renting a place in Nairobi, but when he went to look for one he was appalled at the vulgar suburban feel of the houses. Tania said that the episode depressed him. "He had been in contact with a kind of existence the idea of which was unbearable to him," she wrote. He told her he would be perfectly happy in a tent in the Maasai reserve. Even after Denys had settled to a profession he loved and committed himself to goals he judged worthwhile, he rejected the trappings of worldly success. Most of the time he and Tania still talked as if the future did not exist, as they always had; one had to, with Denys.

In *Out of Africa*, Tania implies that Denys was disturbed at this time, citing the brush with middle-class suburbia and lack of a base as the cause. But he was not troubled, and at forty-four still had no desire to settle. His life was busier than ever, and he was full of plans. He was sorry for her and wanted to help, but he knew that the thing that would really help her was the thing he could not give. They were living in different mental worlds, as unhappy lovers do, coexisting like the twin beaters of a rotary whisk, spinning in time but never touching. His notes are clumsy and awkward; in one, he told her how convenient it was to be in Nairobi because he had a telephone there. Tania's friends concluded that Denys left her, in the end, because he was being suffocated by her possessiveness. But she wasn't possessive. She loved him and he didn't love her—not enough, anyway. It was not a surprise that he left her; she was not shocked. Within days of meeting him twelve years earlier, she had made an observation, writing to her mother, "It is interesting to talk to Britishers who have been to war or who are going to war; none of them are afraid, of course, but somehow you get the impression that this is more due to a certain contempt for life than what we usually call courage. There seems to be no loss in the world which they would really lament as there seems to be nothing they really 'love': not their mothers, their mistresses, their children—

[except] perhaps their dogs!" Before they even began their relationship, she had recognized that Denys did not really love anyone, the implication being that he and his kind never did and never would. In all the years that followed, somewhere in her heart or her mind, or at least swimming in her subconscious like some mysterious deep-sea fish, she knew that he would never be able to give her what she wanted. If only, equipped with such knowledge, one could stop oneself from falling in love.

NOW THAT SHE had lost her two great loves, Denys and the farm, Tania compressed her vision of the world into a mythic saga of tragedy and passion. It was a process long established in her imagination, and now it became a survival mechanism. In time, it was to emerge fully fledged in her stories. In the closing months on the farm, she adopted a magnanimous pose in public, talking with dignity of the "world of poetry" that Africa had opened to her and of her gratitude that her house had been a refuge for wayfarers and the sick. But darker forces were swirling around beneath the surface. Those close to her were worried that she might kill herself, as her father had done. Thomas and her mother cabled encouragement, telling her not to feel that her life had been wasted, and Uncle Aage wrote to say that she was not responsible for the failure of the company. "We realise that you have fought a long battle with exceptional ability and endurance," he said kindly. At Ngong, Ingrid, Rose, and others gathered around. But the "double" in her previously noted by Ingrid was still visible. Tania wrote to Thomas informing him that death was now an attractive option, and that it was preferable to bourgeois life. However, she went on to suggest, her death might in fact be avoided were he prepared to subsidize a new life in Europe—training to be a chef, perhaps, or a journalist (she had started to write a book in English). She stated categorically that a permanent home at Rungstedlund was not on the agenda, and her bald announcement that the alternatives were death or a subsidy was perilously close to blackmail. "I know that I can die happily, and if you are in doubt [about funding a life elsewhere] let me do that," she concluded the bizarrely cheerful letter. "Let me take Ngong, and everything that belongs to it, in my arms and sink with it. . . . Will you please reply to this letter by telegram?"

—

DENYS WAS UNEXPECTEDLY spending time in his old cottage on the grounds of Muthaiga, the one he had taken jointly with Delamere after the war. It was now rented by Beryl. After the departure of the princes in 1928, Beryl had gone back to England alone to have her baby. The Duke of Gloucester met her ship, as he had promised he would. A son was born in February 1929, and soon after, Beryl again took up with her royal consort, hiding in a cupboard at Buckingham Palace when Queen Mary appeared. The cuckolded Markham had been suspicious of the duke for some time, and after a batch of royal love letters surfaced, any lingering doubt disappeared. When the baby was a few months old his parents separated—the boy was brought up by his paternal grandmother—and there was talk of citing the duke in divorce proceedings. Questions were asked in private about the baby's paternity. (Tania said everyone in Kenya was counting on their fingers.) A close examination of dates reveals that Beryl's child could not in fact have been Prince Henry's. But in 1929, to avoid the scandal of a divorce case, and to keep Markham quiet, a capital sum and an annual income were settled on Beryl, the latter to continue until the end of her life. The monies were drawn from the prince's own account. Meanwhile, Beryl returned to Kenya depressed and listless. She went to the farm, telling Tania that her husband was a swine and a blackmailer and that she was unhappy to be separated from her infant son. Tania invited her to stay during race week. But Beryl didn't want to go to the races, as people in Nairobi glared at her. Tania thought she was "the greatest baby I have known, but there is more in her than in most of the people who pretend to be so shocked at her now." With fine proleptic irony she predicted that Beryl was "so young and light hearted that I am sure, sooner or later, she will find something else to live for." Then, suddenly, Beryl fled back to England and another summer as royal mistress. By November, she had returned to Kenya and rented Denys's former cottage.

Now, aged twenty-eight, Beryl was at her most alluring. Nearly six feet tall, slim-hipped and long-fingered, although she was not classically beautiful—she had a strong chin and toothy jaw—she was handsome; her Nordic looks have often been described as Garboesque. She gave the impression that she cared little for anything on two legs, and men found her nonchalance attractive. Beryl was different from Tania in almost every way. Tania was wafty and incorporeal, whereas there was something earthy and physical about Beryl: if her lover disappeared on safari, she would gallop off to someone else's bed rather than pen a treatise on the morality of marriage. Unlike Tania, she was robust and never ill (she admitted that she was "pathologically" afraid of sickness, hers or anyone else's). She was calm where Tania was neurotic. Tania found tomfoolery disgraceful, whereas Beryl was always game for rough-and-tumble—she once raced Ingrid in a furniture steeplechase for a rupee note stowed above the Muthaiga clock. (The race ended in a dead heat, and they tore the note in half.) In 1934, when she had qualified as a pilot, she flew for Blix, scouting elephants from the air. Once she dropped him a message from her plane with reports of tusker positions, ending the dispatch, "Work hard, trust in God, and keep your bowels open—Oliver Cromwell." As her affair with Denys entered the public arena, the bungalow became known as "the way of all flesh." The fact that Tania was her faithful confidante was of no consequence to Beryl. Characteristically, she played down their friendship later. "She was all right," she told an interviewer. "I can't say I thought the world of her. She wasn't my cup of tea really." This was rank ingratitude. Like Denys, Beryl was languid, but she had a harder edge. She often abused the kindness of friends; in particular, she was hopelessly irresponsible with money and seldom repaid loans. "She had charm but no warmth," one hostess said of her. But one detail of Beryl's recollection of the relationship between Tania and Denys rings true. "Tania," she recalled, "was always waiting for him to come back."*

Denys and Beryl rode together and picnicked in the hills, sang duets, and went to parties. If he was preparing for a safari, she went with him in the Hudson to collect supplies. When he took her flying they landed at

---

* Beryl told at least one author that Denys was bisexual. But she was an unreliable source. She claimed a lot of things, many of them contradictory. She suggested that Denys might have had a black child, and that Tania was sleeping with Farah. She said that she'd had an affair with Blix, and also that she hadn't. Self-dramatizing tendencies were a smoke screen for a lack of confidence. The suggestion that Denys was bisexual or homosexual has been repeated down the years, always by people who knew little of him. There is no evidence for either, and both seem to me unlikely. The idea originated, I believe, in a pedestrian misunderstanding of the magnetic effect Denys had on other men and of his capacity for intimacy with a range of figures from Philip Sassoon to J. A. Hunter.

Melela, where Clutt was training. (Markham, Beryl's husband, was in England.) With Beryl, Denys had his freedom back. Unlike her husbands, he did not try to control her, and when he turned his slow rakish smile on her he expected nothing in return. Above all, he opened up a whole new cultural world. He read to her and introduced her to the poetry of Walt Whitman. "He half taught me how to live," she said much later. A close friend thought he was Beryl's first great love, and the only man who competed with her father. She admired him hugely, and to a certain extent she had the measure of him. Someone, she wrote in her autobiography, will say that Denys was a great man who never achieved greatness. She was right; they did say that. "This will not only be trite," she continued, "but wrong; he was a great man who never achieved arrogance." He gave out, Beryl said, "a force that bore inspiration, spread confidence in the dignity of life, and even gave sometimes a presence to silence." And while he was a scholar "of almost classical profundity, he was less pedantic than an untutored boy. There were occasions when Denys, like all men whose minds have encompassed among other things the foibles of their species, experienced misanthropic moments; he could despair of men, but find poetry in a field of rock. As for charm, I suspect Denys invented it . . . it was a charm of intellect and strength, of quick intuition and Voltairian humour."*

Interviewed in 1986, Beryl noted that Denys was "a lovely man, very upright." Then there was a pause. "What makes me so depressed," she continued, "is that I've had so many lovely men who've been very good to me. I don't mean to sound as if I'm bragging. Of course, I was good to them too. Now look at all this!" She swept her arm out to indicate the shabby room and the metal-framed bed propped up on sawn-off tree trunks. This was the price she had paid for her choices: a lonely, impover-

---

* Beryl's 1942 autobiography, *West with the Night*, was her love letter to Africa, just as Tania's *Out of Africa* was hers. To many tastes, *West with the Night* is the better of the two. There is some evidence that the book was written by Beryl's third husband. The narrative regularly departs from the truth, whoever wrote it: key events of Beryl's childhood are reorganized, events are conflated and facts distorted. But it is a brilliant book. Hemingway recommended it to Max Perkins. "This girl," he wrote, "who is, to my knowledge, very unpleasant, and we might even say, a high-grade bitch, can write rings around all of us who consider ourselves writers." He was aware that the book was economic with the *actualité*. "She omits some very fascinating stuff which I know about which would destroy much of the character of the heroine; but what is that anyhow in writing?" he commented.

ished old age, reliant on alcohol and living off her memories as a hibernating animal lives off its fat.

IN FEBRUARY OF 1931, Denys departed on safari with the Sofer Whitburns, an English couple in their fifties. (Like all his clients, they returned to England a little in love with him.) He had been thinking about flying the Moth home shortly after the safari ended, but as the month advanced decided he was too busy. He was planning a solo photographic expedition in June, and before that was flying to the coast, first to work on his house and then to try scouting for elephants from the air around Voi. He knew that he had to visit Tania before he went down to Takaungu, to hold out a faithless arm. She was to leave Kenya for good on June 9, and her family were so anxious about her emotional state that Thomas cabled to say that he would sail out to bring her home. (She cabled back telling him not to bother.) The furniture sale had not been concluded, and she was still busy receiving viewers and packing crates. But the animals had gone. Someone in Nairobi adopted Dinah, Dusk's grandchild, and Tania had ridden her horse, Rouge, into town and seen him loaded, protesting, into the horse van of the Naivasha train. When Denys arrived, she asked if he would take her with him to Takaungu. First he said yes, then he changed his mind on the grounds that the journey onward to Voi would be turbulent and he might have to sleep in the bush; besides which he had to take one of his servants, and the plane seated only two. But she reminded him that he said he had brought the Moth out to fly her over Africa. Yes, he said, he had; if he found elephants around Voi, there would still be time to take her down there when he knew where to find suitable landing strips. Tania said later, to make a story out of it, that it was the only time she ever asked him to take her up that he refused. She wrote of "an unconditional truthfulness which outside of him [Denys] I have only met in idiots." But he was not being honest. He did not want to take her. They quarreled in the end, and he asked for his ring back—the soft gold one he had brought her from Abyssinia. He was afraid (she said later) that she might give it away to Pooran Singh, her bearded Indian blacksmith; Denys complained that whenever he bought her anything she gave it away to her Africans. He put the ring on his own finger and said he would keep it till Pooran Singh had gone.

Denys left the farm on Wednesday, May 6, telling her to look out for him the following Thursday, when he would be back in time to have luncheon with her. He turned for the drive, then went indoors again to collect a volume of poems. It was the book Iris had published. At the end, he stood with one foot on the running board of the Hudson and one on the gravel, and with a finger in the book below a poem they had been discussing. "Here are your grey geese," he said, and read a few of the lines Iris had written for him.

> *I saw grey geese straining over the flat lands,*
> *Wild geese vibrant in the high air,*
> *Saw them as I feel them, symbols,*
> *Felt my soul stiffened out in their throats . . .*
> *And the grey whiteness of them ribboning the enormous skies,*
> *And the spokes of the sun over the crumpled hills.*

Then he swung into the car and drove away. Tania said later that the first servant he asked to go to Takaungu with him refused; she concluded that "The shadow of destiny, which Denys himself had felt during the last days at Ngong, was seen more strongly now, by the native." But this was when she was able to create a piece of theater from the misery. At the time, she went to a friend's house and, according to Thomas, tried to cut her wrists but bungled the attempt. The suicide note she left has vanished from her papers.

On the seventh, Denys dined with his friends Jack Melhuish and Joan Waddington at their house in Nairobi. Joan worked in the telegram office at Government House, and Jack was a dentist and an amateur photographer. He had a darkroom that Denys often used. Nairobi was chilly after the start of the long rains, and Denys appeared that night in a dinner jacket and black tie, with his camel-hair dressing gown on top. During the meal, he asked Joan if she wanted to fly down to Takaungu with him. "Good God, Denys!" she spluttered. "Do you want me to commit suicide?" He had known she would not go. His offer was not serious, because he had already asked Beryl to go to Takaungu and Voi with him. She had agreed immediately. On the morning of the eighth, the day they were due to leave, she was at the airfield with her flying instructor, Tom Campbell Black.

"I'm going down to Voi with Denys," Beryl told Tom. "He wants to see how efficiently elephants can be spotted from the air, and if it would be possible to keep a hunting party more or less in touch with a moving herd."

Tom leaned against a workbench in the newly built Wilson Airways hangar, jotting figures on a scrap of paper. The open hangar looked out on the airfield, on the plains, and on a square of sky lonely for clouds. "It was a flyer's day," Beryl recalled. Tom stuffed the piece of paper in the pocket of his leather jacket.

"Sounds practical enough," he said, "up to a point. You'd find a lot more elephant than places to land after you'd found them."

"I suppose so," Beryl conceded. "But it seems worth trying—Denys's ideas always are. Anyway, we're just going to fly out from Voi and back again. No rough landings. If it works out, there should be a good living in it. When you think of all the people who come out here for elephant, and all the time that's spent, and . . ."

"I know," said Tom. "It's an excellent idea." He moved away from the bench and went out the hangar door and looked at the field. He stood there without moving. Then he came back.

"Make it tomorrow, Beryl," he said.

"Weather?"

"No, the weather's all right. Just make it tomorrow—will you?"

"I suppose I will, if you ask me to, but I don't see why."

"Neither do I," said Tom, "but there it is."

There it was. Beryl let Denys take off without her.* In his haste to find another passenger he went to fetch his cook, the old ruffian Hamisi, and told him they were leaving promptly for the coast. Hamisi began flapping,

---

* Two normally reliable sources told Mary Lovell, Beryl's biographer, that Beryl was pregnant by Denys at the time. One source was Genessie Hamilton, who spoke on condition that what she said would not be attributed in her lifetime (she has died since publication of Lovell's book). Beryl terminated the pregnancy. I have not included this in the text, as it is impossible to substantiate, but I believe it to be true.

complaining that he didn't have time to go home to collect spare clothes or to give his wife her share of his wages. But Denys was in a hurry and said he would give him fresh clothes when they arrived at Takaungu. Kanuthia drove them both to the airstrip.

They took off in radiant good weather. Around Takaungu, the fields rippled with high spiky leaves that looked like the tops of giant pineapples. The sisal had just poled, and a tall, sticklike growth shot up from the heart of each plant. From the air, the neat rows ran across the land like green corduroy. Denys had cleared an airstrip north of the creek, within walking distance of his house, and installed a wind sock. He spent three quiet days on the coast with Hamisi, but when they took off again a wheel dug into soft ground and chipped one of the wooden propeller blades in two places on a block of coral. They landed at Voi and Denys wired Tom Campbell Black from the station asking him to send a new blade down by train. He was sure he could replace it himself, but Tom dispatched an African mechanic with it, just in case. With the fresh blade fitted, Denys and Hamisi took off again on Wednesday, May 13, heading for the hills around Voi. Hamisi was airsick, so they landed twelve miles south of Maktau and remained on the ground for two hours. Then they flew on, spotting a large herd of elephants browsing along the Voi River. Denys was elated at the success of his scheme, which he was convinced would cut out weeks of scouting on foot. Now he planned to spend one night in the district before returning to Nairobi. He knew the area well and often landed on an airstrip at the foot of Mbolo Hill in order to stay with District Commissioner Vernon Cole and his wife, Hilda, or with Stanley and Margaret Layzell, who lived adjacent to a large sisal plantation that Stanley managed for a British company. It was an isolated region—according to Beryl, "Voi presumed to be a town then, but was hardly more than a word under a tin roof"—and social visits were keenly anticipated.

That night the Coles hosted a small party. Guests included J.A., who was starting on safari the next day with an American client named Lee Hudson. Stanley and Margaret Layzell were also present, along with their two elder daughters, Katharine and Anne, aged seven and nine, who adored Denys. Hudson and J.A. left the party early to prepare for a dawn start the next day, and Denys went onto the porch to say good night. As he was standing in the doorway, Hilda came up behind him and gave him an armful of oranges to take back to Nairobi. Kenyan oranges are the color of spring grass, and as Denys stood on the threshold of the bungalow, waving to his friend with his free hand, the electric light reflected amber green on the dimpled skin of the fruit.

THURSDAY MORNING CAME bright and cloudless. Margaret Layzell arrived at seven to drive Denys to the airstrip. She brought Katharine and Anne, who had clamored to see their hero again. It was toward the end of the rains, and the sky was a tender blue. There was no wind. The sisal had been cut and the fields smelled sulfurous, as water was fermenting in the irrigation furrows.

The Coles arrived to see Denys off, bringing their small son, John. Hilda was in the early stages of a second pregnancy.* After refueling, Denys turned to Margaret and invited her up for a spin. She accepted, but Katharine grabbed her hand and begged her not to go. Keen to fly, Margaret tried to calm her daughter, but the girl became irrationally frightened and would not be placated. Margaret reluctantly told Denys the spin would have to be postponed.

Denys buttoned his flying helmet and wrapped his greatcoat around him. Hamisi took the chocks away and swung the propeller. The engine spluttered, and Denys pushed gently on the throttle. Hamisi jumped into the front. Iris's poetry book was stuffed down the side of Denys's seat. As the Moth banked to gain altitude, the wind played tunes on the struts. The plane circled twice and turned in the direction of Nairobi. As it was still gaining height, the engine faltered. The Moth plummeted out of sight of the spectators and crashed a mile away, close to Mwakangale Hill. On impact, it burst into flames. When all the fuel was burned up and the fire began to go cold, three black oranges rolled out of the fuselage.

Tania buried him in the indifferent soil of the Ngong Hills, under the grass where he once lay looking at eagles.

---

* Later that afternoon, she miscarried in shock.

ILLUSTRATIONS

Henry Finch Hatton, Denys's father (family collection)
Nan Finch Hatton with her three children (family collection)
Denys and his mother (family collection)
Toby and Denys at Haverholme (family collection)
Denys golfing (family collection)
Topsy and Denys (family collection)
Haverholme Priory (family collection)
Julian Grenfell and Denys (courtesy of Lord Ravensdale)
Denys as a teenager, photographed by his mother (family collection)
Toby and the Haverholme gamekeeper (family collection)
Denys at Eton (family collection)
Nan, Henry, and Margaretta in 1919 (family collection)
Denys, Nan, and Henry at Haverholme in 1922 (family collection)
Toby, Ossie, and Denys (family collection)
Toby and Denys (family collection)
Denys in 1910, before departure for Africa (family collection)
The Mara Triangle (courtesy of Eco-resorts: www.eco-resorts.com)
Nine hundred and fifty-three elephants (Peter Beard)
Denys with Rose and Algy Cartwright at Lake Naivasha
    (family collection)
Nairobi in the 1920s (Archive of the Rungstedlund Foundation,
    Royal Library, Copenhagen)
Denys, Jack Pixley, Tich Miles, and Lady Colville (by kind permission
    of the Estate of Elspeth Huxley)
Denys with buffalo, Lake Jipe, 1927 (family collection)
Cole's Scouts watering, 1915 (Lord Cranworth, *Kenya Chronicles*, 1939)
Berkeley Cole and Tich Miles (courtesy of Miles family)
Denys interrogating an *askari* during the East Africa campaign, 1915
    (private collection)
Tania with Dawn and Dusk (Archive of the Rungstedlund Foundation,
    Royal Library, Copenhagen)

NOTES

All books published in London unless otherwise indicated.

ABBREVIATIONS

AFH	Anne Finch Hatton (Nan)
BB	Bror Blixen
BM	Beryl Markham
DFH	Denys Finch Hatton
GC	Galbraith Cole
GFH	Guy Finch Hatton (14th Earl of Winchilsea; Toby)
HFH	Henry Finch Hatton (13th Earl of Winchilsea)
KB	Karen Blixen
KR	Kermit Roosevelt
PoW	Edward, Prince of Wales, later Edward VIII
TD	Thomas Dinesen
KC	Lord Cranworth, *Kenya Chronicles*, 1939.
Letters	Frans Lasson, ed., *Isak Dinesen: Letters from Africa*, trans. Anne Born, Chicago, 1981.
OoA	Karen Blixen (Isak Dinesen), *Out of Africa*, New York, 1937. Page numbers refer to 1985 Penguin edition.
SotG	Karen Blixen (Isak Dinesen), *Shadows on the Grass*, 1960. Page numbers refer to 1985 Penguin edition.
WwtN	Beryl Markham, *West with the Night*, New York, 1942. Page numbers refer to 1984 Virago edition.

ARCHIVAL SOURCES USED IN NOTES

Northampton	Winchilsea and Nottingham Family Papers (Finch Hatton Papers), Northamptonshire Record Office
RH	Errol Trzebinski Archive (uncataloged), Bodleian Library of Commonwealth and African Studies, Rhodes House, Oxford
KBA	Karen Blixen Archive, *Det Kongelige Bibliotek* (Royal Library), Copenhagen

LoC   Kermit and Belle Roosevelt Papers, Manuscript Division, Library of Congress, Washington, D.C.

PRONI   Enniskillen Papers, Public Record Office of Northern Ireland, Belfast

PRO   Public Record Office, London

INTRODUCTION

xviii *"the paradise section of":* Introduction to *WwtN,* viii.

xviii *"Charm . . . is the great":* Evelyn Waugh, *Brideshead Revisited,* 1945, 260.

xviii *"The man with about":* KC, 190.

xx *"exceptionally scanty material":* C. Hordern and H. Stacke, *Military Operations in East Africa (History of the Great War Based on Official Documents),* vol. 1, 1941, iii.

xx *"We found accounts of":* KC, 180.

xxi *"It is worth having":* Letters, 168.

xxi *"No one came into":* Ibid., xxv.

CHAPTER 1. OUT OF TRIM

3 *"I saw him first":* Llewelyn Powys, *Black Laughter,* 1925, 168.

3 *"like one of his":* Evening Standard, May 15, 1931.

5 *"But if a man":* Harold Finch Hatton, *Advance Australia!,* 1885, 88.

5 *"only white man who":* Who's Who, 1897–1904.

6 *"getting out of trim":* The Times, August 22, 1864.

6 *"so many imputations of":* Ibid., November 24, 1864.

7 *"began to 'take soundings'":* Edith Craig and Christopher St. John, eds., *Ellen Terry's Memoirs,* 1933, 127.

7 *"He has remained with":* John Craigie, "Memories of Denys Finch Hatton," dictated to Seton Gordon 1969, private collection.

7 *"Everything in the family":* HFH, Diary, January 1, 1887, Northampton.

8 *"to see to things":* Ibid., January 23, 1887.

8 *"Alack, HP is a":* Ibid., February 10, 1887.

8 *"No sale is possible":* Ibid., April 20, 1887.

9 *"Hurrah at last! . . . No":* Ibid., May 10, 1887.

9 *"My darling Nan":* Ibid., August 15, 1887.

9 *"Never had so much":* Ibid., November 12, 1887.

9 *"So ends 1887, and":* Ibid., December 31, 1887.

9 *"Poor dear old W.":* Ibid., June 15, 1887.

10 *"the succession led to":* The Times, September 8, 1898.

12 *"Chix having a fine":* AFH, Diary, June 30, 1891, family collection.

13 *"I wish us all":* AFH, Diary, January 1, 1892, family collection.

13 "Il faut à la": inscribed by King Leopold in 1861 on a paperweight he presented to the anticolonial Belgian finance minister. Paperweight now in Tervuren Museum.

14 *"Oh . . . all the time"*: Christopher St. John, ed., *Ellen Terry & George Bernard Shaw, A Correspondence*, 1931, 104.

15 *"She was so unselfish"*: HFH to Michael Williams, July 3, 1924, family collection.

16 "locus vastae, solitudinis et": Les Gostick, "The Story of the People of Ewerby & Haverholme," n.d., unpublished, 80.

17 *"My God, man"*: Michael Williams, conversation with author, July 2002.

17 *"Last day, last walk"*: AFH, Diary, January 1896, family collection.

17 *"Horrid cold place. It"*: Ibid.

18 *"the 'Avunculus Hector' whose"*: anon., *Eton College Chronicle*, May 21, 1931, 1060.

22 *"Imperialism in the air"*: Beatrice Webb, June 26, 1897, published in *The Diary: 1892–1905—All the Good Things of Life*, 1983.

22 *"a sympathetic, fatherly and"*: Mark Hichens, *West Downs*, Durham, 1992, 9.

23 *"Please, sir, may I"*: Ibid., 15.

23 *"Toby had great charm . . . a wonderful family, quite . . . He had such understanding . . . immense reserves of affection"*: correspondence between Michael Williams and Errol Trzebinski, 1975, RH.

23 *"The Dog was wild"*: Rudyard Kipling, *Just So Stories*, 1902.

CHAPTER 2. TAKE YOUR HAT OFF, HATTON

25 *"Did the sun always"*: anon., *Eton College Chronicle*, May 21, 1931, 1060.

26 *"Most of us know"*: Robert Skidelsky, *John Maynard Keynes, 1883–1946*, 2003, 57.

26 *"So the blow has"*: Wilfrid Blunt, *Lady Muriel*, 1962, 27.

26 *"was something in which"*: Osbert Sitwell, *Left Hand, Right Hand!*, vol. 1, *The Cruel Month*, 1945, 241.

27 *"a gust of Tathalmic"*: anon., *Eton College Chronicle*, May 21, 1931, 1060.

28 *"he might have been"*: Peter Stansky, *The Worlds of Philip and Sybil Sassoon*, 2003, 26.

28 *"that family of fabulous"*: L. E. Jones, *A Victorian Boyhood*, 1955, 93.

31 *"Is it peace?"*: Evelyn Waugh, *The Life of Ronald Knox*, 1959, 62.

31 *"Very grave news. Come"*: Jones, *A Victorian Boyhood*, 179.

32 *"without doubt the handsomest . . . dressing-gown—an unforgettable Antinous"*: Julian Huxley, *Memories*, vol. 1, 1970, 52.

32 *"in full sunshine crossing"*: anon., *Eton College Chronicle*, May 21, 1931, 1060.

33 *"Keir Hardie in his . . . but it could never . . . to be an island"*: Jones, *A Victorian Boyhood*, 219.

33 *"The headmaster used to"*: KC, 190.

33 *"Denys was a great . . . of him like that"*: anon., *Eton College Chronicle*, May 21, 1931, 1060.

34 *"It is very nice"*: Blunt, *Lady Muriel*, 35.

35 *"I remember Denys so"*: Oliver Wynne Hughes, *Every Day Was Summer*, Llandysul, 1989.

36 *"special bond"*: Michael Williams, correspondence with author, 2003; correspondence between Anne Williams and Errol Trzebinski, 1975, RH.

36 *"rotten social life"*: correspondence between Michael Williams and Errol Trzebinski, 1975, RH.

36 *"a breath of fresh air"*: Michael Williams, correspondence with author, 2003.

36 *"There is no good"*: family collection.

38 *"Even as a boy"*: Evening Standard, May 15, 1931.

38 *"Take your hat off"*: Errol Trzebinski, *The Lives of Beryl Markham*, 1993, 88.

38 *"the roomy, uncrowded years"*: L. E. Jones, *An Edwardian Youth*, 1956, 41.

39 *"Remember, you are playing"*: KC, 190.

40 *"He did not appear"*: Evening Standard, May 15, 1931.

40 *"I had myself been"*: Karen Blixen (Isak Dinesen), *Seven Gothic Tales*, New York, 1934, 256 (page number refers to Penguin Classics edition, 2002).

40 *"The Hon. Finch Hatton"*: Eton College Chronicle, April 6, 1905.

40 *"a tiara of hair"*: Craigie, "Memories of Denys Finch Hatton."

41 *"Oxford was always a"*: Waugh, *The Life of Ronald Knox*, 53.

41 *"The only time I . . . idle for a moment"*: Evening Standard, May 15, 1931.

42 *"Denys was such a"*: Craigie, "Memories of Denys Finch Hatton."

42 *"the 52nd heir to"*: Ibid.

42 *"It's 'arf past seven"*: Ibid.

42 *"In a long life"*: Ibid.

43 *"romance was the star"*: Daphne Fielding, *The Rainbow Picnic*, 1974, 13.

43 fn. *"the only true bohemian"*: John Julius Norwich, conversation with author, 2004.

44 *"was a romantic, and"*: Ivan Moffat to Errol Trzebinski, May 30, 1975, RH.

44 *"Denys has taken a"*: Nicholas Mosley, *Julian Grenfell*, 1976, 139.

44 *"for matches"*: Craigie, "Memories of Denys Finch Hatton."

44 *"With his grand physique"*: KC, 191.

45 *"It is surprising how"*: Bertrand Russell, *The Autobiography of Bertrand Russell*, vol. 1, 1967, 70.

47 *"crowd and heat appalling"*: GFH (Toby), Diary, May 20, 1910, family collection.

47 *"England is small, much"*: correspondence between Michael Williams and Errol Trzebinski, 1975, RH.

48 *"What do we mean"*: A. C. Benson and H.F.W. Tatham, eds., *Men of Might*, 1892, 257.

48 *"The thirst for the"*: H. Rider Haggard, *King Solomon's Mines*, 1886, 18.

50 *"It was simply splendid"*: Blunt, *Lady Muriel*, 48.

CHAPTER 3. INTO AFRICA

51 *"London always seemed rather"*: Alan Parsons, *Evening Standard*, May 15, 1931.

53 *"a railway through the"*: Charles Miller, *The Lunatic Express*, 1971, 587.

59 *"Don't waste time turning"*: Elspeth Huxley, *White Man's Country*, vol. 1, 1935, 155.

60 *"destroying any old or"*: Ibid., v.

61 *"He had seen what"*: Frederick B. Patterson, *African Adventures,* New York, 1928, 19.

61 *"Great success though personally"*: GFH (Toby), Diary, February 2, 1906. This volume of the diary has gone missing from the Northampton archive but was read and noted by Errol Trzebinski in 1975.

62 *"hoping to find Denys's"*: GFH (Toby), Diary, July 20, 1912, family collection.

62 *"Went to see 'Post'"*: GFH (Toby), Diary, January 11, 1913, family collection.

63 *THE FLOODGATES OF REVOLUTION: Daily Mail,* August 11, 1911.

63 *"Everything went very well"*: GFH (Toby), Diary, February 5, 1912, family collection.

64 *"panelled slum"*: Viola Parsons, ed., *Alan Parsons' Book,* 1937, 50.

64 *"beautiful and happy chaos"*: Ibid.

64 *"He's such a tonic . . . on champagne and caviare"*: Mosley, *Julian Grenfell,* 202.

64 *"the Valhalla of Julian"*: Parsons, ed., *Alan Parsons' Book,* 294.

66 *"smelt of the sweat"*: Powys, *Black Laughter,* 53.

68 *"With his vast talents . . . Once I remonstrated . . . finally have yielded to"*: KC, 192.

70 *"an unusual outburst of . . . sick of being treated"*: Ibid., 83.

70 *"The very best of"*: Ibid., 191.

70 *"the economic conquest"*: *Leader,* Nairobi, April 9, 1911.

71 *"a sop to the"*: Ibid., March 14, 1914.

71 *"I believe . . . that even"*: Ibid., October 7, 1911.

71 *"Nature had endowed him"*: KC, 192.

71 *"At all times, however"*: *The Times,* April 11, 1934.

73 *"Things very flat . . . Russia"*: GFH (Toby), Diary, February 7, 1913, family collection.

73 *"very good"*: GFH (Toby), Diary, March 7, 1913, family collection.

73 *"fly upside down . . . wonderful"*: GFH (Toby), Diary, September 3, 1913, family collection.

74 *"By Allah, I will"*: Charles Chevenix Trench, *Men Who Ruled Kenya,* 1993, 64.

76 *"True solitude"*: Gerald Hanley, *Warriors,* 1993 edition, 3.

76 *"I have never in . . . more distinction of mind"*: Malcolm Elwin, *The Life of Llewelyn Powys,* 1949, 126.

77 *"It seemed that Galbraith"*: *The Times,* October 12, 1929.

77 *"You will imagine the"*: GC to Adrian and Christine Cave, September 14 [1914], PRONI.

CHAPTER 4. HUNS IN THE JUNGLE

78 *"Finch Hatton could best"*: Powys, *Black Laughter,* 168.

78 *"Men are requested to"*: *Leader,* August 8, 1914.

78 *"This is their country!"*: GC to Adrian and Christine Cave, n.d., PRONI.

79 *"Yes! . . . The Squareheads have"*: GC to Adrian and Christine Cave, April 4, 1914, PRONI.

79 *"There is not the"*: Leader, August 15, 1914.

79 *"Neither I nor anyone"*: Bror von Blixen-Finecke, *African Hunter*, New York, 1986, 274.

79 *"ready cover to conceal"*: Angus Buchanan, *Three Years of War in East Africa*, 1919, 139.

80 *"a strong impression of"*: Judith Thurman, *Isak Dinesen: The Life of Karen Blixen*, 1982, 142 (page number refers to Penguin edition, 1984).

80 *"not human beings"*: Letters, 77.

80 *"made no secret of"*: KC, 191.

80 *"sodjering"*: DFH to KR, November 2, 1918, LoC.

80 *"I can remember thinking"*: Carlos Baker, *Ernest Hemingway*, New York, 1969, 57.

81 *"Once they began to"*: KC, 198.

82 *"On guard on a"*: Leader, October 9, 1915.

82 *"Every known type of"*: Ibid., August 21, 1915.

82 *"In all this campaign"*: Francis Brett Young, *Marching on Tanga*, 1917, 17.

82 *"It has not always"*: DFH to "Pussy" Lucas, September 12, 1915, private collection.

82 *"resplendently coloured stories"*: E.A.T. Dutton, *Lillibullero, or, The Golden Road*, Zanzibar, 1944, 126.

83 fn. *"Lettow-Vorbeck's brilliant campaign"*: John Iliffe, *A Modern History of Tanganyika*, Cambridge, 1979, 241.

84 *"The success at Tanga"*: Paul von Lettow-Vorbeck, *My Reminiscences of East Africa*, 1920, 51.

84 *"This reverse will increase"*: GC to Adrian and Christine Cave, October 3 [1914], PRONI.

85 *"Now the scene should"*: Leader, June 26, 1915.

85 *"the best example I"*: Richard Meinertzhagen, *Army Diary 1899–1926*, Edinburgh and London, 1960, 86.

85 *"On the whole"*: Richard Meinertzhagen, *Kenya Diary 1902–1906*, Edinburgh and London, 1957, 239.

85 fn. *"This was my first"*: Meinertzhagen, *Army Diary*, 93.

86 *"it was touch and"*: GC to Adrian and Christine Cave, March 29, n.y., PRONI.

86 *"We spent long hours"*: KC, 198.

87 *"Steadily the roars approached"*: Ibid., 200.

87 *"Presumably there was some"*: Ibid., 201.

87 *"The damaged, dusty gory"*: Wynn E. Wynn, *Ambush*, 1937, 30.

87 *"We have lost the"*: Meinertzhagen, *Army Diary*, 147.

87 fn. *"Jollie is a decrepit"*: Meinertzhagen, *Army Diary*, 172.

88 *"If the initial attempt"*: DFH to "Pussy" Lucas, September 12, 1915, private collection.

88 *"before the Germans have"*: Ibid.

88 *"Jesus, make it stop"*: Siegfried Sassoon, "Attack," from *The Old Huntsman and Other Poems*, 1918.

88   *"Darling, if I could":* Mosley, *Julian Grenfell,* 251.

89   *"I saw a man":* Ronald Knox, *Patrick Shaw Stewart,* 1920, 159.

89   *"I doubt whether any":* Christen Christensen, ed., *Blockade and Jungle,* Nashville, n.d., 104.

90   *"full of their own . . . left behind in India":* J. R. Gregory, *Under the Sun: A Memoir of Dr R.W. Burkitt,* Nairobi, n.d., 27.

90   *"One hopes that the":* DFH to "Pussy" Lucas, September 12, 1915, private collection.

91   *"as frustrating as teaching":* Elwin, *The Life of Llewelyn Powys,* 126.

91   *"The Pox is so":* Ibid., 131.

91   *"and plug at anything":* GC to Adrian and Christine Cave, October 3 [1914], PRONI.

92   *"It is both the":* Charles Miller, *Battle for the Bundu,* 1974, 197.

94   *"and man the launches":* Ibid., 204.

94   *"His Majesty's congratulations to":* Ibid., 206.

94   NELSON TOUCH ON AFRICAN: Ibid., 211.

94   *"they all seem quite":* Meinertzhagen, *Army Diary,* 163.

94   *"When we arrived at":* Leader, August 5, 1916.

95   *"It is hot, and":* Meinertzhagen, *Army Diary,* 176.

95   *"a hopeless, rotten soldier":* Ibid., 171.

95   *"If General Smuts considers":* General Sir J. M. Stewart, WO 95/5335, PRO.

95   *"I still have those":* General Sir J. M. Stewart to DFH, August 20, 1916, Stewart Papers, National Army Museum, London.

96   *"perhaps the most gifted":* KC, 220.

96   *"Never in my experience . . . Such was his charm":* Ibid., 191.

97   *"Their boats ran aground":* Leonard Mosley, *Duel for Kilimanjaro,* 1963, 137.

98   *"I had a farm":* OoA, 15.

98   *"Never did* floreat etona*":* KC, 223.

99   *"When we had read":* Young, *Marching on Tanga,* 87.

99   *"Suddenly, the news came":* Alfred Johansen, "The Kenya I Knew," unpublished memoir, RH.

100   *"one of the few":* Hordern and Stacke, *Military Operations in East Africa,* 306.

100   *"One can only think":* Leader, August 12, 1916.

100   *"Mere superiority in numbers":* Hordern and Stacke, *Military Operations in East Africa,* 516.

100   *"Many men are almost":* General Sheppard, WO 95/5335, PRO.

100   *"On every piece of":* KC, 231.

101   *"a campaign against nature":* J.H.V. Crowe, *General Smuts' Campaign in East Africa,* 1918, viii.

101   *"Picture the difficulty of":* Buchanan, *Three Years of War in East Africa,* 138.

101   *"Colonel furious, I furious":* H. Moyse-Bartlett, *The King's African Rifles,* Aldershot, 1956, 315.

102   *"Rations were so green":* Miller, *Battle for the Bundu,* 238.

102   *"rats' alley/Where the":* T. S. Eliot, *The Waste Land,* New York, 1922.

102 *"I feel with one":* General R. Hoskins, WO 95/5335, PRO.

102 *"the mutual personal esteem":* Lettow-Vorbeck, *My Reminiscences of East Africa,* 170.

104 *"An order issued in":* Ibid., 194.

104 *"The German army was so":* Christensen, ed., *Blockade and Jungle,* 203.

104 *"The enemy is evidently":* General R. Hoskins, WO 339/120999, PRO.

105 *"He had done awfully":* GC to Adrian and Christine Cave, April 8, 1917, PRONI.

105 *"He had managed to":* C. P. Fendall, *The East African Force 1915–1919,* 1921, 100.

105 *"In view of the":* War Office to General R. Hoskins, WO 339/120999, PRO.

105 *"lost grip of the":* Ross Anderson, *The Forgotten Front,* Stroud, 2004, 210.

105 *"All the military folk":* GC to Lady Eleanor Cole, n.d., RH.

105 *"If they had left":* DFH to KR, November 2, 1918, LoC.

106 *"We are all depressed":* GC to Lady Eleanor Cole, n.d., RH.

CHAPTER 5. BABYLON, MESPOT—IRAQ

107 *"When I think of":* KC, 195.

107 *"world grown old and":* Rupert Brooke, "Peace," *New Numbers* 4 (1915).

108 *"stacked like straw":* Blunt, *Lady Muriel,* 111.

109 *"As one who has":* The Times, November 12, 1914.

110 *"Will you convey to":* DFH to "Pussy" Lucas, August 8, 1917, private collection.

110 *"murder, not only to":* Edmund Blunden, *Undertones of War,* 1928.

111 *"Christmas feed in this":* Ann Crichton-Harris, *Seventeen Letters to Tatham,* Toronto, 2002, 49.

111 *"Very few outsiders care":* Sylvia Jukes Morris, *Edith Kermit Roosevelt,* New York, 1980, 298.

112 *"the one with the":* Ibid., 399.

112 *"Finch Hatton and I":* Kermit Roosevelt, *War in the Garden of Eden,* New York, 1919, 8.

113 MADE IN THE USA: Ibid., 18.

113 *"the Mesopotamian picnic":* Ibid., 223.

113 fn. *"Hostile . . . Very":* A. J. Barker, *The Neglected War,* 1967, 234.

114 *"I slipped behind my":* Roosevelt, *War in the Garden of Eden,* 16.

114 *"The trenches were a":* Ibid., 20.

115 fn. *"Is this the land":* Barker, *The Neglected War,* 63.

116 *"Dear K":* DFH to KR, December 1917, LoC.

118 *"frantic wiring to all":* DFH to KR, n.d., LoC.

118 *"A very attractive person":* Lady Eleanor Cole to her mother, May 19, 1918, RH.

119 *"It was nice to":* DFH to KR, n.d., LoC.

119 *"an unusually charming person":* Letters, 66.

119 *"It is seldom that":* Ibid., 67.

119 *"for I have been":* Ibid., 89.

119 *"quite a nice piece":* DFH to KR, n.d., LoC.

120   "I heard elephant all": Ibid.

121   "About eight in a": Ibid.

121   "I may have to": Ibid.

121   "had rather fun meeting": DFH to KR, July 17, 1918, LoC.

122   "He was in good": Ibid.

122   "So far it is": DFH to KR, n.d., LoC.

122   "They work us morn": DFH to KR, July 17, 1918, LoC.

122   "We keep going by . . . winter there these days . . . don't get killed": Ibid.

122   "after chopping and burning": DFH to KR, November 2, 1918, LoC.

122   "It begins to look": Ibid.

123   "in wonderful form": Ibid.

123   "I am very glad": Ibid.

123   "The Boche in defeat": Ibid.

123   "If my toe had": Ibid.

123   "Von Lettow has now": Ibid.

124   "very satisfactory lately": Ibid.

124   "What in the name": Ibid.

125   "again shown itself in": Ibid.

125   "As things are pretty": Ibid.

125   "The Nile played up": DFH to KR, January 27, 1919, LoC.

125   "comfortable climate": Ibid.

125   "a real Swahili ruffian": Ibid.

126   "though in what capacity": Meinertzhagen, Army Diary, 115.

126   "emits hot air by": Ibid., 116.

126   "Old Kitchener": DFH to KR, January 27, 1919, LoC.

126   "It was just as": Ibid.

126   "furious wiring, relays of": Ibid.

126   "I am very sorry . . . You ought to . . . I feel that": DFH to KR, January 27, 1919, LoC.

126   fn. "Young lady . . . in my": KC, 183.

127   "All our troops, native": Lettow-Vorbeck, My Reminiscences of East Africa, 318.

CHAPTER 6. MY WIFE'S LOVER

128   "As for charm, I": WwtN, 192.

128   "The sun rose and": Powys, Black Laughter, 172.

129   "They are at peace": Laurence Binyon, "For the Fallen," The Times, September 21, 1914.

129   "Among the white community": Leader, November 11, 1918.

129   "When you sat down": Nellie Grant, Nellie: Letters from Africa, 1980, 82.

130   "Lots of women were": Trzebinski, The Lives of Beryl Markham, 68.

130   "One of the things": Frans Lasson, ed., Isak Dinesen: Her Life in Pictures (originally published as The Life and Destiny of Isak Dinesen, New York, 1970), Rungsted Kyst, 1994, 153.

130   "strange beauty": Bunny Allen, The Wheel of Life, Long Beach, 2002, 34.

131 *"full of magnetism and"*: Elspeth Huxley, *East African Annual 1958–59*, Nairobi, 60.

131 *"all awry"*: Ibid.

131 *"never significantly silent"*: *WwtN*, 209.

131 *"I would have been"*: Baker, *Ernest Hemingway*, 803.

131 *"Blickie is in hell"*: Carlos Baker, ed., *Ernest Hemingway: Selected Letters 1917–1961*, New York, 2003, 839.

132 *"How desperately she longed"*: Lasson, ed., *Isak Dinesen: Her Life in Pictures*, 54.

132 *"without any petty attention"*: Thomas Dinesen, *My Sister, Isak Dinesen*, 1975, 53.

132 *"Gold meant coffee"*: Blixen-Finecke, *African Hunter*, 14.

132 *"I was on my"*: Blixen, *Seven Gothic Tales*, 244.

133 *"a person who had"*: *OoA*, 78.

133 *"I find that nation"*: *Letters*, 24.

133 *"decent"*: Ibid., 10.

133 *"like brothers"*: Ibid., 26.

133 *"If I cannot be"*: Ibid., 381.

133 *"The Danish character"*: Thurman, *Isak Dinesen: The Life of Karen Blixen*, 70.

133 *"ecstasy"*: Dinesen, *My Sister, Isak Dinesen*, 55.

134 *"My fingers itched to"*: Blixen-Finecke, *African Hunter*, 3.

134 *"So far . . . the tourist"*: Gustav Kleen, ed., *Bror Blixen: The Africa Letters*, New York, 1988, 129.

134 *"sleep on one's shoulder"*: Ibid., 129.

135 *"extraordinarily sure"*: *Letters*, 47.

135 *"If I should wish"*: Thurman, *Isak Dinesen: The Life of Karen Blixen*, 162.

135 *"If it did not"*: *Letters*, 281.

135 *"It was Africa distilled"*: *OoA*, 15.

136 *"I don't think I"*: *Letters*, 97.

136 *"one of the old . . . a much better type"*: Ibid., 66.

136 *"I think it is"*: Ibid.

136 *"in the same restricted"*: Ibid., 67.

137 *"my good friend, and"*: Thurman, *Isak Dinesen: The Life of Karen Blixen*, 197.

138 *"all wild with the"*: *OoA*, 251.

139 *"the ache for those"*: W. S. Churchill, *The World Crisis: The Aftermath*, 1929, 19.

139 *"The war did not"*: Parsons, ed., *Alan Parsons' Book*, 88.

139 *"Everything I had known"*: Siegfried Sassoon, *Memoirs of a Fox-Hunting Man*, 1928, 294.

140 *"unsociable and shy"*: Thurman, *Isak Dinesen: The Life of Karen Blixen*, 232.

141 *"Nothing exciting has taken"*: *Leader*, October 9, 1920.

142 *"a sort of futuristic idea"*: Ibid., October 11, 1919.

142 *"where erstwhile we were"*: Ibid., January 10, 1920.

142 *"What is Bolshevism?"*: Ibid., February 21, 1920.

144 *"all the ghastly lozenges"*: GFH (Toby), Diary, March 4, 1922, Northampton.

145 *"And yet I really"*: Undated poem handwritten by DFH, private collection.

145 *"pretty exciting"*: GFH (Toby), Diary, December 30, 1921, Northampton.

147 *"Tanne sat as if"*: Dinesen, *My Sister, Isak Dinesen*, 68.

147 *"I will never be"*: Letters, 58.

147 *"It seems likely that"*: Dinesen, *My Sister, Isak Dinesen*, 59.

147 *"She couldn't do any"*: Thomas Dinesen to Knud W. Jensen, *Karen Blixen—Storyteller* (subtitled Danish film by Christian Braad Thomsen).

147 *"a Bolshevik"*: Letters, 138.

147 *"And they were right"*: Dinesen, *My Sister, Isak Dinesen*, 76.

149 *"There is so much"*: Letters, 108.

149 *"the greatest sorrow in . . . but I do not"*: Ulf Aschan, *The Man Whom Women Loved*, New York, 1987, 63.

149 fn. *"Her species has become"*: Daily Telegraph, December 19, 1988.

149 *"harassed her about it . . . By his vicious lies . . . for money and assistance"*: Anders Westenholz, *The Power of Aries*, Baton Rouge, 1987, 25.

150 *"But she does have"*: Letters, 131.

150 *"Father understood me as"*: Ibid., 110.

150 *"I have suffered all . . . person in the world"*: Ibid., 110–11.

151 *"He has a great"*: Ibid., 139.

151 *"subject to special kinds"*: OoA, 244.

151 *"bad temper"*: DFH to KB, March 19 [1924], KBA.

CHAPTER 7. DANIEL

152 *"He never did but"*: OoA, 158.

152 *"door handles both inside"*: Kenya Observer, February 10, 1923.

152 *"sucking the lifeblood of"*: Leader, December 20, 1919.

152 *"I think the Government"*: Ibid., January 18, 1919.

153 *"India for the Indians"*: Ibid., August 14, 1920.

153 *"the interests of the"*: white paper, "Indians in Kenya," 1923, quoted in Huxley, *White Man's Country*, vol. 2, 275.

154 *"worn-down and frustrated"*: Introduction to Peter Beard, ed., *Longing for Darkness: Kamante's Tales from Out of Africa*, New York, 1975 (no page numbers).

154 *"I would be so"*: Letters, 146.

154 *"ready to burst when"*: Ibid., 147.

155 *"near to the sun"*: OoA, 15.

156 *"Bedar is on his"*: Ibid., 146.

156 *"starved of talk"*: Ibid., 117.

156 *"Let us drive as"*: Ibid., 248.

157 *"as if courteously making"*: Ibid., 160.

157 *"I would like Beethoven"*: Ibid.

157 *"That such a person"*: Letters, 171.

157 *"He was happy on"*: OoA, 159.

158 *"never reliable, but in"*: Ibid., 26.

158 fn. *"Swahili as She Is": Leader*, February 14, 1920, and elsewhere.

159 *"our house . . . our horses"*: *SotG*, 288.

159 *"so fat he had"*: Beard, ed., *Longing for Darkness*, chapter 12 (no page numbers).

159 *"it was as if"*: *OoA*, 155.

160 *"It would be reasonable"*: *Letters*, 165.

160 *"No one knows how"*: Ibid., 168.

160 *"There have been many"*: Ibid.

160 *"This time I mean"*: Westenholz, *The Power of Aries*, 30.

160 *"I think we have"*: *Letters*, 172.

162 *"not your run-of-the-mill"*: Introduction to *WwtN*, vii.

163 *"I really do believe"*: *Letters*, 194.

163 *"the most wonderful being"*: Ibid., 196.

163 *"Goodbye . . . and thank you"*: DFH to KB, March 19 [1924], KBA.

163 *"I believe that for"*: *Letters*, 224.

164 *"I'd give most of the Rue"*: DFH to KR, April 21, 1924, LoC.

164 *"Rammed a thorn in"*: GFH (Toby), Diary, May 23, 1924, family collection.

164 *"It is sad to"*: DFH to KR, June 17, 1924, LoC.

165 *"Tiny, are you asleep . . . It was always a . . . Read the Bible"*: Michael Williams, conversations with the author, 2003–2004.

165 *"I have often found"*: DFH to KR, June 17, 1924, LoC.

166 *"I am so sorry"*: GFH (Toby), Diary, October 15, 1924, family collection.

166 *"All sorrows can be"*: Else Brundbjerg, *Isak Dinesen: Karen Blixen, Woman, Heretic and Artist*, Charlottenlund, 1997, 20.

166 *"without the support of"*: Karen Blixen, *On Modern Marriage and Other Observations*, 1987, 56.

166 *"which takes the form"*: *Letters*, 270–71.

166 *"the love relationship could"*: Olga Anastasia Pelensky, *Isak Dinesen: The Life and Imagination of a Seducer*, Athens (Ohio), 1991, 90.

166 *"I do not think"*: *Letters*, 321.

167 *"so little sexual"*: Ibid.

167 *"a mirthful forbearance with"*: Karen Blixen (Isak Dinesen), *Last Tales*, 1957, 96 (page number refers to Penguin Classics edition, 2001).

167 *"sweat and stable"*: Ibid., 98.

167 *"slightly moist"*: Ibid.

167 *"mystically she had become"*: Ibid., 96.

168 *"I sure reckon I"*: DFH to KR, March 21, 1924, LoC.

168 *"and yet he came"*: Le Comte de Janzé, *Vertical Land*, 1928, 116.

170 *"In those days people"*: Mary Lovell, *Straight on Till Morning*, 1987, 72 (page number refers to Arena edition, 1988).

171 fn. *"a very clear inverse"*: Frank McLynn, *Hearts of Darkness*, 1992, 187.

172 *"You know that Denys"*: *Letters*, 384.

172 *"When you saw them"*: Allen, *The Wheel of Life*, 34.

172 *"Do you know Norman"*: This anecdote has been handed down the generations by many among Denys's family and friends, in each case with a different name

after "Do you know. . . ." I have included it because it rings true; and William "Norman" Tod was a close friend of Denys's at Eton.

173 *"My rotten heart has"*: Berkeley Cole to John Cole, March 25 [1925], PRONI.

173 *"a vista of success"*: GC to John Cole, March 3, 1925, PRONI.

173 *"Funeral everything you all"*: Hugh Martin to John Cole, April 28, 1925, PRONI.

173 *"The more I reflect"*: GC to John Cole, March 3, 1925, PRONI.

174 *"nothing more to ask"*: Letters, 242.

174 *"I will not and"*: Ibid., 249.

174 *"One has freedom and"*: Ibid., 270.

175 *"The reason for my"*: Ibid., 281.

175 *"Don't drive fast when"*: DFH to KB, n.d., Karen Blixen Museum, Rungsted-lund.

175 CLASS WAR SPLITS BRITAIN: *Daily Express*, May 1, 1926.

176 *"The elderly Liberal leaders"*: A. J. Taylor, *English History 1914–1945*, Oxford, 1965, 320.

176 *"Strongly urge you cancel"*: This cable, dated May 21, 1926, is quoted by Thurman in her biography *Isak Dinesen: The Life of Karen Blixen* (246). She cites as her source the Karen Blixen Archive in Copenhagen. But the cable has vanished from the archive and my inquiries as to its whereabouts were not answered. It is inconceivable that a researcher as scrupulous as Thurman did not see and accurately transcribe this first cable, so I quote it here without fear of inaccuracy.

176 *"Reference your cable and"*: DFH to KB, May 21, 1926, KBA.

177 *"Thanks cables never meant"*: written on reverse of DFH to KB, May 21, 1926, KBA.

177 *"I am rather depressed"*: Another document that has mysteriously vanished from the Karen Blixen Archive in Copenhagen. The telegram, dated June 15, is quoted in full in Brundbjerg, *Isak Dinesen: Karen Blixen, Woman, Heretic and Artist* (230). I believe this source to be reliable.

177 *"the foul rag and"*: W. B. Yeats, "The Circus Animals' Desertion," *Last Poems*, 1938.

177 *"on sentimental grounds"*: GFH (Toby), Diary, August 1, 1925, Northampton.

178 *"In spite of his"*: DFH to KB, September 12, 1926, KBA.

178 *"I shall be glad"*: Ibid.

178 *"so that we can"*: Ibid.

178 *"to say whether you"*: Ibid.

178 *"charming letter . . . I have got your"*: DFH to KB, September 23, 1926, KBA.

179 *"to keep this icy"*: DFH to KB, June 15, n.y., KBA.

179 *"Oh that I had"*: Iris Tree, *The Traveller and Other Poems*, New York, 1927.

179 *"Men are cumbersome"*: Fielding, *The Rainbow Picnic*, 101.

180 *"17 days prison"*: DFH to KB, September 12, 1926, KBA.

180 *"Homeward bound I feel"*: Letters, 297.

181 *"That man died at"*: OoA, 160.

181 *"Denys was a loveable"*: Trzebinski, *The Lives of Beryl Markham*, 84.

182 *"She was difficult, but"*: Thurman, *Isak Dinesen: The Life of Karen Blixen*, 234.

182   *"Tanne liked to use"*: Pelensky, *Isak Dinesen: The Life and Imagination of a Seducer*, 125.

182   *"I hope we're not . . . I wouldn't mind"*: Aschan, *The Man Whom Women Loved*, 97.

182   *"She was double"*: Pelensky, *Isak Dinesen: The Life and Imagination of a Seducer*, 125.

CHAPTER 8. STUNTING

183   *"Denys could, like the"*: Mrs. Kit Taylor to Errol Trzebinski, June 30, 1975, RH.

184   *"wish to transplant and"*: Evelyn Waugh, *Remote People*, 1931, 140–41.

185   *"They were a group"*: Aidan Hartley, *Literary Review*, April 2002.

185   *"I had many a"*: R. E. Dear to Michael Williams, April 24, 1986, family collection.

186   *"I bless you whenever"*: Letters, 302.

186   *"quite pleasant"*: DFH to KR, June 3, 1927, LoC.

186   *"a wonderful road, rising"*: Ibid.

186   *"They have a madman"*: Ibid.

186   *"If I have ever"*: Letters, 316.

187   *"Do you know aught"*: DFH to KR, August 14, 1926, LoC.

187   *"a walking encyclopedia . . . rattle"*: Frederick B. Patterson, *African Adventures*, New York, 1928, 8.

187   *"Hatton . . . seemed eight feet"*: Ibid., 19.

188   *"We waited for an"*: Ibid., 49.

189   *"Oh . . . it just happened"*: Ibid., 9.

189   *"I never knew two . . . I was aware of . . . clear steady eyes, with . . . He began to weave"*: Mrs. Kit Taylor to Errol Trzebinski, July 8, 1975, RH.

190   *"miles of damn-all"*: Edward Paice, *Lost Lion of Empire*, 2001, 33.

190   *"zest"*: Patterson, *African Adventures*, 58.

190   *"a pandemonium of trumpetings"*: Ibid., 60.

191   *"He looked v. peaceful"*: GFH (Toby), Diary, August 14, 1927, Northampton.

191   *"Hatton was talking of . . . Till we meet again"*: Patterson, *African Adventures*, 82.

191   *"civilisation"*: Ibid.

191   *"healthful wonderland"*: Ibid., 4.

191   *"Every tale I have"*: Ibid., 5.

191   *"I could not have"*: Ibid., 8.

191   *"Never once did I"*: Ibid., 20.

193   *"horribly thin"*: Letters, 328.

193   *"a sudden quelling smell"*: OoA, 161.

194   *"twelve or fifteen yards"*: Ibid.

194   *"was a declaration of"*: Ibid., 162.

194   *"the lions or family"*: Letters, 365.

194   *"gets just as much"*: Ibid., 367.

194   *"Who can judge . . . I myself think that"*: Ibid., 371–72.

194   *"being let down"*: Ibid., 348.

195 *"Oh yes, vive la"*: Elizabeth Harlan, *George Sand*, 2004.

195 *"accompanied, unfortunately . . . by his"*: *Letters*, 352.

196 *"fine desperado"*: James Fox, *White Mischief*, 1982, 33.

196 *"the fastest gun in"*: Bunny Allen to Mary Lovell, 1986, Mary Lovell Archive.

197 *"I knew her very"*: Genesta Hamilton, *A Stone's Throw*, 1986, 92.

197 *"a wonderful person without"*: Errol Trzebinski, *Silence Will Speak*, 1977, 215–16.

199 *"so she is pretty . . . Beryl and I could"*: Lovell, *Straight on Till Morning*, 53.

199 *"Beryl would never have"*: Ibid., 312.

199 *"She was always up"*: Trzebinski, *The Lives of Beryl Markham*, 95.

199 *"I was so sorry"*: Lovell, *Straight on Till Morning*, 56–7.

199 *"dressed like Solomon in"*: Ibid., 58.

200 *"the most momentous occasion"*: *East African Standard*, June 30, 1928.

200 *"absolute despair"*: *Letters*, 361.

200 *"It is true that"*: *The Times*, June 29, 1929.

202 *"old illness"*: *Letters*, 214.

202 *"We could have done"*: Thurman, *Isak Dinesen: The Life of Karen Blixen*, 323.

202 *"You will be the"*: Trzebinski, *Silence Will Speak*, 182.

204 *"merely an existence"*: PoW to Mrs. Humphrey Butler, September 6, 1920, collection of Mohamed Al Fayed.

204 *"these foul tours"*: PoW to Mrs. Humphrey Butler, November 16, 1921, collection of Mohamed Al Fayed.

204 *"I've got four terrible"*: Ibid.

204 *"I've not had any"*: PoW to Mrs. Humphrey Butler, September 4, n.y., collection of Mohamed Al Fayed.

204 *"I suppose there are"*: PoW to Mrs. Humphrey Butler, September 6, 1920, collection of Mohamed Al Fayed.

204 *"Darling Poots, well here"*: PoW to Mrs. Humphrey Butler, October 6, 1920, collection of Mohamed Al Fayed.

205 *"the most unpleasant and"*: Lady Grigg's diary, October 12, 1928, private collection.

205 *"absolutely charming . . . I am so much"*: *Letters*, 384.

205 *"Harry is enjoying himself"*: PoW to Mrs. Humphrey Butler, October 6, 1920, collection of Mohamed Al Fayed.

206 *"the farmyard morals . . . the"*: Duff Hart-Davis, ed., *In Royal Service: The Letters and Journals of Sir Alan Lascelles, 1920–1936*, vol. 2, 1989, 101.

206 *"were tight before the"*: Ibid., 97.

206 *"Though I have little"*: Ibid., 201.

208 *"Memsahib, they are coming"*: *SotG*, 298.

208 *"that all I felt"*: Vivienne de Watteville, *Speak to the Earth*, New York, 1935, 161.

208 *"absolutely ravishing"*: *Letters*, 387.

208 *"a very strange fish"*: Beard, ed., *Longing for Darkness: Kamante's Tales from Out of Africa*, chapter 4 (no page numbers).

208 *"for we all think"*: *SotG*, 299.

209 *"I fiche myself completely"*: Hart-Davis, ed., *In Royal Service*, 101.

209 *"practically everyone in Nairobi"*: Patrick R. Chalmers, *Sport and Travel in East*

Africa 1928–30, compiled from the Private Diaries of HRH the Prince of Wales, 1934, 101.

210 *"How dare you shoot":* Trzebinski, *Silence Will Speak,* 242.

210 *"Your Royal Highness":* Ibid.

211 *"I'm the Prince":* Blixen-Finecke, *African Hunter,* 179.

211 *"You could not":* Ibid.

212 *"There was something ominous":* Chalmers, *Sport and Travel,* 146.

212 *"I remember sitting, one":* Hart-Davis, ed., *In Royal Service,* 109.

212 *"I don't believe a"* et seq.: Ibid.

213 *"Imagine . . . I could be":* Trzebinski, *Silence Will Speak,* 268.

213 *"One sat and waited":* Chalmers, *Sport and Travel,* 147.

213 *"What a mess up . . . a curious":* PoW to DFH, December 4, 1928, family collection.

214 *"It was very sad . . . I do not":* Piers "Joey" Legh to DFH, December 5, 1928, family collection.

CHAPTER 9. ARIEL

215 *"A man never forgotten":* Elspeth Huxley, *Forks and Hope,* 1964, 87.

215 *"a law against nature . . . so would it be":* Trzebinski, *Silence Will Speak,* 271. This postcard has vanished from KBA.

215 *"left a reserve of ":* Lovell, *Straight on Till Morning,* 101.

215 *"He often wondered":* Blixen (Dinesen), *Last Tales,* 265 (page number refers to Penguin Classics edition, 2001).

216 *"Learn as much mathematics":* DFH to Michael Williams, January 12, 1929, family collection.

216 *"not get far with":* Michael Williams, conversation with author, 2004.

217 *"an orgy of slaughter":* The Times, January 21, 1928.

217 *"Is it too much":* Ibid.

218 *"A treacherous eddy of ":* Ibid., June 29, 1929.

218 *"hideous abuse":* Ibid., July 3, 1929.

218 *"the beginning of the end":* Ibid., July 10, 1929.

218 *"In Nyasaland in my":* Ibid., July 13, 1929.

218 *"Mr Finch Hatton's crusade":* Ibid., July 18, 1929.

219 *"Within a few years":* Julian Huxley, *Memories,* 196.

220 *"It is a terribly":* East African Standard, January 29, 1927.

220 *"Few portions of the":* Leader, January 31, 1919.

221 *"epoch-making":* East African Standard, October 20, 1926.

221 *"too abominable for words":* Trzebinski, *Silence Will Speak,* 158.

222 *"If I don't move":* Trzebinski, *The Lives of Beryl Markham,* 144.

222 *"enough to make a":* Sporting Times, April 1, 1922.

222 *"to be secured by":* Westenholz, *The Power of Aries,* 31–2.

224 *"twelve unclouded years of ":* Eleanor Cole to Christine Cave, November 6, 1929, PRONI.

224 *"the beauty of the":* OoA, 244.

225 *"The scenery was of"*: Ibid., 243.

225 *"and in the porous"*: Ibid.

225 *"a great hero"*: Allen, *The Wheel of Life*, 4.

225 *"I was always ready"*: Ibid., 35.

225 *"And what a difference"*: Ibid., 47–8.

226 *"put up with it"*: Bunny Allen, *The First Wheel*, n.d., 108.

226 *"weak, self-absorbed, futureless"*: Dinesen, *My Sister, Isak Dinesen*, 117.

226 *"Locust eggs are hatching"*: W. H. Dickens to KB, May 21, 1929, KBA.

227 *"I think it is"*: W. H. Dickens to KB, September 26, 1929, KBA.

227 *"Farah I am sorry"*: W. H. Dickens to KB, August 17, 1929, KBA.

227 *"The whole of the"*: W. H. Dickens to KB, July 4, 1929, KBA.

227 *"everything is looking very"*: W. H. Dickens to KB, September 2, 1929, KBA.

227 *"in tip-top condition"*: W. H. Dickens to KB, October 3, 1929, KBA.

227 *"The Somalis . . . are generally"*: OoA, 230.

228 *"for having raised and"*: Westenholz, *The Power of Aries*, 33.

228 *"I am longing to"*: PoW to DFH, November 13, 1929, family collection.

228 *"my new hobby"*: Duke of Windsor, *A King's Story*, 1951, 235 (page number refers to Prion edition, 1988).

229 *"We sat down where"*: Blixen-Finecke, *African Hunter*, 194.

229 *"If I wanted to . . . I am sorry that . . . I will do anything . . . You are having a"*: DFH to KB, n.d., KBA.

230 *"But I thought that"*: Westenholz, *The Power of Aries*, 77.

230 *"a scene of the"*: Letters, 407.

230 *"Your talk disturbed me"*: DFH to KB, n.d., KBA.

231 *"This was our Eden"*: Gloria Vanderbilt and Thelma, Lady Furness, *Double Exposure*, 1959, 265.

231 *"What [the creatures] left"*: Chalmers, *Sport and Travel*, 200.

232 *"Darling . . . I've got to"*: Vanderbilt and Furness, *Double Exposure*, 268.

232 *"responsibility to the empire"*: Ibid.

232 *"perhaps the most beautiful"*: Chalmers, *Sport and Travel*, 216.

232 *"Finch Hatton was responsible"*: Ibid., 170.

233 *"Everyone says they are"*: DFH to KB, May 11, 1930, KBA.

233 *"The trouble is that . . . which is very exhilarating . . . Shall be quite ready"*: Ibid.

234 *"Christ has risen . . . and"*: Philip Ziegler, *Diana Cooper*, 1981, 29.

235 *"pestilential . . . This is a cursed country . . . This afternoon I have . . . I feel it would . . . One could land it"*: DFH to KB, May 11, 1930, KBA.

236 *"My black brother here"*: Letters, 407.

237 *"I am finding it"*: Ibid., 409.

237 *"You were up very"*: et seq., OoA, 172.

238 *"You knew then"*: WwtN, 38.

238 *"the competence which he"*: Ibid., 193.

238 *"Flying suits Denys . . . There is a good"*: Letters, 413.

240 *"Denys and I could"*: J. A. Hunter, *Hunter's Tracks*, 1957, 66.

240 *"Denys opened up the"*: Ibid., 70.

240 *"But Denys was quicker"*: et seq., ibid., 69.

CHAPTER 10. TOO CLOSE TO THE SUN

241   *"Denys would have greeted"*: WwtN, 192.

242   *"No friend, brother or"*: SotG, 300.

242   *"And during this time"*: OoA, 233.

243   *"He himself looked upon"*: Ibid., 242.

243   *"He had been in"*: Ibid., 243.

243   *"It is interesting to"*: unpublished trans. (by Lars Kaaber) of Else Brundbjerg, "Kœrlighed og Økonomi" ("Love and Finance"), *Kritik* 66 (1984), Copenhagen.

244   *"world of poetry"*: Letters, 416.

244   *"We realise that you"*: Westenholz, *The Power of Aries*, 35.

244   *"I know that I"*: Letters, 421.

245   *"the greatest baby I"*: Lovell, *Straight on Till Morning*, 92.

245   *"so young and light"*: Ibid.

246   *"Work hard, trust in"*: WwtN, 241.

246   *"the way of all flesh"*: Trzebinski, *The Lives of Beryl Markham*, 155.

246   *"She was all right"*: Ibid., 92.

246   *"She had charm but"*: Lovell, *Straight on Till Morning*, 261.

246   *"Tania . . . was always waiting"*: Trzebinski, *The Lives of Beryl Markham*, 92.

247   *"He half taught me"*: Ibid., 91.

247   *"This will not only . . . a force that bore . . . of almost classical profundity"*: WwtN, 192–93.

247   *"a lovely man, very"*: interviews with BM by Mary Lovell, March 1986, transcripts in Mary Lovell Archive.

247   fn. *"This girl who is"*: Carlos Baker to Mary Lovell, December 23, 1983, Mary Lovell Archive.

248   *"an unconditional truthfulness which outside"*: OoA, 247.

249   *"Here are your grey"*: Ibid., 245.

249   *"I saw grey geese"*: Tree, *The Traveller and Other Poems*.

249   *"The shadow of destiny"*: OoA, 245.

249   *"Good God, Denys! . . . Do"*: Joan Waddington to Errol Trzebinski, n.d., RH.

250   *"I'm going down to"*: et seq., WwtN, 193–94.

251   *"Voi presumed to be"*: Ibid.

SELECTED BIBLIOGRAPHY

All books published in London unless otherwise indicated.

Allen, Bunny. *The Wheel of Life*. Long Beach, 2002.

Anderson, Ross. *The Battle of Tanga 1914*. 2002.

————. *The East African Front*. 2003.

Aschan, Ulf. *The Man Whom Women Loved*. New York, 1987.

Barker, A. J. *The Neglected War*. 1967.

Beard, Peter, ed. *Longing for Darkness: Kamante's Tales from Out of Africa*. New York, 1975.

Bjørnvig, Thorkild. *The Pact: My Friendship with Isak Dinesen*. Trans. Ingvar Schousboe and William Jay Smith. Baton Rouge, 1983.

Blixen, Karen (Isak Dinesen). *Seven Gothic Tales*. New York, 1934.

————. *Out of Africa*. 1937.

————. *Winter's Tales*. 1942.

————. *The Angelic Avengers*. 1946.

————. *Last Tales*. 1957.

————. *Anecdotes of Destiny*. 1958.

————. *Shadows on the Grass*. 1960.

————. *Ehrengard*. 1963.

————. *On Modern Marriage and Other Observations*. Trans. Anne Born. 1987.

Blixen-Finecke, Bror von. *African Hunter*. Trans. F. H. Lyon. New York, 1937.

Blunt, Wilfrid. *Lady Muriel*. 1962.

Brundbjerg, Else. *Isak Dinesen: Karen Blixen, Woman, Heretic and Artist*. Trans. Lars Kaaber. Charlottenlund, 1997.

Buchanan, Angus. *Three Years of War in East Africa*. 1919.

Buchanan, Sir George. *The Tragedy of Mesopotamia*. 1938.

Chalmers, Patrick R. *Sport and Travel in East Africa 1928–30*. Compiled from the Private Diaries of HRH the Prince of Wales. New York, n.d.

Christensen, Christen, ed. *Blockade and Jungle*. Trans. Eleanor Arkwright. Nashville, n.d.

Craig, Edith, and Christopher St. John, eds. *Ellen Terry's Memoirs*. 1933.

Lord Cranworth. *Kenya Chronicles*. 1939.

Crichton-Harris, Ann. *Seventeen Letters to Tatham*. Toronto, 2002.

Crowe, J.H.V. *General Smuts' Campaign in East Africa*. 1918.

Dinesen, Thomas. *My Sister, Isak Dinesen*. Trans. Joan Tate. 1975.

Dutton, E.A.T. *Lillibullero, or, The Golden Road*. Zanzibar, 1944.

Elwin, Malcolm. *The Life of Llewelyn Powys*. 1949.

Farwell, Byron. *The Great War in Africa*. 1987.

Fielding, Daphne. *The Rainbow Picnic: A Portrait of Iris Tree*. 1974.

Finch Hatton, Harold. *Advance Australia!* 1885.

Fox, James. *White Mischief*. 1982.

Gregory, J. R. *Under the Sun: A Memoir of Dr R.W. Burkitt*. Nairobi, n.d.

Hamilton, Genesta. *A Stone's Throw: Travels from Africa in Six Decades*. 1986.

Hart-Davis, Duff, ed. *In Royal Service: The Letters and Journals of Sir Alan Lascelles, 1920–1936*, vol. 2. 1989.

Hemsing, Jan. *Then and Now: Nairobi's Norfolk Hotel*. Nairobi, 1975.

Herne, Brian. *White Hunters*. New York, 1999.

Hordern, C., and H. Stacke. *Military Operations in East Africa (History of the Great War Based on Official Documents)*, vol. 1, Aug. 1914–Sept. 1916. 1941.

Hunter, J. A. *Hunter*. 1952.

———. *Hunter's Tracks*. 1957.

———. *White Hunter*. n.d.

Huxley, Elspeth. *White Man's Country—Lord Delamere and the Making of Kenya*. 2 vols. 1935.

———. *The Flame Trees of Thika*. 1959.

———. *Forks and Hope: An African Notebook*. 1964.

———. *The Mottled Lizard*. 1982.

———. *Out in the Midday Sun*. 1985.

Huxley, Elspeth, ed. *Nellie: Letters from Africa*. 1980.

Huxley, Julian. *Memories,* vol. 1. 1970.

Jones, L. E. *A Victorian Boyhood*. 1955.

———. *An Edwardian Youth*. 1956.

Ker, Donald I. *Through Forest and Veldt*. 1958.

Kleen, G.F.V., ed. and trans. *Bror Blixen: The Africa Letters*. New York, 1988.

Knox, Ronald. *Patrick Shaw Stewart*. 1920.

Lasson, Frans, ed. *Isak Dinesen: Letters from Africa*. Trans. Anne Born. Chicago, 1981.

———. *Isak Dinesen: Her Life in Pictures* (originally published as *The Life and Destiny of Isak Dinesen*, New York, 1970). Rungsted Kyst, 1994.

Lovell, Mary. *Straight on Till Morning*. 1987.

Markham, Beryl. *West with the Night*. New York, 1942.

McLynn, Frank. *Hearts of Darkness*. 1992.

Meinertzhagen, Richard. *Kenya Diary 1902–1906*. Edinburgh and London, 1957.

———. *Army Diary 1899–1926*. Edinburgh and London, 1960.

Miller, Charles. *The Lunatic Express*. 1971.

———. *Battle for the Bundu*. 1974.

Mosley, Leonard. *Duel for Kilimanjaro*. 1963.

Mosley, Nicholas. *Julian Grenfell: His Life and the Times of His Death*. 1976.

Moyse-Bartlett, H. *The King's African Rifles*. Aldershot, 1956.

Nicholls, Christine. *Elspeth Huxley*. 2002.

Oliver, Roland. *The African Experience*. 1991.

Page, William, ed. *The Victoria History of the Counties of England: A History of Lincolnshire*, vol. 2. 1906.

Paice, Edward. *Lost Lion of Empire*. 2001.

Pakenham, Thomas. *The Scramble for Africa*. 1991.

Parsons, Viola, ed. *Alan Parsons' Book*. 1937.

Patterson, Frederick B. *African Adventures*. New York, 1928.

Powys, Llewelyn. *Black Laughter*. 1925.

Roosevelt, Kermit. *War in the Garden of Eden*. New York, 1919.

Setright, L.J.K. *Drive On! A Social History of the Motor Car*. 2004.

Shankland, Peter. *The Phantom Flotilla*. 1968.

Thurman, Judith. *Isak Dinesen: The Life of Karen Blixen*. 1982.

Tidrick, Kathryn. *The Empire and the English Character*. 1990.

Tree, Viola. *Castles in the Air*. 1926.

Trzebinski, Errol. *Silence Will Speak*. 1977.

———. *The Kenya Pioneers*. 1985.

———. *The Lives of Beryl Markham*. 1993.

Vanderbilt, Gloria, and Thelma, Lady Furness. *Double Exposure*. 1959.

Visram, M. G. *On a Plantation in Kenya* (subsequently retitled *Red Soils of Tsavo*). Mombasa, 1987.

Von Lettow-Vorbeck, Paul. *My Reminiscences of East Africa* (U.S. edition titled *East African Campaigns*). 1920.

Watteville, Vivienne de. *Speak to the Earth*. New York, 1935.

Waugh, Evelyn. *Remote People*. 1931.

———. *The Life of Ronald Knox*. 1959.

Westenholz, Anders. *The Power of Aries*. Trans. Lise Kure-Jensen. Baton Rouge, 1987.

Wilkinson, Louis, ed. *Letters of Llewelyn Powys*. 1943.

Wynn, Wynn E. *Ambush*. 1937.

Wynne Hughes, O. *Every Day Was Summer*. Llandysul, 1989.

Young, Francis Brett. *Marching on Tanga*. 1917.

———. *Jim Redlake*. 1930.

Ziegler, Philip. *Edward VIII*. 1990.

———. *Diana Cooper*. 1981.

SELECTED UNPUBLISHED SOURCES

Cole, Berkeley. Correspondence, various dates, Enniskillen Papers, Public Record Office of Northern Ireland, Belfast.

Cole, Galbraith. Correspondence, various dates, Enniskillen Papers, Public Record Office of Northern Ireland, Belfast.

Errol Trzebinski Archive (uncataloged and restricted), Bodleian Library of Commonwealth and African Studies, Rhodes House, Oxford.

Finch Hatton, Anne (Nan). Diary, Finch Hatton Papers, Northamptonshire Record Office; and private collection.

Finch Hatton, Guy (Toby). Diary, Finch Hatton Papers, Northamptonshire Record Office; and private collection.

Finch Hatton, Henry. Diary, Finch Hatton Papers, Northamptonshire Record Office.

Karen Blixen Archive, *Det Kongelige Bibliotek* (Royal Library), Copenhagen.

Kermit and Belle Roosevelt Papers, Manuscript Division, Library of Congress, Washington, D.C.

Oates. "Titus," *Muthaiga Club* (private collection).

Rice, Brian. *Memoirs of the Rices of Dane Court*, privately printed, 2002.

Stewart Papers, National Army Museum, London.

ACKNOWLEDGMENTS

WITH SO FEW PRIMARY SOURCES, I WAS OBLIGED TO SEEK THE ADVICE of strangers. In the very first months of my research I approached Errol Trzebinski, who wrote about Denys thirty years ago. She immediately opened her archive to me and has been on hand ever since to answer questions and track down leads. I am in awe of her unstinting generosity of spirit, and I wish to record my profound gratitude. Denys's family were wonderfully helpful. His nephew Sir Michael Williams gave me both time and wisdom. Rupert Finch Hatton also offered valuable practical assistance, as well as warm encouragement. Shirley, Dowager Countess of Winchilsea, cheerfully watched me drive off with the car trunk crammed with precious family diaries.

In Denmark, I benefited enormously from the advice, hospitality, and friendship of Tore and Betty Dinesen. I also want to thank Marianne Wirenfeldt Asmussen at the Karen Blixen Foundation, and the formidable Blixen scholars Else Brundbjerg and Clara Selborn.

In Kenya, Edward and Anne Clay offered sanctuary while I plowed through the Nairobi archives. M. G. Vikram, known just as M.G., showed me everything I needed to see in the Voi area, including the spot where he unearthed part of Denys's crumpled Gypsy Moth. Thanks also in Africa to Tobina Cole, Aidan Hartley, Rory McGuiness (who took me flying), Melinda Rees, Monty Brown, Sadiq Ghalia, Hamish Grant, and Tony Valentine.

In England and America, I wish to thank Mohamed Al Fayed for allowing me to read letters from Edward, Prince of Wales; Peter Beard for talk and hospitality in Montauk; Richard Cohen; Jamie Fergusson; James Fox; Emma Grove; Michael Holroyd; Patrick Kerwin in the Manuscript Division of the Library of Congress, Washington, D.C.; Phil Kolvin; Mary Lovell for generously opening her Beryl Markham archive; Lucy McCann, archivist at

Rhodes House; Alexander Maitland; David Marx for gun lessons; Douglas Matthews for another index; Reginald Piggott for maps; Brian Rice; Caspar and Sue Tiarks; John Richens at University College Hospital in London for syphilis tuition; Martin Village for golfing insights; David Yaxley; and Jenny York. And, as always, the indefatigable staff of the London Library.

I owe much to my publisher, Dan Franklin; my editor, Ellah Allfrey; my agent, Gillon Aitken; and my editor at Random House in New York, Susanna Porter. I relied, as always, on two valiant and insightful readers who battled through early scripts: Lucinda Riches and Jeremy Lewis. But my greatest editorial thanks go to Peter Graham. He read every line of every draft and set me right so often that *Too Close to the Sun* would have been a different book without him. It is a debt that, while deeply appreciated, I shall never be able to repay.

I am grateful to the following for permission to quote from published and unpublished works: the Library of Congress, Washington, D.C. (Kermit and Belle Roosevelt Papers); Mary Lovell (*Straight on Till Morning*); the Provost and Fellows of Eton College (the *Eton College Chronicle*); Jonathan Moffat (*The Traveller and Other Poems* by Iris Tree); Nicholas Mosley, Lord Ravensdale (*Julian Grenfell*); the Northamptonshire Record Office (Finch Hatton Papers); Pollinger Limited (*West with the Night* by Beryl Markham); the Public Record Office of Northern Ireland (Enniskillen Papers); the Rungstedlund Foundation (*On Modern Marriage, Seven Gothic Tales, Out of Africa,* and *Shadows on the Grass,* all by Karen Blixen); George Sassoon (*Memoirs of a Fox-Hunting Man* and "Attack," from *The Old Huntsman and Other Poems,* © Siegfried Sassoon, by kind permission of George Sassoon); Sheil Land Associates (extracts from *In Royal Service: The Letters and Journals of Sir Alan Lascelles, 1920–1936,* volume 2, by Duff Hart-Davis, © Duff Hart-Davis, 1989, are reproduced by permission of Sheil Land Associates on behalf of Duff Hart-Davis); the Society of Authors and the Estate of Laurence Binyon ("For the Fallen (September, 1914)"); Errol Trzebinski (*Silence Will Speak* and *The Lives of Beryl Markham*); the University of Chicago Press (Isak Dinesen, *Letters from Africa 1914–1931*); and the Dowager Countess of Winchilsea and Sir Michael Williams (family diaries and letters).

INDEX

Like Denys Finch Hatton, SARA WHEELER was
educated at Brasenose College, Oxford. Her books include
Terra Incognita: Travels in Antarctica; Travels in a Thin Country;
and *Cherry: A Life of Apsley Cherry-Garrard*, all available from
the Modern Library. When not traveling, Wheeler lives with
her family in London.